THE ANNUAL DIRECTORY OF AMERICAN
AND CANADIAN BED & BREAKFASTS

The Midwest

Includes

MIDWESTERN CANADA

2000 EDITION • VOLUME IV

THE ANNUAL DIRECTORY OF AMERICAN AND CANADIAN BED & BREAKFASTS

The Midwest

Includes

MIDWESTERN CANADA

2000 EDITION • VOLUME IV

Tracey Menges, *Compiler*

PUBLISHING, INC.
Uhrichsville, Ohio

ISBN 1-57748-774-5

Published by Barbour Publishing, Inc., P.O. Box 719, Uhrichsville, Ohio 44683
http://www.barbourbooks.com

Cover design and book design by Harriette Bateman
Page composition by Roger A. DeLiso, Rutledge Hill Press®

Printed in the United States of America.

1 2 3 4 5 6—02 01 00 99

Contents

Introduction

The 2000 edition of *The Annual Directory of Midwestern Bed & Breakfasts* is one of the most comprehensive directories available today. Whether planning your honeymoon, a family vacation or reunion, or a business trip (many bed and breakfasts provide conference facilities), you will find what you are looking for at a bed and breakfast. They are all here just waiting to be discovered.

Once you know your destination, look for it, or one close by, to see what accommodations are available. Each state has a general map with city locations to help you plan your trip efficiently. There are listings for all 50 states, Canada, Puerto Rico, and the Virgin Islands. Don't be surprised to find a listing in the remote spot you thought only you knew about. Even if your favorite hideaway isn't listed, you're sure to discover a new one.

How to Use This Guide

The sample listing below is typical of the entries in this directory. Each bed and breakfast is listed alphabetically by city and establishment name. The description provides an overview of the bed and breakfast and may include nearby activities and attractions. *Please note that the descriptions have been provided by the hosts. The publisher has not visited these bed and breakfasts and is not responsible for inaccuracies.*

Following the description are notes that have been designed for easy reference. Looking at the sample, a quick glance tells you that this bed and breakfast has four guest rooms, two with private baths (PB) and two that share a bath (SB). The rates are for two people sharing one room. Tax may or may not be included. The specifics of "Credit Cards" and "Notes" are listed at the bottom of each page.

GREAT TOWN_____

Favorite Bed and Breakfast

123 Main Street, 12345
(800) 555-1234

This quaint bed and breakfast is surrounded by five acres of award-winning landscaping and gardens. There are four guest rooms, each individually decorated with antiques.

It is close to antique shops, restaurants, and outdoor activities. Breakfast includes homemade specialties and is served in the formal dining room at guests' leisure. Minimum stay of two nights.

Hosts: Sue and Jim Smith
Rooms: 4 (2 PB; 2 SB) $65-80
Full Breakfast
Credit Cards: A, B
Notes: 2, 5, 8, 10, 11, 12, 13

For example, the letter A means that MasterCard is accepted. The number 10 means that tennis is available on the premises or within 10 to 15 miles.

In many cases, a bed and breakfast is listed with a reservation service that represents several houses in one area. This service is responsible for bookings and can answer other questions you may have. They also inspect each listing and can help you choose the best place for your needs.

Before You Arrive

Now that you have chosen the bed and breakfast that interests you, there are some things you need to find out. You should always make reservations in advance, and while you are doing so you should ask about the local taxes. City taxes can be an unwelcome surprise. Make sure there are accommodations for your children. If you have dietary needs or prefer nonsmoking rooms, find out if these requirements can be met. Ask about check-in times and cancellation policies. Get specific directions. Most bed and breakfasts are readily accessible, but many are a little out of the way.

When You Arrive

In many instances you are visiting someone's home. Be respectful of their property, their schedules, and their requests. Don't smoke if they ask you not to, and don't show up with pets without prior arrangement. Be tidy in shared bathrooms, and be prompt. Most places have small staffs or may be run single-handedly and cannot easily adjust to surprises.

With a little effort and a sense of adventure you will learn firsthand the advantages of bed and breakfast travel. You will rediscover hospitality in a time when kindness seems to have been pushed aside. With the help of this directory, you will find accommodations that are just as exciting as your traveling plans.

We would like to hear from you about any experiences you have had or any inns you wish to recommend. Please write us at the following address:

Barbour Publishing, Inc.
P.O. Box 719
Uhrichsville, Ohio 44683

THE ANNUAL DIRECTORY OF AMERICAN
AND CANADIAN BED & BREAKFASTS

The Midwest

Includes
MIDWESTERN CANADA

2000 EDITION   •   VOLUME IV

Illinois

Illinois

Victorian Rose Garden

ALGONQUIN

Victorian Rose Garden Bed & Breakfast

314 Washington Street, 60102
(847) 854-9667; (888) 854-9667
FAX (847) 854-3236; e-mail: roses@mc.net
www.7comm.com/rosegarden

Built in 1886, the Victorian Rose Garden invites guests to come and relax on its wrap-around porch and enjoy the garden. Rooms are decorated with a mix of antiques and much-loved furniture. Play the baby grand piano or Baldwin organ, or just relax by the fireplace. The area provides golfing, antiquing, bike trail, acclaimed restaurants, and is only one hour from Chicago. "Let us pamper you!" Packages are available.

Hosts: The Brewers
Rooms: 4 (PB) $70-139
Full Breakfast
Credit Cards: A, B, C
Notes: 2, 5, 7, 12, 14

ALTON

B & B MidWest Reservations

2223 Crump Lane, Columbus, IN 47203-2009
(812) 378-5855; (800) B AND B (342-2632)
FAX (812) 378-5822
e-mail: reservations@bandbmidwest.com
www.BandBmidwest.com

02019. "Elegant" well describes this lovely mansion in this northern suburb of St. Louis, Missouri. Most of the five rooms offer double whirlpools (one is even heart-shaped) and private baths. Some also offer fireplaces in the room. One room has king-size bed while the others offer double in beautiful antique furnishings. Unique offering—breakfast may be served in the dining room or in bed, if guests prefer. $119-179.

ANTIOCH

B & B MidWest Reservations

2223 Crump Lane, Columbus, IN 47203-2009
(812) 378-5855; (800) B AND B (342-2632)
FAX (812) 378-5822
e-mail: reservations@bandbmidwest.com
www.BandBmidwest.com

26118. Enjoy a leisurely Continental breakfast on the sun porch of this stylized contemporary country home overlooking seven acres of fields and woods near the Illinois-Wisconsin border. A short drive to Gurnee Mills, Six Flags, Fox Lake, Milwaukee, and Kenosha. Three lovely guest rooms include a four-poster queen-size

NOTES: Credit cards accepted: A MasterCard; B Visa; C American Express; D Discover; E Diner's Club; F Other; 2 Personal checks accepted; 3 Lunch available; 4 Dinner available; 5 Open all year; 6 Pets welcome; 7 No smoking; 8 Children welcome; 9 Social drinking allowed; 10 Tennis nearby; 11 Swimming nearby; 12 Golf nearby; 13 Skiing nearby; 14 May be booked through a travel agent; 15 Handicapped accessible.

bed in a country American motif. Rooms include TV with remote, ceiling fan, and detached private bath. Two other large rooms offer a king-size bed with a shared bath and a suite with two queen-size beds and shared bath. $60-85.

ARLINGTON HEIGHTS

B & B MidWest Reservations

2223 Crump Lane, Columbus, IN 47203-2009
(812) 378-5855; (800) B AND B (342-2632)
FAX (812) 378-5822
e-mail: reservations@bandbmidwest.com
www.BandBmidwest.com

06098. In the historic district of this popular Northwest suburb, enjoy the charm and decor this Dutch Victorian-style home. This redecorated home is convenient to commuter rail service and an easy walk to neighborhood shops. The host couple will serve not only a delightful Continental breakfast but lots of hospitality. The accommodations include a Victorian-style room with double bed with an 1800s German Walnut headboard, a faux fireplace, and private bath. The second large room has more California influence with a four-poster bed and white wicker furnishings with shared bath. The third room has a white wrought iron bed, hardwood floor, and shared bath. $65-85.

BELLEVILLE

Victory Inn Bed & Breakfast

712 South Jackson Street, 62220
(618) 277-1538; (888) 277-8586
FAX (618) 277-1576
www.victoryinn.com

The stately home, built in 1877, offers an inviting picture from first sight. Guests often feel transformed back in time while sipping tea in the dining room or sharing experiences in the parlor. Modern conveniences are also present,

including two whirlpool tubs, private telephones, fax, computer, electronic entry, and modem access.

Hosts: Tom and Jo Brannan
Rooms: 3 (PB)
Suite: 1
Continental Breakfast
Credit Cards: A, B, C
Notes: 2, 5, 7, 9, 10, 12, 14

BERWYN

B & B MidWest Reservations

2223 Crump Lane, Columbus, IN 47203-2009
(812) 378-5855; (800) B AND B (342-2632)
FAX (812) 378-5822
e-mail: reservations@bandbmidwest.com
www.BandBmidwest.com

1903901. Convenient access to downtown Chicago (20 minutes) or Oak Park (5 minutes) makes this apartment-style accommodation a pleasant experience. The apartment has a very large living room, dining room, and kitchen facilities as well as a queen-size bed and full bath. The decor is eclectic and the neighborhood is friendly and safe. Breakfast items are provided for a self-serve breakfast. Use of the kitchen for additional meals is acceptable. Two-night minimum. $99.

BISHOP HILL

B & B MidWest Reservations

2223 Crump Lane, Columbus, IN 47203-2009
(812) 378-5855; (800) B AND B (342-2632)
FAX (812) 378-5822
e-mail: reservations@bandbmidwest.com
www.BandBmidwest.com

03118. Enjoy the feeling of days gone by in this Colonial-style bed and breakfast. Originally built as a colony hospital, the home has been beautifully refurbished with hardwood floors and period furnishings. The home offers three accommodations. One has recently been

---

NOTES: Credit cards accepted: A MasterCard; B Visa; C American Express; D Discover; E Diner's Club; F Other; 2 Personal checks accepted; 3 Lunch available; 4 Dinner available; 5 Open all year; 6 Pets welcome;

completed with queen-size bed, kitchenette, and Jacuzzi in the private bath. The second room has a queen-size bed, private bath, and kitchenette. The third is a two-bedroom suite with kitchen and bath. All guests may enjoy the large porch and front hallway. A Continental breakfast is provided in each kitchenette with fresh breads delivered in the morning. $75-115.

CHICAGO

Amber Creek's Chicago Connection

122 South Bench Street, Galena, 61036 (mailing)
10 West Elm, 60610 (location)
(815) 777-8400; FAX (815) 777-8446

Charming apartment in quiet secure building on Chicago's Gold Coast in the heart of the restaurant and entertainment district. Walk to Michigan Avenue shopping, Water Tower Place, and Lake Michigan. Spacious living room with lake and city views, antique decor, fully equipped kitchen, bath with tub and shower. Romantic, master bedroom with king-size bed, second bedroom with double bed, TV, telephone, answering machine, air conditioned. One block to airport limousine and public transportation. Parking garage across the street. Ideal for one or two couples or a small family.

Hosts: Doug and Kate Freeman
Apartment: 1 (PB) $109-169
Continental Breakfast
Credit Cards: A, B, C, D, E
Notes: 2, 3, 4, 5, 7, 8, 9, 11, 12, 14

City Scene Bed & Breakfast

2101 North Clifton Avenue, 60614
(773) 549-1743; FAX (773) 529-4711
e-mail: cityscene@aol.com
www.citysenebb.com

A cozy, private suite with one or two bedrooms, sitting room, kitchen, and bath in a Vic-

torian four-flat. The furnishings are an interesting mix of antiques and collectibles. Each bedroom has one double bed and the well-stocked kitchen allows guests to prepare breakfast at their leisure. On a quiet residential street in a historic Lincoln Park neighborhood, three miles from downtown Chicago. Nearby are a variety of restaurants, unusual shops, beautiful homes, gardens, and parks.

Host: Mary A. Newman
Suite: $100-190
Continental Breakfast
Credit Cards: None
Notes: 2, 5, 7

COLLINSVILLE

Maggie's Bed & Breakfast

2102 North Keebler Road, 62234
(618) 344-8283

Maggie's sits atop a wooded hill overlooking a quiet lane. This historic former mine superintendent's home features five bedrooms, three have baths en suite, and two share a bath. One private room is accessible to physically challenged guests, and two feature fireplaces. The bed and breakfast is filled with an intriguing collection of unique antiques gathered during Maggie's many years of world-wide travel.

Rooms: 5 (3 PB; 2 SB) $45-100
Full Breakfast
Credit Cards: None
Notes: 2, 5, 7, 9, 11, 12, 15

DANVILLE

B & B MidWest Reservations

2223 Crump Lane, Columbus, IN 47203-2009
(812) 378-5855; (800) B AND B (342-2632)
FAX (812) 378-5822
e-mail: reservations@bandbmidwest.com
www.BandBmidwest.com

11036. This classic Tudor Revival-style home features gabled dormers, side porches, antiques

7 No smoking; 8 Children welcome; 9 Social drinking allowed; 10 Tennis nearby; 11 Swimming nearby; 12 Golf nearby; 13 Skiing nearby; 14 May be booked through a travel agent; 15 Handicapped accessible.

galore, and two and one-half acres of wooded surroundings. Within an easy drive to University of Illinois, Indianapolis activities, Chicago, and Rockville's Covered Bridge Festival, this home has four guest rooms with private or shared baths. Full breakfast. Ten dollars per additional person. $85-115.

DU QUOIN

Francie's Inn On-Line

104 South Line Street, 62832
(618) 542-6686; (877) 877-2657 (toll-free)
FAX (618) 542-4534; e-mail: bbinn@midwest.net
www.midwest.net/bbinn

This inn is the place for a perfect getaway vacation, a romantic adventure, or business retreat. With a full breakfast served, the hosts offer five rooms for guests' pleasure. All rooms are decorated in a Victorian tone, with writing desks and lounging chairs. Meeting/banquet facilities for birthdays, anniversaries, reunions, etc. Within walking distance to shops, dining, movies, fairgrounds. Proud members of the Illinois Bed and Breakfast Association. "Try us—you'll love us!"

Hosts: Benny and Cathy Trowbridge
Rooms: 5 (3 PB; 2 SB) $60-100
Full Breakfast
Credit Cards: A, B, C, D
Notes: 2, 5, 7, 8, 9, 10, 12.

Francie's Inn On-Line

ELDRED

Bluffdale Vacation Farm

Rural Route 1, 62027
(217) 983-2854

Hosts' new hideaway cottage in the woods and log cabin are secluded and luxurious. Soak in the whirlpool while watching the sun set or gazing at the stars, then pop on a robe and enter the guest room where the fireplace is blazing. At the base of the bluff, guests have 200 acres of woodlands to explore.

Hosts: Bill and Lindy Hobson
Rooms: 2 (PB) $95
Full Breakfast
Credit Cards: None
Notes: 2, 5, 7, 8, 9, 12

EVANSTON

B & B MidWest Reservations

2223 Crump Lane, Columbus, IN 47203-2009
(812) 378-5855; (800) B AND B (342-2632)
FAX (812) 378-5822
e-mail: reservations@bandbmidwest.com
www.BandBmidwest.com

04125. Just two blocks from Northwestern University's campus, the immaculate home is the upper level of a two-flat home. A very comfortable day porch and living room are available for guest use. The owner excitedly shares his extensive music library for guests' enjoyment. The accommodations include a king-size bed (side-by-side twins on king headboard) and shared bath with the owner. Very convenient for Evanston or downtown Chicago activities. Continental plus breakfast is served. $75.

16115. In the Evanston Lakeshore Historic District, this grand old Victorian-style home offers antiques, a beautiful wrap-around veranda, and a short walk to Lake Michigan. Accommodations include a queen-size bed with brass headboard, wood-burning fireplace

NOTES: Credit cards accepted: A MasterCard; B Visa; C American Express; D Discover; E Diner's Club; F Other; 2 Personal checks accepted; 3 Lunch available; 4 Dinner available; 5 Open all year; 6 Pets welcome;

in the room, circular bay window, window air conditioner, and private bath. Two additional rooms share a hallway bath. An extended breakfast is served in the morning. $70-115.

GALENA

Accommodations and Reservations In and Around Galena

122 South Bench Street, 61036
(815) 777-8400; FAX (815) 777-8446
www.lodgings@galenareservations.com

Anna's Suite. Vintage townhouse in the heart of Galena's historic district with one-bedroom apartment available for overnight guests. Fireplace, antique decor, queen-size bed, full bath, TV/VCR, telephone, stereo/CD/tape player, fully equipped kitchen. Walk to most of Galena. No smoking. Sleeps two. $89-139.

The Blue Heron. A very private, one-bedroom cottage with a great view of the Mississippi River at Savanna. Five minutes from the Mississippi Palisades State Park and 30 minutes on the Great River Road to Galena. Fireplace, two-person whirlpool, loft with king-size bed, bath with shower, fully equipped kitchen, deck, charcoal grill, spacious yard with outdoor campfire circle. TV/VCR, stereo/CD/tape player, telephone. Walk to downtown for fishing, boating, terrific antique shopping, restaurants, and the movies. Pets permitted by request. No smoking. Sleeps two. $99-179.

Cottage at Amber Creek. This one-bedroom guest cottage on a 300-acre horse ranch was once the summer kitchen for the main house. Secluded in the hills, 20 minutes from Galena, it offers hiking, bird watching, stargazing and wildlife for nature lovers. Fireplace, two-person whirlpool, queen-size bed, fully equipped kitchen. Telephone, stereo/CD/tape player, deck, charcoal grill, small private garden with fountain, campfire circle. Pets permitted by request. No smoking. Sleeps two. $99-139.

Council Hill Guest House. One-room school house tucked into the hills 10 miles east of Galena; nicely restored and furnished in antique-country decor. Fireplace, TV/VCR, stereo/CD/tape player, telephone, fully equipped kitchen, bath with shower and two-person whirlpool. Spiral staircase leads to sleeping loft with queen-size bed. Deck with picnic table and charcoal grill overlooking a beautiful valley. No smoking or pets. Sleeps two. $109-149.

The Eagle's Nest. A delightful 1842 brick cottage tucked into a private wooded hillside in Galena's historic district. Faithfully restored and decorated with period antiques. Master bedroom with queen-size four-poster bed, second bedroom with full bed. Fireplace, TV/VCR, telephone, stereo, full bath with two-person tub, totally equipped kitchen, patio, charcoal grill, landscaped yard with small garden and fountain. Walk to most of Galena. Perfect for antique and history buffs. Children welcome. Pets permitted by request. No smoking. Note: Steep, narrow stairs and walkways in house and on property. Sleeps two to four. $99-169.

Hanover House. Luxurious one-bedroom apartment, over a gift shop, in the small town of Hanover just 15 minutes from Galena on the Great River Road. Spacious living room with fireplace, lots of windows, fully equipped kitchen, bedroom with queen-size bed and double whirlpool bath with two-person shower. TV/VCR, stereo/CD/tape player. Children welcome. No smoking. Sleeps two to four. $129-189.

Harvest Lane. Get back to nature in this casual home surrounded by woods and meadows. Stone fireplace, loft with window seat, and two-person whirlpool, TV/VCR,

7 No smoking; 8 Children welcome; 9 Social drinking allowed; 10 Tennis nearby; 11 Swimming nearby; 12 Golf nearby; 13 Skiing nearby; 14 May be booked through a travel agent; 15 Handicapped accessible.

stereo/CD/tape player, telephone, fully equipped kitchen, washer/dryer. Master bedroom has king-size bed, second bedroom with queen-size bed, two bathrooms. Deck, charcoal grill, spacious yard, excellent hiking, and cross-country skiing. Access to Galena Territory Resort amenities. Children welcome. Pets permitted by request. No smoking. Sleeps two to four. $119-189.

Hazelwood Farm. Beautifully restored and furnished 1860s farmhouse set on a country acre, with lovely gardens just west of Galena. Three bedrooms, two baths, large country kitchen, formal dining room, living room, den with TV/VCR, stereo/CD/tape player, wood-burning fireplace, washer/dryer. Master bedroom has sleigh bed, private staircase, and balcony. Perfect for a family or group of friends. Children welcome. No smoking or pets. Sleeps eight. $225-250.

Logan House Inn. Comfortable suites and rooms at reasonable prices, discounts at the popular restaurant/bar on the main level and the downtown location make the Logan House a good value. All suites and rooms have a queen-size bed, private bath, and TV. Suites also have sleeper-sofas. Continental breakfast is served in the lounge area which has a refrigerator and microwave available for guests' use. Children welcome. Smoking permitted in designated areas only. $75-90.

O'Rourke's Garden Apartment. Contemporary home with one-bedroom garden apartment. Twin beds, antiques, fully equipped kitchen, bath with shower, den with TV/VCR, walking distance to downtown, and most of Galena. Sleeps two. By the week only. $349.

Pine Hollow Inn. The peace and quiet of this beautiful wooded valley just outside of Galena give Pine Hollow a special appeal. Hike along wildflower-lined streams. Enjoy the deer, wild turkeys, blue herons, and other wildlife that share the gorgeous surroundings with human

visitors. The large guest rooms decorated in warm, country style, have queen-size four-poster beds, fireplaces, and private baths, several have whirlpool. Hearty, fresh-baked Continental breakfast. No smoking, children, or pets. $85-125.

Rosebud. This 1842 stone house with two suites is just steps away from Galena's downtown shops and restaurants. Each suite has a queen-size bed, gas fireplace, two-person whirlpool, and private bath. Full breakfast is served in the parlor which is furnished with eclectic antiques from the owner's family. No children, pets, or smoking. $109-149.

Tuk-A-Way Center. A spacious, comfortable lodge nestled on 80 acres of rolling meadows and woodland between Stockton and Mount Carroll. Five bedrooms, two and one-half baths. Fireplace, fully equipped kitchen, washer/dryer, TV/VCR, telephone, fax, copier, stereo/CD/tape player. Large deck area and spacious lawn for outdoor activities. Great for meetings, retreats, family reunions, or a group of friends. Children welcome. No smoking. Sleeps up to 15. $195-245.

The Victorian Mansion. An elegant three-story Victorian home on Quality Hill surrounded by spacious lawns and tree-lined gardens. Antique furnishings, library, formal dining room, double parlor, porches with rocking chairs, and a full gourmet breakfast make staying here a first-class bed and breakfast experience. Each of the eight guest rooms has a private bath, antique marble-top dressers; one bedroom has a fireplace. No children, smoking, or pets. $130-165.

Avery Guest House

606 South Prospect Street, 61036
(815) 777-3883

This pre-Civil War home, within Galena's historic district, is a short walk from antique shops and historic buildings. Enjoy the scenic

Avery Guest House

view from the porch swing. Breakfast is served in the sunny dining room with a bay window overlooking the Galena River valley. Two-night minimum stay required for weekends and holidays.

Hosts: Gerry and Armon Lamparelli
Rooms: 3 (1 PB; 2 SB) $65-90
Full Breakfast
Credit Cards: A, B, D
Notes: 2, 5, 7, 9, 11, 12, 13

B & B MidWest Reservations

2223 Crump Lane, Columbus, IN 47203-2009
(812) 378-5855; (800) B AND B (342-2632)
FAX (812) 378-5822
e-mail: reservations@bandbmidwest.com
www.BandBmidwest.com

06059. A restored cottage secluded in the hills near Galena. This accommodation has air conditioning and beautiful views of the countryside. The Early American decor is carried throughout the suite. Suite consists of queen-size bed, living room with fireplace, Jacuzzi, loft, and private porch. Two-night minimum required on weekends. $125.

06205. A cabin-like suite five miles north of Galena, sitting in 17 acres of pine trees. Suite has deck and private entrance, living room with Franklin fireplace and picture windows, bedroom with queen-size bed, bath with sauna, and small kitchenette. Two-night minimum. $95.

Belle Aire Mansion Guest House

11410 Route 20 West, 61036
(815) 777-0893; e-mail: belleair@galenalink.com
www.galena-bnb.com/belleaire

Belle Aire Mansion is a pre-Civil War home set on 11 beautiful acres just minutes from Galena. Three of the rooms feature gas fireplaces, and the two suites each have a double whirlpool. Two-night minimum stay for weekends is required. Closed Christmas. Guests say, "It's just like visiting friends." The hosts say, "Welcome home—to our home."

Hosts: Jan and Lorraine Svec
Rooms: 5 (PB) $87.20-179.85
Full Breakfast
Credit Cards: A, B, D
Notes: 2, 7, 8, 9, 11, 12, 13, 14

Belle Aire Mansion

Bielenda's Mars Avenue Guest House

515 Mars Avenue, 61036
(815) 777-2808; FAX (815) 777-1157
e-mail: bmarsbb@galenalink.net

This 1855 Federal-style home in Galena's historic district is within walking distance of downtown. One suite with additional bed (can accommodate three) and two large guest rooms. King-, queen-size, and twin beds, private baths, fireplaces in all guest rooms and parlor, antique decor, and porch swing. Full breakfast, evening

7 No smoking; 8 Children welcome; 9 Social drinking allowed; 10 Tennis nearby; 11 Swimming nearby; 12 Golf nearby; 13 Skiing nearby; 14 May be booked through a travel agent; 15 Handicapped accessible.

Bielenda's Mars Avenue Guest House

desserts, central air, and bikes available. "Come let us make you feel special."

Room: 3 (PB) $85-110
Full Breakfast
Credit Cards: A, B, D
Notes: 2, 5, 7, 11, 12, 13

Brierwreath Manor Bed & Breakfast

216 North Bench Street, 61036
(815) 777-0608

Circa 1884 Queen Anne house with wrap-around porch only one short block from historic Main Street. Cable TV, early morning coffee buffet, and full breakfast are only a few of the comforts guests will experience. The manor has three large suites with sitting rooms,

Brierwreath Manor

gas log fireplaces, and private baths. Each room is furnished with antiques and modern comforts. Special packages available.

Hosts: Mike and Lyn Cook
Suites: 3 (PB) $95-105
Full Breakfast
Credit Cards: None
Notes: 2, 5, 7, 9, 11, 12, 13

Captain Harris Guest House

Captain Harris Guest House

713 South Bench Street, 61036
(815) 777-4713; FAX (815) 777-4723
www.galena-bnb.com/CptnHarris

Robert Scribe Harris, steamboat captain and lead mine owner, built this 1836 home that was enhanced with the addition of 50 leaded-glass windows in the 1920s. Within walking distance of downtown Galena, with three guest rooms, one guest suite, and detached honeymoon cottage. Guest living room and library, color TV in every room.

Rooms: 5 (PB) $90-175
Full Breakfast
Credit Cards: A, B, D
Notes: 2, 5, 7, 11, 12, 13

Grandview Guest Home

113 South Prospect Street, 61036
(815) 777-1387; (800) 373-0732

A 129-year-old brick traditional on Quality Hill, overlooking the city and countryside. Vic-

NOTES: Credit cards accepted: A MasterCard; B Visa; C American Express; D Discover; E Diner's Club; F Other; 2 Personal checks accepted; 3 Lunch available; 4 Dinner available; 5 Open all year; 6 Pets welcome;

Grandview Guest Home

countryside, four guest rooms, queen-size beds, private baths, full breakfast, central air, stained- and beveled-glass windows, coal burning and gas fireplaces, antique decor. IBBA, ABBA (three-crown rating 1994-1997), and Mobil inspected and approved. Children over 10 welcome. Discounts for senior citizens. No smoking. No pets.

Hosts: Roger and Evelyn Bird
Rooms: 4 (PB) $99-149
Full Breakfast
Credit Cards: None
Notes: 2, 5, 7, 9, 10, 11, 12, 13, 14

torian furnishings. The full breakfast features home-baked goods and European coffees. Two blocks from Main Street shops, museums, and restaurants.

Hosts: Harry and Marjorie Dugan
Rooms: 3 (1 PB; 2 SB) $70-90
Full Breakfast
Credit Cards: A, B, C, D
Notes: 2, 5, 7, 8, 9, 10, 11, 12, 13

Hellman Guest House

318 Hill Street, 61036
(815) 777-3638

An 1895 Queen Anne Victorian home with wraparound porch overlooking downtown and

Hellman Guest House

Park Avenue Guest House

Park Avenue Guest House

208 Park Avenue, 61036
(815) 777-1075; (800) 359-0743

An 1893 Queen Anne "painted lady," with wraparound screened porch and shaded garden with gazebo. Original woodwork, queen-size beds, and antique furniture. Central air conditioning. In-room fireplaces and TV. Twelve full Christmas trees for viewing during November, December, and January. Walk to town; ample parking.

Host: Sharon Fallbacher
Rooms: 4 (PB) $75-125
Full Breakfast
Credit Cards: A, B, C, D
Notes: 2, 5, 7, 9, 10, 11, 12, 13

7 No smoking; 8 Children welcome; 9 Social drinking allowed; 10 Tennis nearby; 11 Swimming nearby; 12 Golf nearby; 13 Skiing nearby; 14 May be booked through a travel agent; 15 Handicapped accessible.

Pine Hollow Inn

4700 North Council Hill Road, 61036
(815) 777-1071

This cottage-style country home, on 120 acres, is secluded in a wooded valley two minutes north of Main Street Galena. The inn contains four suites and one guest room. All bedrooms have private bedside wood-burning fireplaces. Rooms are furnished in country decor and includes four-poster queen-size beds, private whirlpool and conventional baths, sky lights, stained-glass windows. This home includes a wraparound porch, giving guests a chance to put their feet up and enjoy the peace and quiet of this country setting. Pine Hollow also provides guests with access to cross-country skiing, wildlife, hiking, and streams to walk along.

Hosts: Sally and Larry Priske
Rooms: 5 (PB) $75-125
Continental Breakfast
Credit Cards: A, B, D
Notes: 2, 5, 7, 9, 10, 11, 12, 13

GENEVA

B & B MidWest Reservations

2223 Crump Lane, Columbus, IN 47203-2009
(812) 378-5855; (800) B AND B (342-2632)
FAX (812) 378-5822
e-mail: reservations@bandbmidwest.com
www.BandBmidwest.com

19068. Large, restored estate mansion in a country setting surrounded by seven acres of gardens and grounds. Outdoor swimming pool available (weather permitting). Seven master guest rooms offer a large range of accommodations with period furniture and some antiques. Large living room with fireplace available for guests. Some private baths and some rooms can accommodate up to four people. Nearby shopping at antique and craft shops. Lower rates Sunday through Thursday. Full country breakfast. $119-140.

GURNEE

B & B MidWest Reservations

2223 Crump Lane, Columbus, IN 47203-2009
(812) 378-5855; (800) B AND B (342-2632)
FAX (812) 378-5822
e-mail: reservations@bandbmidwest.com
www.BandBmidwest.com

10030. "Wonderful" describes this cozy country farmhouse, one-half mile from Six Flags Great America theme park. Handmade quilts, feather comforters, and antiques throughout make staying in one of the three guest rooms a special experience. Accommodations include two rooms with private baths; family two-room suite sleeping up to four; and separate cottage with kitchenette. Living room fireplace. Short drive to outlet mall, Lake Michigan, horseback riding, and other sports. Llama and sheep on premises. Full breakfast. Fifteen dollars per each additional person. $95-125.

Sweet Basil Hill
Bed & Breakfast Inn

15937 West Washington Street, 60031
(847) 244-3333

Sitting atop a hill on seven and one-half wooded acres, this inn is midway between Chicago and Milwaukee. Sheep and llamas,

Sweet Basil Hill

paths, gardens, hammock, and a lawn swing all offer a more restful pace. The common room, with English pine antiques and fireplace, make a cozy winter retreat. Full breakfast, beverages, and snacks served in the knotty-pine breakfast room. Featured in the August 1991 *Country Home* magazine, April 1993 *Country Inns*, and *The Romance of Country Inns* by Gail Greco. Private telephones, TV, VCR, video library, and individual air conditioning in all rooms.

Hosts: Teri and Bob Jones
Rooms: 3 (PB) $95-150
Full Breakfast
Credit Cards: A, B, C, D, E
Notes: 2, 5, 7, 8, 9, 10, 11, 12, 13, 14

The 258 Inn

HIGHLAND PARK

B & B MidWest Reservations

2223 Crump Lane, Columbus, IN 47203-2009
(812) 378-5855; (800) B AND B (342-2632)
FAX (812) 378-5822
e-mail: reservations@bandbmidwest.com
www.BandBmidwest.com

16048. Nestled in the ravines of the North Shore in the Highland Park area, this 1926 English Colonial-style brick home sits quietly on a wooded lot. Conveniently located just two blocks from Ravinia Music Park and a private neighborhood beach on Lake Michigan, guests will enjoy the warmth and hospitality from the host couple. Guests rave about the TLC exuded during their stays at this fine location. Two rooms with double beds and private baths. One room has an additional sleeping area for an extra person ($20 a night). Third room has a king-size bed with a bath shared with the owners. An extensive gourmet full breakfast is served in the dining room. All kinds of extras. $120-130.

JACKSONVILLE

The 258 Inn Bed & Breakfast

258 West Morton Road, 62650
(217) 245-2588

This 1840 house restored with a bridal suite and antique country rooms. A Quilt shop downstairs with a Bed-Bath and Kitchen shop. There are 450 bolts of calico and patterns. A Continental plus breakfast of fruits and homemade breads. Smoking is not permitted indoors. No pets. Children over 12 are welcome. Smoking permitted on outside porch only.

Host: Rosalee McKinley
Rooms: 3 (PB) $60-70
Continental Breakfast
Credit Cards: None
Notes: 2, 7, 9, 10, 11, 12

JERSEYVILLE

The Homeridge Bed & Breakfast

1470 North State Street, 62052
(618) 498-3442

Beautiful brick Italianate Victorian private home, circa 1867, on 18 acres in comfortable country atmosphere. Drive through stately iron gates and pine-tree-lined driveway to the 14-room historic estate of Senator Theodore Chapman. Beautiful, expansive pillared front porch. Hand-carved stairway to spacious guest rooms and third floor. Large swimming pool.

7 No smoking; 8 Children welcome; 9 Social drinking allowed; 10 Tennis nearby; 11 Swimming nearby; 12 Golf nearby; 13 Skiing nearby; 14 May be booked through a travel agent; 15 Handicapped accessible.

Homeridge

Central air conditioning. Between Springfield, Illinois, and St. Louis, Missouri.

Hosts: Sue and Howard Landon
Rooms: 4 (PB) $75-85
Full Breakfast
Credit Cards: A, B, C
Notes: 2, 5, 7, 10, 11, 12

MAEYSTOWN

Corner George Inn

Corner of Main and Mill, P.O. Box 103, 62256
(618) 458-6660; (800) 458-6020
FAX (618) 458-7770; e-mail: cornrgeo@htc.net

Built as a frontier Victorian hotel and saloon in 1884, the Corner George Inn is 45 minutes south of St. Louis in a quaint 19th century German village. Seven guest rooms with private baths include a guest cottage, log cabin, and claw-foot whirlpool suite. Area offers shops, restaurants, horse-drawn carriages, biking, hiking, and golf. Nearby are Fort de

Corner George Inn

Chartres, Fort Kaskaskia, and the scenic Mississippi bluff road.

Hosts: David and Marcia Braswell
Rooms: 7 (PB) $77-149
Full Breakfast
Credit Cards: A, B, C, D
Notes: 2, 5, 7, 12, 14, 15

METROPOLIS

Isle of View/Bed & Breakfast

205 Metropolis Street, 62960
(618) 524-5838; (800) 566-7491
FAX (618) 524-2978; e-mail: kimoff@hcis.net
www.bbonline.com/il/isleofview

Elegant Victorian mansion one block from riverboat casino, offers five spacious guest rooms. Private baths feature antique claw-foot tubs and showers. Three rooms also have extra-large whirlpool tubs and two working fireplaces. A full gourmet breakfast is served at guests' convenience. Two hours north of Nashville, Tennessee, and two and one-half hours southeast of St. Louis, Missouri. Area offers hunting, fishing, antiquing, theater, and museums.

Hosts: Kim and Gerald Offenburger
Rooms: 5 (PB) $65-125
Full Breakfast
Credit Cards: A, B, C, D, E, F
Notes: 2, 5, 6, 9, 12, 14

MINONK

Victorian Oaks Bed & Breakfast

435 Locust Street, 61760
(309) 432-2771; FAX (309) 432-3309
e-mail: victorian@davesworld.net

This 1895 Victorian home is nestled in a small Midwestern town where peace and quiet abound. Guests select a full breakfast from an extensive menu at a time they choose. All meals, homemade from scratch

---

NOTES: Credit cards accepted: A MasterCard; B Visa; C American Express; D Discover; E Diner's Club; F Other; 2 Personal checks accepted; 3 Lunch available; 4 Dinner available; 5 Open all year; 6 Pets welcome;

Victorian Oaks

on the premises, are served by candlelight on fine china with gold flatware atop a table covered with linen tablecloths and crisp linen napkins. In the winter, guests may choose to dine in front of a roaring fire in front of the marble fireplace.

Host: Sharon Kimzey
Rooms: 5 (3 PB; 2 SB) $60-115
Full Breakfast
Credit Cards: A, B, D
Notes: 3, 4, 5, 6, 9, 11, 12, 14, 15

MORRISON

B & B MidWest Reservations

2223 Crump Lane, Columbus, IN 47203-2009
(812) 378-5855; (800) B AND B (342-2632)
FAX (812) 378-5822
e-mail: reservations@bandbmidwest.com
www.BandBmidwest.com

23063. This 102-year-old bed and breakfast was built by E. A. Smith for his bride. Ten guest rooms with private baths, some with Jacuzzis. Separate cottage with gas-log fireplace, oversize spa for two, and deck. Breakfast, 7-9 A.M., includes a full range of home-cooked and baked items. Near the Quad Cities and riverboat gambling in Clinton, Iowa,

there are many cultural and scenic activities available to guests. $60-160.

MOUNT CARMEL

B & B MidWest Reservations

2223 Crump Lane, Columbus, IN 47203-2009
(812) 378-5855; (800) B AND B (342-2632)
FAX (812) 378-5822
e-mail: reservations@bandbmidwest.com
www.BandBmidwest.com

19056. This historic landmark home is along the Wabash River. Travelers enjoy a warm, friendly atmosphere found in earlier days. Browse through historic artifacts on display or sing around the antique player piano. Four guest accommodations include two two-bedroom suites, each with private bath. Each of the two other rooms has a double bed and private bath. Full breakfast served. Twenty-five-acre park with well-stocked lake adjacent to bed and breakfast, and lots more. $45-85.

MUNDELEIN

B & B MidWest Reservations

2223 Crump Lane, Columbus, IN 47203-2009
(812) 378-5855; (800) B AND B (342-2632)
FAX (812) 378-5822
e-mail: reservations@bandbmidwest.com
www.BandBmidwest.com

12049. This grand old house, built in the early 1900s, features 44 windows throughout. Halfway between Chicago and Milwaukee, this location is convenient to Long Grove Village, Ravinia Park, Lamb's Farm, and more. Old-fashioned decor and a musical theme are woven together throughout this Victorian home. Three guest rooms share full bath. Two rooms have private baths. Two bedrooms with a bath booked as a suite. Another suite with one bedroom, a private bath, sitting area, and fireplace. Rates include Continental plus breakfast. $60-120.

7 No smoking; 8 Children welcome; 9 Social drinking allowed; 10 Tennis nearby; 11 Swimming nearby; 12 Golf nearby; 13 Skiing nearby; 14 May be booked through a travel agent; 15 Handicapped accessible.

NAPERVILLE

B & B MidWest Reservations

2223 Crump Lane, Columbus, IN 47203-2009
(812) 378-5855; (800) B AND B (342-2632)
FAX (812) 378-5822
e-mail: reservations@bandbmidwest.com
www.BandBmidwest.com

08057. Nestled in historic Naperville, this circa 1904 home has been restored to reflect the elegance of the past. The home has unique antique furnishings and period fixtures and yet offers color TV and central air conditioning. Enjoy the luxury of monogrammed fluffy overside towels, fresh flowers, and complimentary refreshments and hearty full breakfast. Four guest rooms offer private baths. In addition, one suite also offers a Jacuzzi and shower. Antique quilts, feather beds, and lace curtains make this a bed and breakfast that guests never forget. $118-158.

OAK BROOK

B & B MidWest Reservations

2223 Crump Lane, Columbus, IN 47203-2009
(812) 378-5855; (800) B AND B (342-2632)
FAX (812) 378-5822
e-mail: reservations@bandbmidwest.com
www.BandBmidwest.com

01043. Contemporary suburban home sits nestled in surprisingly quiet wooded acreage convenient to Drury Lane Theater, Oakbrook Shopping Center, many corporate centers, and thoroughfare highways. Three newly decorated guest accommodations offer queen-size beds and private baths. Guests have access to fully equipped kitchen to prepare other meals on their own and very large common great room with fireplace and lounge. Continental breakfast served. $70.

04044. Lovely sprawling home, conveniently near interstates and public transportation, offers four guest rooms with private baths. The master suite boasts a double Jacuzzi and queen-size bed. Two other rooms offer a queen-size bed with detached private bath. Fourth room has a single bed with detached private bath for one. A formal Continental plus breakfast served. $45-95.

OAKLAND

Inn on the Square

3 Montgomery, P.O. Box 945, 61943
(217) 346-2289

This 1878 restored Colonial inn offers a potpourri of the "village experience." Antiques, flowers, gifts, and ladies' apparel shops all pique guests' curiosity. The tea room offers simple but luxurious luncheons. Dinner is available Friday and Saturday, 5-8 P.M., and Sunday, 11 A.M.-2 P.M. Golf, swimming, conservation park, Amish settlement, and Lincoln historical sites nearby. Inquire about accommodations for children.

Hosts: Gary and Linda Miller
Rooms: 3 (PB) $50-55
Full Breakfast
Credit Cards: A, B
Notes: 2, 3, 4, 5, 7, 10, 11, 12, 14, 15

Inn on the Square

OAK PARK

B & B MidWest Reservations

2223 Crump Lane, Columbus, IN 47203-2009
(812) 378-5855; (800) B AND B (342-2632)
FAX (812) 378-5822
e-mail: reservations@bandbmidwest.com
www.BandBmidwest.com

02116. This newly refurbished Victorian-style home offers comfort, style, and hospitality galore. Two rooms sharing a bath on the main level are tastefully decorated with antiques. The hosts offer warmth and hospitality to each guest. The morning Continental breakfast during the week or the full breakfast on weekends is elegantly served in the dining room. $70.

04118. Large Victorian brick home offers one guest accommodation with a king-size bed and detached private bath. Collections and furnishing from the 70s make this a unique location. Full Breakfast. $65.

13096. A 1909 English-style home furnished with Victorian antiques, oriental rugs, and Laura Ashley wallpapers. Two of the three guest rooms have entrance to a lovely second-floor screened porch with wicker furniture. The largest room has a queen-size bed with private bath, fireplace, and comfortable reading chaise lounge. The second room offers two beds, a reading chair, and shared bath. The third room has a four-poster bed, chair, and shared bath. A full breakfast is served in the paneled dining room with its restored mural border. $65-100.

15099. Queen Anne Victorian home in a prominent historic suburb one block from Frank Lloyd Wright's home and studio and 20 minutes from Chicago. The home, built in 1885, is air conditioned. One room has a large queen-size bed with private bath and Victorian-style antiques; two other rooms offer either twin beds with a desk work area and TV or a king-size bed with shared bath just steps from the room. Enjoy a family-style Continental breakfast or sit on the veranda when weather permits. Children an additional $10. $65-75.

19111. Truly for the followers and admirers of Frank Lloyd Wright, this home is one of Mr. Wright's architectural creations. Furnished entirely with his signatured pieces and in keeping with his choice of decor. Stay in one of two suites in the lower level of this remarkable home with private entrances. Each suite includes two bedrooms, dining area, bar sink, refrigerator, microwave, gas fireplace. Jacuzzis in large baths. Stocked refrigerator provides food for a light Continental self-serve breakfast. Two-night minimum stay most weekends. Additional $25 for second couple in same suite. $155.

PEORIA (MOSSVILLE)

Old Church House Inn Bed & Breakfast

1416 East Mossville Road, Mossville, 61552
(309) 579-2300
e-mail: church.house@MCIone.com

Come take sanctuary from the cares of life in this 1869 country church. Includes historic building, 18-foot ceilings, library loft, Victorian antiques, classical music, afternoon tea, crackling fire, pillow chocolates, featherbeds, and flower gardens. Nearby are Rock Island

Old Church House Inn

---

7 No smoking; 8 Children welcome; 9 Social drinking allowed; 10 Tennis nearby; 11 Swimming nearby; 12 Golf nearby; 13 Skiing nearby; 14 May be booked through a travel agent; 15 Handicapped accessible.

Bike Trail, tearooms, antiquing, riverboat cruises, fine dining, scenic drives, and sweet memories. Continental plus breakfast. IBBA inspected and approved.

Hosts: Dean and Holly Ramseyer
Rooms: 2 (1 PB; 2 SB) $75-109
Continental Breakfast
Credit Cards: A, B, D
Notes: 2, 5, 7, 10, 11, 12, 13, 14

PINCKNEYVILLE

Oxbow Bed & Breakfast

3967 State Route 13/127, 62274
(618) 357-9839; (800) 929-6888

The Oxbow Bed and Breakfast, a 16-room brick country home, has six lovely guest rooms with private baths and queen-size beds covered with pretty quilts. The honeymoon suite is in a 1915 restored barn. Guests can find the charm of the Old South and Civil War period on these 10 acres in a peaceful rural area. Enjoy antique furniture, Arabian horses, restored barns, a woodworking shop, windmills, and fountain. Delicious full country breakfast is served. Covered swimming pool. Children over six welcome.

Hosts: Al and Peggy Doughty
Rooms: 6 (PB) $50-65
Full Breakfast
Credit Cards: A, B
Notes: 2, 5, 7, 10, 11, 12, 14

ROCHESTER

B & B MidWest Reservations

2223 Crump Lane, Columbus, IN 47203-2009
(812) 378-5855; (800) B AND B (342-2632)
FAX (812) 378-5822
e-mail: reservations@bandbmidwest.com
www.BandBmidwest.com

13047. Newly constructed country getaway is just 10 miles from Springfield. Beautifully furnished with country antiques, the home offers a huge wraparound porch for guests to marvel over gorgeous sunsets and farm fields. Relax while star gazing in the late evening or sipping fresh coffee while smelling the fresh dew on the surrounding fields in the morning. Four guest rooms offer private baths, queen-size beds, and TVs. The romantic suite offers a gas fireplace and large double whirlpool tub also. Gracious hosts offer a hearty self-serve breakfast on weekdays; full breakfast on weekends. $75-125.

Country Dreams Bed & Breakfast

3410 Park Lane, 62563
(217) 498-9210; FAX (217) 498-8178
e-mail: host@countrydreams.com
www.countrydreams.com

Wide-open spaces and friendly faces. Country Dreams is a new bed and breakfast, built from ground up in 1997 to be a cozy, comfortable, country hideaway. Only 10 miles from downtown Springfield, Illinois. Country Dreams Bed and Breakfast is close enough to the city to be convenient and rural in all the best ways. On 16 acres of beautiful rural Illinois farmland, Country Dreams provides panoramic views of a small lake with swans, ducks, and geese and miles of fertile fields. View acres of green grass, flowers by the thousands, vegetable gardens, fruit orchards, and cattle. Continental breakfast is served Monday through Thursday. Full breakfast is served on weekends.

Hosts: Ralph and Kay Muhs
Rooms: 4 (PB) $60-135
Continental and Full Breakfast
Credit Cards: A, B, C
Notes: 2, 5, 7, 9, 12, 14, 15

ROCK ISLAND

Bed and Breakfasts of the Quad City Area Room Availability Cooperative

P.O. Box 3464, 61201
(319) 322-5055

Leisure Harbor Leisure Inn. (309) 654-2233. Pre-Victorian home. Four guest rooms with private baths plus library, sitting room, and sun porch, on the Mississippi River, will make guests' stay enjoyable. The river offers fantastic views of eagles in the winter as well as a peaceful summer resting spot. $69-79.

Top o' the Morning. (309) 786-3513. This 18-room brick mansion was originally built by Hiram S. Cable, president of Rock Island Railroad, in 1912. It sits in a central location overlooking the Mississippi River. $40-100.

Victorian Inn. (800) 728-7068. In the heart of old Rock Island. Antiques adorn six spacious guest rooms with private baths. Enjoy a formal breakfast on fine china and sterling silver. Step back in time to gracious living in this treasure, which is listed in the National Register of Historic Places. $65 and up.

Top o' the Morning

1505 19th Avenue, 61201
(309) 786-3513

Sam and Peggy welcome guests to this brick mansion on the bluffs overlooking the Mississippi River. Fantastic view day or night. Three-acre wooded estate with winding drive, orchard, and gardens. Air-conditioned bedrooms, whirlpool tub, and natural fireplaces in the dining area and parlor.

Hosts: Sam and Peggy Doak
Rooms: 3 (PB) $40-100
Full Breakfast
Credit Cards: A, B
Notes: 2, 5, 7, 8, 9, 10, 11, 12, 13

Victorian Inn Bed & Breakfast

702 20th Street, 61201
(309) 788-7068; (800) 728-7068
FAX (309) 788-7086

Light from the windows of the stained-glass tower welcomes guests to the Victorian Inn Bed and Breakfast. In the Broadway historic

Victorian Inn

area near riverboat gambling and festival attractions. Antiques adorn the five spacious guest rooms with private baths. Close to Augustana College. Built with Old World charm in 1876. Step back in time to gracious living in this home listed in the National Register of Historic Places. Enjoy the black squirrels and birds in the sanctuary on the grounds. Inquire about accommodations for children. AAA three-diamond-rated.

Hosts: David and Barbara Parker
Rooms: 5 (PB) $65-85
Full Breakfast
Credit Cards: A, B, C
Notes: 2, 5, 7, 10, 11, 12, 13

ST. CHARLES

B & B MidWest Reservations

2223 Crump Lane, Columbus, IN 47203-2009
(812) 378-5855; (800) B AND B (342-2632)
FAX (812) 378-5822
e-mail: reservations@bandbmidwest.com
www.BandBmidwest.com

07076. A very special hideaway near St. Charles offers a large grotto accommodation with a double bed, kitchenette, fireplace, private bath with oversize whirlpool, telephone, TV, and VCR. Nestled in a picturesque

7 No smoking; 8 Children welcome; 9 Social drinking allowed; 10 Tennis nearby; 11 Swimming nearby; 12 Golf nearby; 13 Skiing nearby; 14 May be booked through a travel agent; 15 Handicapped accessible.

pine-covered courtyard with French doors leading to this quiet retreat. The property includes two acres and borders a forest preserve. Nearby entertainment includes canoeing, bike trails, and sports. Continental plus breakfast is served. $125.

floating spindle staircase, gleaming chandeliers, and magnificent French doors. Four guest rooms with private baths. Full breakfast and evening treats greet all the lucky guests. Saturday gourmet dinners are available for additional fee. $75-150.

SANDWICH

B & B MidWest Reservations

2223 Crump Lane, Columbus, IN 47203-2009
(812) 378-5855; (800) B AND B (342-2632)
FAX (812) 378-5822
e-mail: reservations@bandbmidwest.com
www.BandBmidwest.com

13039. This 1930 English Cape Cod-style home in rural Sandwich will remind guests of New England with its stone wall fence and English perennial gardens. Three guest accommodations include a king-size bed suite with private bath and fireplace decorated in wedgewood blues. Each the other two guest rooms, decorated in the English and Victorian traditions, includes a queen-size bed with private bath (shower only). Beautifully manicured grounds. Continental breakfast weekdays; full breakfast on weekends. $95-125.

SHEFFIELD

B & B MidWest Reservations

2223 Crump Lane, Columbus, IN 47203-2009
(812) 378-5855; (800) B AND B (342-2632)
FAX (812) 378-5822
e-mail: reservations@bandbmidwest.com
www.BandBmidwest.com

02046. "The perfect bed and breakfast" is the comment often heard by satisfied guests after leaving this beautiful classic New England-style country inn built in 1845 in Sheffield just off I-80. The home offers gracious accommodations in the English tradition, a three-story

SPRINGFIELD

B & B MidWest Reservations

2223 Crump Lane, Columbus, IN 47203-2009
(812) 378-5855; (800) B AND B (342-2632)
FAX (812) 378-5822
e-mail: reservations@bandbmidwest.com
www.BandBmidwest.com

11037. Visit the hometown of the Abraham Lincoln family and enjoy this historic inn with four guest accommodations. Built in the 1860s, the Italianate-style national historic home offers three rooms with queen-size beds and one with twin beds. Each room has a private bath. The home has been decorated in Traditional, Early 19th-Century, Art Deco, and Empire styles with antiques and historical artifacts of the capital's political influences. Continental breakfast is served. $65-75.

Inn at 835

835 South Second Street, 62704
(217) 523-4466; FAX (217) 523-4468
www.innat835.com

Experience Old World charm, while enjoying the conveniences of a modern hotel. Private verandas, cozy fireplaces, and Jacuzzis await visitors. Guests are treated to delicious wines and cheeses upon arrival, as well as a sumptuous gourmet breakfast each morning. This grand 1909 structure was placed in the National Register of Historic Places in 1995. Recently renovated, the building retains period features and elegant character. Refined Arts and Crafts details include oak and cherry woodwork. Restored wood floors are accented

---

NOTES: Credit cards accepted: A MasterCard; B Visa; C American Express; D Discover; E Diner's Club; F Other; 2 Personal checks accepted; 3 Lunch available; 4 Dinner available; 5 Open all year; 6 Pets welcome;

In at 835

by lush Robert Morris-inspired rugs. Plump queen-size beds in each guest room inspire visitors to linger, while period antiques add warmth to the professionally decorated rooms. The Inn at 835 also offers eight elegant and versatile meeting rooms to accommodate groups from 10 to 150.

Hosts: Court and Karen Conn
Rooms: 7 (PB) $92.50-135
Full Breakfast
Credit Cards: A, B, D, E
Notes: 2, 5, 7, 9, 10, 11, 12, 14, 15

TAYLORVILLE

B & B MidWest Reservations

2223 Crump Lane, Columbus, IN 47203-2009
(812) 378-5855; (800) B AND B (342-2632)
FAX (812) 378-5822
e-mail: reservations@bandbmidwest.com
www.BandBmidwest.com

08015. Filled with antiques, this 1892 historic home was fully restored in 1994. The Victorian-style home offers eight guest rooms with private baths. Five rooms have double Jacuzzis; some have fireplaces. Beautifully decorated throughout the home with lovely antiques. Taylorville is an easy 30-minute drive

to Springfield and Decatur. Full gourmet breakfast is served. $75-95.

WEST DUNDEE

B & B MidWest Reservations

2223 Crump Lane, Columbus, IN 47203-2009
(812) 378-5855; (800) B AND B (342-2632)
FAX (812) 378-5822
e-mail: reservations@bandbmidwest.com
www.BandBmidwest.com

08040. Guests step back into the early 1900s when visiting this newly renovated historical site. This mansion is filled with antiques and royal hospitality while convenient shopping malls, interstate highways, and business districts are within a few minutes drive. The eight uniquely decorated rooms range from smaller country style to formal Colonial doubles to Victorian suites with Jacuzzis and private baths. Some rooms have shared baths with Jacuzzis for guests. Central air conditioning. Full breakfast is served. Small weddings and seminars are welcome. $49-179.

WINNETKA

Chateau des Fleurs

552 Ridge Road, 60093
(847) 256-7272 (phone/FAX)

This authentic French country home, built in 1936, is filled with antiques and has been

Chateau des Fleurs

featured in two newspapers. It offers elegant respite from the world, welcoming guests with light, beauty, warmth, and lovely views from every window. Near a private road for walking and jogging. The inn is four blocks from the Northwestern train commuting to the Chicago Loop. Antique shops and stores of all kinds are only blocks away. Lake Michigan is 10 blocks east and O'Hare Airport 30 minutes west. Two-night minimum stay on weekends. Children over 15 are welcome.

Host: Sally Ward
Rooms: 3 (PB) $130
Full Breakfast
Credit Cards: None
Notes: 2, 5, 7, 9, 10, 11, 12, 13

WOODSTOCK

B & B MidWest Reservations

2223 Crump Lane, Columbus, IN 47203-2009
(812) 378-5855; (800) B AND B (342-2632)
FAX (812) 378-5822
e-mail: reservations@bandbmidwest.com
www.BandBmidwest.com

11112. A lovely Victorian-style home near the square of Woodstock provides a charming getaway. Enjoy the older small town with its quaint shops and the Woodstock Opera theater. Two guest rooms are available each with queen-size bed and private bath. A Continental plus breakfast will be provided. Lovely antiques throughout the home. $75.

NOTES: Credit cards accepted: A MasterCard; B Visa; C American Express; D Discover; E Diner's Club; F Other; 2 Personal checks accepted; 3 Lunch available; 4 Dinner available; 5 Open all year; 6 Pets welcome;

Indiana

ANDERSON

Plum Retreat Bed & Breakfast

926 Historic West 8th Street, 46016
(765) 649-7586

Come experience the ambiance of an 1892 Queen Anne Victorian home nestled in Anderson's historic district. Gaslights lining the streets and candle-lit windows welcome the weary traveler. Stained and leaded glass windows and doors, beautiful fireplace mantels, chandeliers, antiques, tapestries, a library, breakfast gazebo room, wraparound porch filled with wicker furniture, yard and gardens with willow furniture are all for guests enjoyment when they stay at the Plum Retreat.

Hosts: John and Marilyn Bertacchi
Rooms: 3 (1 PB; 2 SB) $70-120
Full Breakfast
Credit Cards: None
Notes: 2, 5, 7, 10, 11, 12

ANGOLA

Sycamore Hill Bed & Breakfast

1245 Golden Lake Road, 46703
(219) 665-2690

This two-story Colonial pillared home was built in 1963 by master craftsmen. Tucked away amid 26 acres of rolling hills and woods. Great for bird watching. Shady back yard with two picnic tables at guests' disposal. Sumptuous breakfast. Gas grill in the back yard. Six minutes from Pokagon State Park beaches, nature trails, canoeing, and golfing.

Host: Betsey Goranson
Rooms: 4 (1 PB; 3 SB) $40-60
Full Breakfast
Credit Cards: A, B
Notes: 2, 5, 7, 8, 10, 11, 12, 13, 14

BETHLEHEM

Inn at Bethlehem

101 Walnut and Riverview, 47104
(812) 293-3975 (phone/FAX); (888) 293-9195
e-mail: bethinn@aye.net

An elegant historic country inn overlooking the mighty Ohio River. The 1830 home is listed in the National Register of Historic Places. Located in a remote river valley in the hills of southern Indiana, the decorator designed inn and lodge provide a quiet retreat from the cares of the world. It is a beautiful setting for a business conference, family getaway, or intimate wedding. Boat dock, rocking chairs, outstanding scenery, peace and quiet in abundance.

Hosts: Chester and Jeanne Browne;
    Gloria J. Childers, manager
Room: 9 (PB) $75-200
Full Breakfast
Credit Cards: A, B
Notes: 2, 3, 4, 5, 7, 8, 9, 12, 14

BEVERLY SHORES

Dunes Shore Inn

33 Lake Shore County Road, Box 807, 46301-0807
(219) 879-9029

A casual bed and breakfast in secluded Beverly Shores, open since 1985. Surrounded by the

Indiana

Indiana Dunes State and National Lakeshore Parks. Miles of beaches and trails, spectacular sunrises and sunsets, and an ever-changing lake await guests. One block off Lake Michigan, one hour from Chicago, three hours from Indianapolis. Whether a party of one, a small group, or a family reunion, this is a great place to relax in a four-season oasis. Continental plus breakfast served. Open mid-April through mid-November.

Hosts: Rosemary and Fred Braun
Rooms: 12 (4 SB) $60-70
Continental Breakfast
Credit Cards: None
Notes: 2, 7, 8, 9, 10, 11, 12

BLUFFTON

The Washington Street Inn

220 East Washington Street, 46714
(219) 824-9070

The Washington Street Inn is an 1896 Queen Anne-style home. Charming guest rooms have TVs, telephones, and clock radios. (Three queen-size beds and one full-size bed.) The inn features a guest kitchen with a refrigerator and microwave. Common areas include living and dining room and a study. Sit by either of two cherry fireplaces and relax or admire the family heirlooms and antiques throughout the inn. Continental breakfast served Monday through Friday; full breakfast served weekends.

The Washington Street Inn

Rooms: 4 (4 SB)
Continental and Full Breakfast
Credit Cards: A, B
Notes: 2, 5, 7, 9, 11, 12

COLUMBUS

B & B MidWest Reservations

2223 Crump Lane, Columbus, IN 47203-2009
(812) 378-5855; (800) B AND B (342-2632)
FAX (812) 378-5822
e-mail: reservations@bandbmidwest.com
www.BandBmidwest.com

15058. A Greek Revival-style home stately sits encompassed with a black wrought iron fence in the heart of architecturally famous Columbus. The property consumes an entire city block of grounds and tall shade trees. This home was recently renovated throughout and turned into a bed and breakfast. Four guest rooms offer a king-size bed, a small sitting area, and private bath with old-fashioned tub; queen-size bed, gas fireplace, whirlpool tub; and two rooms with queen-size beds and private baths. All rooms have TV, VCR, and telephones. A full candlelight breakfast is served. $65-85.

CONNERSVILLE

Maple Leaf Inn Bed & Breakfast

831 Grand Avenue, 47331
(765) 825-7099; e-mail: dorrper@si-net.com

This lovely 1860s brick home has been an established bed and breakfast since 1989. Across from the public library and within walking distance to the downtown Connersville area. Decorated comfortably with antiques and local artwork, this is the perfect place for a quiet getaway. Nearby are attractions such as Brookville Reservoir, Antique Alley, Mary Gray Bird Sanctuary, and the

Maple Leaf Inn

charming canal/tourist destination of Metamora. The Whitewater Valley Railroad will begin leaving from its new depot in the Spring of 1999—only a few blocks from the Maple Leaf Inn Bed and Breakfast.

Rooms: 3 (PB) $55-65
Full Breakfast
Credit Cards: A, B, C
Notes: 2, 5, 7, 8, 10, 12, 14

COVINGTON

Green Gables Bed & Breakfast

504 Fancy Street, 47932
(765) 793-7164

Covington's first bed and breakfast offers three guest rooms, each with private bath, including the spacious loft with two queen-size beds. Each room has a TV; the entire house is air conditioned. Home-cooked breakfasts are served by the private in-ground pool or by one of two fireplaces in this hilltop home near I-74 in western Indiana. Only five miles from Indiana's finest steak house. Apple Fest in October on the courthouse lawn.

Hosts: Bill and Marsha Wilkinson
Rooms: 3 (PB) $70
Full Breakfast
Credit Cards: A, B, C
Notes: 2, 5, 7, 10, 11, 12

DARLINGTON

Our Country Home Bed & Breakfast, Stable, and Carriage Company

Rural Route Box 103 (CR 550 North), 47940
(765) 794-3139; e-mail: ochome@indy.tds.net

Packages include private candlelight dinners, country carriage or sleigh rides, hot tub under the stars and full country breakfast. Enjoy horseback riding, swimming, or take a ride on a bicycle-built-for-two. All of this and more is just waiting for guests at Our Country Home. Walk along the creek or just relax on the porch and watch the Belgian draft horses graze. Sip coffee and enjoy colorful sunsets, beautiful sunrises, or watch for a falling star. Step back in time and relax. "Come as a guest, leave as a friend." Gift certificates are available. Packages start at $165. Smoking permitted outside only.

Hosts: Jim and Deb Smith and family
Rooms: 3 (SB) $85
Full Breakfast
Credit Cards: A, B, C, D
Notes: 3, 4, 5, 7, 8, 9, 10, 11, 12

FORT WAYNE

At the Herb Lady's Garden

8214 Maysville Road, 46815-6617
(219) 493-8814; FAX (219) 749-8093

Beautiful renovated Civil War farmhouse decorated with antiques and turn-of-the-century family heirlooms. Original art throughout house. Entire house air conditioned; guests rooms with individual controls. Choice of breakfast served in the formal dining room or on the enclosed porch overlooking extensive gardens and beautiful grounds. Welcome reception each afternoon. Indiana's largest mall, major attractions, Amish area—20 minutes. The guest rooms each have a private modern bath, TV, telephone. Breakfast choice will

---

NOTES: Credit cards accepted: A MasterCard; B Visa; C American Express; D Discover; E Diner's Club; F Other; 2 Personal checks accepted; 3 Lunch available; 4 Dinner available; 5 Open all year; 6 Pets welcome;

At the Herb Lady's Garden

affect rates. Extended stay/senior discounts. Smoking permitted in designated areas. Inquire about accommodations for children.

Hosts: Louise and Ralph Rennecker
Rooms: 2 (PB) $60-75
Full or Continental Breakfast
Credit Cards: A, B, D
Notes: 2, 5, 9, 12

FOWLER

Pheasant Country Bed & Breakfast

900 East 5th Street, 47944-1518
(765) 884-0908 (phone/ FAX)
e-mail: june@pheasant.com

Circa 1940 Colonial in historic district on a brick street. Twenty-five minutes to Purdue University. King- or queen-size beds with designer linens. European and Oriental antiques throughout. TV/VCR, telephone, clock/radio cassette players. Turndown with mints on pillow. Afternoon refreshments. Fresh flowers in room. Fresh fruit and bottled water. Gourmet breakfast in formal dining room. Bicycles provided. Antique auctions every weekend in area. Tennis and golf are nearby. Open-to-the-public country club. Antique shop and gallery on premises. Take I-65 to exit 188 west on Highway 18 to Fowler or U.S. 41 to U.S. 52S.

Host: June Gaylord
Rooms: 3 (1 PB; 2 SB) $50-65
Full Breakfast
Credit Cards: A, B
Notes: 2, 3, 4, 5, 7, 8, 9, 10, 11, 12, 14

GOSHEN

The Checkerberry Inn

62644 County Road 37, 46526
(219) 642-4445

At the Checkerberry Inn, in the heart of northern Indiana Amish country, guests will find a unique atmosphere, different from anywhere else in the Midwest. Each individually decorated room has a breathtaking view of the unspoiled countryside. Outdoor pool, tennis court, and croquet green. Cycling, jogging, and walking area. Shopping and golf within 10 to 15 minutes. Award-winning restaurant. Closed January.

Hosts: John, Susan, and Kelly Graff
Rooms: 14 (PB) $140-325
Continental Breakfast
Credit Cards: A, B, C
Notes: 2, 4, 7, 10, 11, 12

Indian Creek Bed & Breakfast

20300 C.R. 18, 46528-9513
(219) 875-6606; FAX (219) 875-3968
e-mail: 71224.1462@compuserve.com

Come visit Amish country and enjoy Hoosier hospitality in a new Victorian home, with gracious architecture and modern amenities. There are four tastefully decorated antique-filled bedrooms with private baths. Guests can enjoy the spacious 42-foot dining, kitchen, and great room combination where they can relax, visit, and watch TV. Watch deer and wildlife from a large deck while taking in the countryside, or guests can stroll back to the woods.

Rooms: 4 (PB) $79
Full Breakfast
Credit Cards: A, B, C, D
Notes: 2, 5, 7, 8, 12, 15

7 No smoking; 8 Children welcome; 9 Social drinking allowed; 10 Tennis nearby; 11 Swimming nearby; 12 Golf nearby; 13 Skiing nearby; 14 May be booked through a travel agent; 15 Handicapped accessible.

Prairie Manor

turn of the century. It recently has been renovated throughout into a lovely bed and breakfast with three guest rooms. The largest has a queen-size bed, high-back cherry headboard, and large private bath. The second has a light and airy motif with a queen-size bed and private bath. The third, ideal for a single, has a 3/4 bed and private bath. All have cable TV and air conditioning. A full formal breakfast is served. $75-95.

Prairie Manor

66398 US 33 South, 46526
(219) 642-4761; (800) 791-3952
FAX (219) 642-4762; e-mail: jeston@npcc.net
www.prairiemanor.com

This English country manor-style home, on 12 acres, was built in the 1920s by a Wall Street banker. The living room replicates his favorite painting of an English baronial hall featuring a fireplace big enough to walk into. Guests will enjoy the wood-paneled library with inviting window seats and fireplace. Interesting architectural details include arched doorways and hidden compartments! Refreshments. Prairie Manor is in the center of northern Indiana Amish country.

Hosts: Jean and Hesston Lauver
Rooms: 4 (PB) $69-95
Full Breakfast
Credit Cards: A, B, D
Notes: 2, 5, 7, 8, 10, 11, 12

GREENBURG

B & B MidWest Reservations

2223 Crump Lane, Columbus, IN 47203-2009
(812) 378-5855; (800) B AND B (342-2632)
FAX (812) 378-5822
e-mail: reservations@bandbmidwest.com
www.BandBmidwest.com

02118. Half-way between Indianapolis and Cincinnati on I-74 is a growing community of Greensburg—the historic "Tower Tree Square" city. Enjoy this rural home built at the

INDIANAPOLIS

Boone Docks on the River

7159 Edgewater Place, 46240
(317) 257-3671

A 1920s English Tudor home on the White River, just north of Broad Ripple village, Boone Docks has a resortlike setting overlooking the river. Enjoy the comforts and charm of the River Room Suite, gracefully decorated in blue, white eyelet, and lace. A hearty breakfast is enjoyed seasonally in the sunroom or on the screened porch. Convenient to dining, entertainment, sporting events, shopping, museums, antiquing, and many downtown attractions.

Hosts: Lynne and Mike Boone
Room: 1 (PB) $55-75
Full Breakfast
Credit Cards: C, D
Notes: 2, 5, 7, 8, 9, 10, 11, 12

Speedway Bed & Breakfast

1829 Cunningham Road, 46224
(317) 487-6531; (800) 975-3412
e-mail: speedwaybb@msn.com

In the little town of Speedway, surrounded by the city of Indianapolis, guests will find a feeling of home at the Speedway. Through the doors walk race enthusiasts, wedding guests, convention and conference attendants. Easy access to the race tracks, museums, stadiums, shops, theaters, churches, and I-465. Honeymoon suite is available for special occasions.

NOTES: Credit cards accepted: A MasterCard; B Visa; C American Express; D Discover; E Diner's Club; F Other; 2 Personal checks accepted; 3 Lunch available; 4 Dinner available; 5 Open all year; 6 Pets welcome;

Hosts: Pauline and Robert Grothe
Rooms: 5 (PB) $65-125
Full and Continental Breakfast
Credit Cards: A, B, D
Notes: 2, 5, 7, 10, 11, 12

JAMESTOWN

Oakwood Bed & Breakfast

9530 West U.S. Highway 136, 46147
(765) 676-5114; FAX (765) 676-5802

New antique-filled Victorian on nine acres.
Peaceful, quiet rural setting. Relax on porches,
deck, or gazebo. Flower gardens, lily pond,
birds. Full breakfast and refreshments. Billiard
room adjoins one guest room. Convenient to I-
74, 25 miles northwest of Indianapolis, 15
miles east of Crawfordsville.

Hosts: Bob and Marilyn Kernodle
Rooms: 2 (PB) $65-70
Full Breakfast
Credit Cards: A, B
Notes: 2, 5, 7, 9, 12

Oakwood

KNIGHTSTOWN

B & B MidWest Reservations

2223 Crump Lane, Columbus, IN 47203-2009
(812) 378-5855; (800) B AND B (342-2632)
FAX (812) 378-5822
e-mail: reservations@bandbmidwest.com
www.BandBmidwest.com

12121. A historic country home midway
between Indianapolis and Richmond provides
three rooms for guests with easy access to I-70.
Guest rooms include queen-size bed with fireplace, queen-size and twin beds, each with pri-

vate bath. Overlook Hoosier farmland and a
beautiful golf course available for guests' use,
with a short drive to a quaint small town. Home
in "Antique Alley." Continental plus breakfast.
$60-70.

LAFAYETTE

B & B MidWest Reservations

2223 Crump Lane, Columbus, IN 47203-2009
(812) 378-5855; (800) B AND B (342-2632)
FAX (812) 378-5822
e-mail: reservations@bandbmidwest.com
www.BandBmidwest.com

14096. A grand Italianate home built in 1882
in the Centennial Historic District of
Lafayette boasts of its original chandeliers
and five guest accommodations with private
baths with old-fashioned claw-foot tubs.
Some rooms also offer whirlpools. Turndown
service in the evening and a full formal breakfast in the morning is served by candlelight,
making this a visit long to be remembered.
Nearby enjoy Purdue University activities,
historic Lafayette, the Wabash River, or historic battlefields. $79-175.

Historic Loeb House Inn

708 Cincinnati Street, 47901
(765) 420-7737

An elegant and comfortable luxury inn in
Lafayette's Centennial Historic District features
ornate plaster, walnut woodwork, and antique
chandeliers. This 1996 decorator showhouse is
restored and furnished to period. Spacious
guest rooms have private baths, telephones, and
cable TVs. Some rooms include whirlpool tubs
and fireplaces. Guests are treated to many
amenities. Turndown with apéritif at the bedside. Breakfast served in the formal dining
room. Near Purdue University, downtown
restaurants, museums, and antique shops. Exercise room and swimming pool available.

7 No smoking; 8 Children welcome; 9 Social drinking allowed; 10 Tennis nearby; 11 Swimming nearby;
12 Golf nearby; 13 Skiing nearby; 14 May be booked through a travel agent; 15 Handicapped accessible.

Historic Loeb House Inn

Hosts: Janice Alford and Dick Nagel
Rooms: 5 (PB) $79-175
Full Breakfast
Credit Cards: A, B, C
Notes: 2, 5, 7, 8, 9, 10, 11, 12, 14

LAGRANGE

The 1886 Inn

212 Factory Street, P.O. Box 5, 46761
(219) 463-4227; www.kuntrynet.com/1886inn

The 1866 Inn bed and breakfast is filled with historical charm and elegance and glows with old-fashioned beauty in every room. The finest lodging, but affordable, this inn is 10 minutes from the Shipshewana flea market. Continental plus breakfast served.

Hosts: Duane and Gloria Billman
Rooms: 3 (PB) $89-129
Continental Breakfast
Credit Cards: A, B
Notes: 2, 5, 7, 12

LEAVENWORTH

The Leavenworth Inn

930 West State Road 62, 47137
(888) 739-2120; FAX (812) 739-2012
e-mail: wyancorp@theremc.com

The Leavenworth Inn, a country inn, is a beautifully renovated turn of the century house perfect for that romantic getaway, family outing, or business retreat. The newest addition to the inn is the newly renovated Scott's House, which gives us a total of 10 bedrooms with private baths. While visiting the inns, enjoy the walking and bicycle paths, tennis court, library, sunroom, outdoor gazebo (perfect for weddings), and a country breakfast at the Overlook Restaurant.

Host: Crystal Day
Rooms: 10 (PB) $59-95
Continental Breakfast
Credit Cards: A, B, C, D
Notes: 3, 4, 7, 8, 9, 10, 11, 12, 13, 15

LEESBURG

Prairie House Bed & Breakfast

495 East 900 North, 46538
(219) 658-9211

Whether travelers have planned tranquil days or non-stop activities touring northern Indiana, the hosts invite them to experience the many delights of staying at the Prairie House where guests come as a stranger and leave as friends. On a working farm amid rolling cornfields and wild flowers. Enjoy the gazebo in summer, or curl up by the fire in the winter. Full breakfast and bedtime snacks.

Hosts: Everet and Marie Tom
Rooms: 4 (2 PB; 2 SB) $45-65
Full Breakfast
Credit Cards: A, B
Notes: 2, 5, 7, 10, 11, 12

Prairie House

MADISON

Ghent House Bed & Breakfast

411 Main Street (US 42), P.O. Box 478,
   Ghent, KY 41045
(502) 347-5807
www.bbonline.com/ky/ghent/

Ghent House, in Ghent, Kentucky, is a gracious reminder of the antebellum days of the Old South. Federal style with a beautiful fantail window, two slave walls, rose and English gardens, gazebo, crystal chandeliers, fireplaces, outdoor hot tub, and whirlpool. Ghent House has a spectacular view of the Ohio River halfway between Cincinnati and Louisville, and one can almost visualize the steamboats. Go back in time and stay at the Ghent House. Come as a guest—leave as a friend.

Hosts: Wayne and Diane Young
Rooms: 3 (PB) $60-120
Full Breakfast
Credit Cards: A, B, C, D
Notes: 2, 5, 7, 8, 9, 10, 11, 12, 14

Schussler House Bed & Breakfast

514 Jefferson Street, 47250
(812) 273-2068; (800) 392-1931

Experience the quiet elegance of a circa 1849 Federal Greek Revival home tastefully combined with today's modern amenities. Madison's historic district, antique shops, restaurants, historic sites, and the Ohio River are within a pleasant walk. This gracious home offers spacious rooms decorated with antiques and reproductions and carefully selected fabrics and wall coverings. A sumptuous breakfast in the sun-filled dining room is a relaxing beginning to the day.

Hosts: Judy and Bill Gilbert
Rooms: 3 (PB) $99
Full Breakfast
Credit Cards: A, B, D
Notes: 2, 5, 7, 9, 10, 11, 12, 14

MCCORDSVILLE

B & B MidWest Reservations

2223 Crump Lane, Columbus, IN 47203-2009
(812) 378-5855; (800) B AND B (342-2632)
FAX (812) 378-5822
e-mail: reservations@bandbmidwest.com
www.BandBmidwest.com

09057. This renovated 1916 circular barn was recently transformed into a bed and breakfast. This historic site offers three guest rooms. One room has a king-size bed, queen-size sleeper sofa, TV, and private bath. The second room offers a queen-size bed with shared bath, and the third room offers two double beds with shared bath. A hearty buffet-style breakfast is served. The common areas offer a wide-screen TV and VCR, game room with pool table, picnic area, enclosed porch, and library/study area. Just 19 miles to downtown Indianapolis. $72-96.

METAMORA

Thorpe House Country Inn

19049 Clayborn Street, P.O. Box 36, 47030-0036
(765) 647-5425; www.bestinns.net/usa/in

Circa 1840s, this peaceful, easy-feeling inn is only one block from the restored Whitewater Canal. Enjoy a hearty breakfast before exploring 100 plus shops, galleries, and museums in this quaint historic village. Transportation

Thorpe House Country Inn

---

options include excursion train, horsedrawn carriage, and canal boat. Recreational diversions—canoeing, hiking, bicycling, fishing, water sports, golf, exploring Indian mounds—are nearby. "Although we are 150 years away, we're conveniently located between Indianapolis and Cincinnati."

Hosts: Mike and Jean Owens
Rooms: 5 (PB) $70-125
Full Breakfast
Credit Cards: A, B, C, D
Notes: 2, 3, 6, 8, 9, 10, 11, 12, 14

MIDDLEBURY

Bee Hive Bed & Breakfast

Box 1191, 46540
(219) 825-5023; FAX (219) 825-5023

Welcome to this cozy country bed and breakfast built with rough-sawn timber and open beams. In the evenings, chat with Herb as he tells about the Amish community, gift shops, museums, parks, and flea markets, or enjoy an old-fashioned sing-along as Herb plays the accordion. Enjoy the old tractors and steam engine. Snuggle under handmade quilts, wake to the smell of a country breakfast being prepared. A great way to start the day. Guest cottage also available.

Hosts: Herb and Treva Swarm
Rooms: 4 (1 PB; 3 SB) $54-70
Full Breakfast
Credit Cards: A, B
Notes: 2, 5, 7, 8, 10, 11, 12, 13

MIDDLETOWN

B & B MidWest Reservations

2223 Crump Lane, Columbus, IN 47203-2009
(812) 378-5855; (800) B AND B (342-2632)
FAX (812) 378-5822
e-mail: reservations@bandbmidwest.com
www.BandBmidwest.com

12034. In the country between Anderson and Muncie, this bed and breakfast offers two guest

accommodations, including a cozy room within the main house with queen-size bed and shared bath. Larger accommodation includes small apartment with kitchenette, dining room, living room with TV and Hide-a-Bed, bath, queen-size bed in bedroom , and patio. Twenty dollars per additional person. Five golf courses in surrounding area, Mounds State Park, and Basketball Hall of Fame all minutes from home. Handicapped accessible. Full breakfast. $55-75.

MILLERSBURG

The Big House in the Little Woods

4245 South 1000 West, 46543
(219) 593-9076; e-mail: bighouse@ligtel.com

Recently built 4,000-square-foot Colonial-style home in a quiet country setting is in the heart of a large Amish community. Four spacious guest rooms have TVs, some antique furniture, handmade quilts, and air conditioning. Take a stroll down the quiet country road or relax in a guest room, living room, or in the quiet woods and watch for birds or woodland animals. Only nine miles to Shipshewana. King- and queen-size beds available. Small conference room available and can sleep 14 people.

Hosts: Sarah and Jacob Stoltzfus
Rooms: 4 (PB) $65-75
Full Breakfast
Credit Cards: A, B, C, D
Notes: 2, 5, 7, 10, 12

NAPPANEE

Market Street Guest House

253 East Market Street, 46550
(219) 773-2261; (800) 497-3791

Feel right at home in the heart of Amish country in this Georgian Colonial built in 1922. Antiques, stained-glass windows, open stairway, fireplace, and baby grand piano compliment the decor. Just two blocks from arts and

Market Street Guest House

hills of southern Indiana. The mood and decor reflect the relaxed lifestyle of the region and the innkeeper. The emphasis is on cleanliness, comfort, and charm.

Host: Tammy Galm
Rooms: 5 (PB) $95
Full Breakfast
Credit Cards: None
Notes: 2, 7, 10, 11, 12, 13

PAOLI

B & B MidWest Reservations

2223 Crump Lane, Columbus, IN 47203-2009
(812) 378-5855; (800) B AND B (342-2632)
FAX (812) 378-5822
e-mail: reservations@bandbmidwest.com
www.BandBmidwest.com

23064. Bordering the beautiful Hoosier National Forest, the town of Paoli is nestled off the beaten trail in southern Indiana. The owners of this historic 1830 landmark tell how the home was moved and turned on the lot and incorporated into the lovely Queen Anne Victorian structure seen today. Six guest accommodations offered, all with private baths. Full breakfast is served. $60-65.

craft and antique shops. Notre Dame and the Shipshewana flea market are 45 minutes away. Visit Amish Acres only one mile away with live theater productions. "Hospitality that remains in your memory long after your visit."

Host: Sharon Bontrager
Rooms: 5 (PB) $65-75
Full Breakfast
Credit Cards: A, B, D
Notes: 2, 5, 7, 8, 9, 10, 11, 12, 14

NASHVILLE

Allison House Inn

90 South Jefferson Street, P.O. Box 1625, 47448
(812) 988-0814

The Allison House is the perfect complement to the charm of Brown County in the rolling

Allison House Inn

RISING SUN

The Jelley House Country Inn

222 South Walnut, 47040
(877) 429-0695; e-mail: jmoore@seidatk.com
www.bbonline.com/in/jelley

Welcome to the Jelley House Country Inn, Rising Sun's first and finest bed and breakfast. Built as a residence in 1847 and in operation as a bed and breakfast since 1986, choose from five guest rooms furnished with antiques, quilts, and local crafts. We offer a full breakfast, guided fishing excursions, and boat cruises. Located on the Ohio River Scenic Route, we are one block from the Ohio River and five blocks from the Grand Victoria Casino.

7 No smoking; 8 Children welcome; 9 Social drinking allowed; 10 Tennis nearby; 11 Swimming nearby; 12 Golf nearby; 13 Skiing nearby; 14 May be booked through a travel agent; 15 Handicapped accessible.

Hosts: Jeff and Jennifer Moore
Rooms: 5 (2-3 PB; 2-3 SB) $100-130
Full Breakfast
Credit Cards: A, B
Notes: 2, 5, 6, 7, 8, 9, 11, 12, 13

ROCKPORT

Trail's End

5931 Highway 56, Owensboro, KY 42301
(502) 771-5590; FAX (502) 771-4723
e-mail: jramey@mindspring.com
www.mindspring.com/~jramey

A condo cottage in Indiana, furnished with antiques and gas-log fireplace, has three bedrooms, fully equipped kitchen with stocked refrigerator of breakfast fixings, laundry facilities, patio, and stables for lessons or trail riding on the property. A second condo cottage in Kentucky has three bedrooms. Guests may enjoy indoor/outdoor tennis, Nautilus fitness, and a sauna. Country-style breakfast served at the tennis club on property. Pool and a fireplace. Cottages are air conditioned. Also available is a two-bedroom trailer with two baths. Weekly rates available. Ten dollars for additional persons over two.

Host: Joan G. Ramey
Condo: 2 (PB) $50-75
Trailer: 2 (PB) $35
Full Breakfast
Credit Cards: A, B, D
Notes: 2, 5, 7, 8, 9, 10, 11, 12, 14, 15

ROCKVILLE

Suits Us Bed & Breakfast

514 North College Street, 47872
(765) 569-5660; (888) 4 SUITSUS

This classic plantation-style home, with its widow's walk and a generous front porch, dates to the early 1880s. In scenic Parke County with 32 covered bridges and just 10 minutes away from Turkey Run State Park. Spacious rooms include TVs and VCRs. All with private baths. Guests can sightsee or hike

all day and relax later on the front porch with a book. Guests may even borrow a bike for a ride around the historic town.

Hosts: Andy and Lianna Willhite
Rooms: 4 (PB) $55-125
Full Breakfast
Credit Cards: None
Notes: 2, 5, 7, 8, 9, 10, 11, 12, 13, 14

RUSHVILLE

Greystone Inn

525 North Main Street, 46173
(765) 932-5922; (888) 276-0022
FAX (765) 932-2192; e-mail: rmgrady@comsys.net
www.thegreystoneinn.com

The Greystone Inn is dedicated to providing a romantic, charming, unique place of hospitality where married couples and singles can find the time to be refreshed. It is dedicated to Jesus Christ. Elegantly decorated with fine antiques, this 25-room mansion is a haven for WCP (world class pampering). Six rooms are available, each one named after a flower. Finest beds money can buy. A breakfast that guarantees guests won't face the day hungry. Nestled in an antique Mecca.

Hosts: Ranny and Denise Grady
Rooms: 6 (3 PB; 3 SB) $80-125
Full Breakfast
Credit Cards: A, B, F
Notes: 2, 5, 7, 10, 11, 12

SCHERERVILLE

Sunset Pines Bed & Breakfast

862 Sunset Drive, 46375
(219) 322-3322; (800) 458-0919 ext. 19
FAX (219) 322-9794
e-mail: sunset@comnetcom.net
www.comnetcom.net/~sunset

Lake County, Indiana's only bed and breakfast is hidden away on the edge of a 50-acre forest and yet is only one-half mile from US 30 and 41, the "Crossroads of America." Charming rooms, delicious and generous full-service breakfast. Mini-suite with private entrance also available. Nonsmoking policy. Queen-size beds, whirlpool tubs, cable TVs. Outdoor pool open during the summer season. Sunset Pines is recommended by the Lake County Visitors Center. Discounts available.

Hosts: Clay and Nikki Foster
Rooms: 3 (PB) $75-95
Full and Continental Breakfast
Credit Cards: A, B, C, D, E
Notes: 2, 5, 7, 8, 9, 10, 11, 12

SHIPSHEWANA

Morton Street Bed & Breakfast

140 Morton Street, P.O. Box 775, 46565
(219) 768-4391; (800) 447-6475
www.shipsewanalodging.com

In the heart of Amish country, our three turn-of-the-century homes provide a restful place after a day of shopping. Morton Street offers ten rooms, all with private baths, queen-size beds, wraparound front porch, gazebos, Victorian garden, full hot breakfast, etc. Surrounded by Shipshewana's shops, flea market, and restaurants, makes this a perfect place for church retreats, family reunions, couples getaways, workshops, etc.

Hostesses: Peggy Scherger and Kelly McConnell
(mother and daughter)
Rooms: 10 (PB) $49-99
Full and Continental Breakfasts
Credit Cards: A, B, C, D
Notes: 2, 5, 7, 8, 12, 13, 14

Morton Street

Poverty Acres Bed & Breakfast

7455 West 350 North, 46565
(219) 768-7457; (219) 768-4422
FAX (219) 768-7457

Come visit one of the most peaceful places in Shipshewana. At Poverty Acres Bed and Breakfast guests can relax on the screened porch or the deck and watch the deer play by the two ponds. The bed and breakfast is also in the heart of Amish Country. Poverty Acres is a stone's throw away from all the exciting activities that Shipshewana has to offer.

Hosts: Becky and Burt Mawhorter
Rooms: 3 (PB) $70-75
Full Breakfast
Credit Cards: A, B
Notes: 2, 7, 8, 10, 12

TRAFALGAR

B & B MidWest Reservations

2223 Crump Lane, Columbus, IN 47203-2009
(812) 378-5855; (800) B AND B (342-2632)
FAX (812) 378-5822
e-mail: reservations@bandbmidwest.com
www.BandBmidwest.com

18098. Perfectly nestled in the woods with a fishing lake nearby and golf courses across the road, this tremendous home was constructed in sections by the owners while they lived on the premises. Just 20 minutes from Columbus, Nashville, and Indianapolis. Richly appointed with fine decorating, cherry woodwork, and numerous fireplaces, guests may relax with a book on the front porch rocking chairs or in front of a blazing fire. Or enjoy a game of pool or Ping-Pong after a full breakfast. Four guest rooms offer a variety of accommodations. Two large suites have private baths and large double Jacuzzis. One has a wood-burning fireplace and the other has a private porch overlooking the woods. Another two rooms both share an adjoining bath. $65-150.

7 No smoking; 8 Children welcome; 9 Social drinking allowed; 10 Tennis nearby; 11 Swimming nearby; 12 Golf nearby; 13 Skiing nearby; 14 May be booked through a travel agent; 15 Handicapped accessible.

VALPARAISO

The Inn at Aberdeen, Ltd.

3158 South State Road 2, 46385
(219) 465-3753; FAX (219) 465-9227
e-mail: innaberd@netnitco.net
www.valpomall.com/theinn

Original home dates to the 1800s with a new addition in 1995 providing 11 guest suites, each with king-size or two queen-size beds, private bath, Jacuzzi, fireplace, ceiling fan, and balcony. Gourmet breakfast, evening snack and beverages included. Library, solarium, and parlor available. Executive Conference Center for business retreats, weddings, receptions, or family gatherings. Gazebo and gardens complement the peace and tranquility of the Inn at Aberdeen. Eighteen-hole championship golf, pool, tennis, and recreation fields adjacent.

Hosts: Bill Simon (Executive Chef & Innkeeper);
   Linda and John Johnson (Proprietors)
Rooms: 11 (PB) $94-157
Full Breakfast
Credit Cards: A, B, C, D, E
Notes: 5, 7, 8, 9, 10, 11, 12, 13, 14, 15

The Inn at Aberdeen

VERNON

B & B MidWest Reservations

2223 Crump Lane, Columbus, IN 47203-2009
(812) 378-5855; (800) B AND B (342-2632)
FAX (812) 378-5822
e-mail: reservations@bandbmidwest.com
www.BandBmidwest.com

08049. An 1840 Greek Revival-style home in the small, historic town of Vernon—30 minutes from Columbus and Madison. This home offers three guest rooms. The home has three baths for guests—shared or private, depending on arrangements. One bath has a Jacuzzi, one room has a private deck, and two rooms have fireplaces. A full breakfast is served. $85-105.

VEVAY

Rosemont Inn

806 West Market Street, 47043
(812) 427-3050

This 1881 Victorian Italianate home, on the banks of the Ohio River, is on more than two acres. Eleven rooms, an open grand entrance stairway with stained glass, beautiful woodwork, and original chandeliers. Large front porch faces the river. Antiquing, casino, and scenic drives/hikes in the area. Grounds are planted in perennial and rose gardens. Riverview and garden-view rooms are available. Queen-size beds (one room with twin beds), private baths, robes for guest use, complimentary refreshments, full hot breakfast.

Rooms: 5 (PB) $85-95
Full Breakfast
Credit Cards: None
Notes: 2, 5, 7, 9, 12

NOTES: Credit cards accepted: A MasterCard; B Visa; C American Express; D Discover; E Diner's Club; F Other; 2 Personal checks accepted; 3 Lunch available; 4 Dinner available; 5 Open all year; 6 Pets welcome;

WABASH

Lamp Post Inn Bed & Breakfast

261 West Hill Street, 46992
(219) 563-3094

A uniquely warm and inviting Romanesque-style home. Built in 1896. The Pink room with private bath extends across the front of the house and features a turret window, a true Grandfather four-poster bed, and lounging area. The blue Wicker Room and green Captain's Room have queen-size beds. All have TV, telephones, and air. Corporate rates available for extended stays.

Innkeeper: Janet Conner
Rooms: 4 (1 PB: 3 SB) $50-60
Full and Continental Breakfast
Credit Cards: None
Notes: 2, 5, 7, 11, 12

WEST BADEN SPRINGS

E. B. Rhodes House Bed & Breakfast

Rhodes Avenue, Box 7, 47469
(812) 936-7378; (800) 786-5176

A spacious first-edition Victorian, built in 1901, with beautiful hand-carved wood and stained-glass windows. Two large porches complete with rockers for guests to enjoy southern Indiana vistas and just plain relaxing. Entertainment for all seasons and tastes includes gracious dining, historical tours, steam locomotive rides, antiquing, museums, and theater. For the more adventurous there are water or snow skiing, nearby state parks, and caving. A carriage house with full bath and fireplaces is also available. Inquire about accommodations for pets. Smoking permitted in designated areas only.

Hosts: Frank and Marlene Sipes
Rooms: 3 (PB) $45-85
Full Breakfast
Credit Cards: A, B, C, D
Notes: 2, 5, 8, 10, 11, 12, 13

7 No smoking; 8 Children welcome; 9 Social drinking allowed; 10 Tennis nearby; 11 Swimming nearby; 12 Golf nearby; 13 Skiing nearby; 14 May be booked through a travel agent; 15 Handicapped accessible.

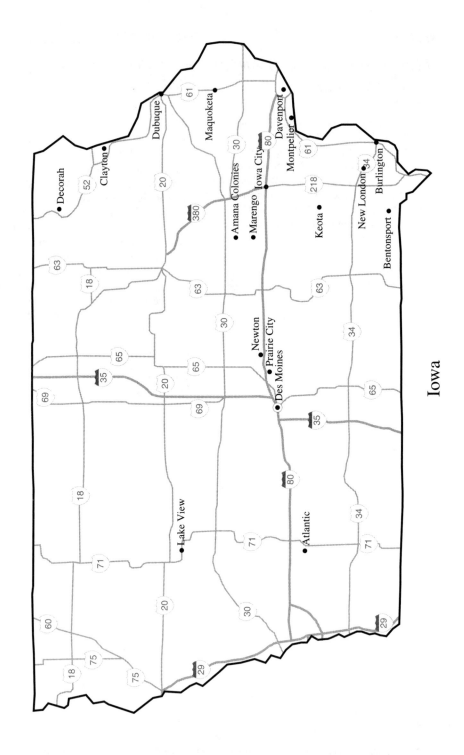

Iowa

Iowa

Die Heimat Country Inn

AMANA COLONIES

Die Heimat Country Inn

Amana Colonies, 1 Main Street, Homestead, 52236
(319) 622-3937

Choose the Amana Colonies' original bed and breakfast for quiet relaxation. A national register 1854 stage coach stop, now a 19-room restored inn with reasonable rates, Amana furniture, canopied beds, quilts, private baths, TV, air conditioning, and full hot breakfast. The hosts combine Australian charm and midwestern hospitality. Inquire about accommodations for pets.

Hosts: Warren and Jackie Lock
Rooms: 19 (PB) $48-70
Full Breakfast
Credit Cards: A, B, D
Notes: 2, 5, 7, 8, 9, 10, 11, 12

ATLANTIC

Chestnut Charm Bed & Breakfast

1409 Chestnut Street, 50022
(712) 243-5652; e-mail: chestnut@netins.net
www.netins.net/showcase/chestnut

This is one of Iowa's finest country inns. An enchanting 1898 Victorian mansion with romantic carriage house suites. Private baths, Jacuzzis, in-room fireplaces, sauna, sunrooms, fountained patio, 12-foot gazebo, natural hardwood floors, and ornate woodwork. Full breakfast with gourmet coffee and fresh home-baking. Air conditioned. Just a short drive to the famous bridges of Madison County, Walnut's Antique City, a Danish windmill with museum, championship golf courses, and many other Iowa treasures. Gift certificates.

Host: Barbara Stensvad
Rooms: 4 (PB) $70-105
Suites: 5 (PB) $140-250
Full Breakfast
Credit Cards: A, B
Notes: 2, 5, 7, 10, 11, 12, 14, 15

BENTONSPORT

Mason House Inn of Bentonsport

Route 2, Box 237, Keosauqua, 52565
(800) 592-3133; e-mail: mhibprt.netins.net

The Mason House Inn was built in 1846, the year Iowa became a state, by Mormon craftsmen making their famous trek to Utah. It is the oldest steamboat river inn still serving overnight guests in the Midwest. The inn has the only fold-down copper bathtub in the state. Oral tradition has it that Abraham Lincoln and

NOTES: Credit cards accepted: A MasterCard; B Visa; C American Express; D Discover; E Diner's Club; F Other; 2 Personal checks accepted; 3 Lunch available; 4 Dinner available; 5 Open all year; 6 Pets welcome; 7 No smoking; 8 Children welcome; 9 Social drinking allowed; 10 Tennis nearby; 11 Swimming nearby; 12 Golf nearby; 13 Skiing nearby; 14 May be booked through a travel agent; 15 Handicapped accessible.

Mason House

Mark Twain slept here. The entire village is listed in the National Register of Historic Places. Guests will find a full cookie jar in every room. AAA-approved.

Hosts: Sheral and William McDermet III
Rooms: 9 (PB) $64-79
Full Breakfast
Credit Cards: A, B
Notes: 2, 3, 4, 5, 7, 8, 9, 11, 12, 15

BURLINGTON

The Schramm House Bed & Breakfast

616 Columbia Street, 52601
(319) 754-0373; (800) 683-7117
e-mail: visit@schramm.com
www.visit.schramm.com

Step into the past when entering this restored 1870s Victorian in the heart of the historic district. Unique architectural features and antique furnishings create the mood of an era past. Four guest rooms, all with private baths, offer queen-size or twin beds, quilts, and more.

The Schramm House

Experience Burlington hospitality while having lemonade on the porch or tea by the fire with the gracious hosts. Walk to the Mississippi River, antique shops, restaurants, and more.

Hosts: Sandy and Bruce Morrison
Rooms: 4 (PB) $65-125
Full Breakfast
Credit Cards: A, B, C, D
Notes: 2, 5, 7, 8, 9, 10, 11, 12, 14

CLAYTON

The Claytonian Bed & Breakfast Inn

100 South Front Street, 52049
(319) 964-2776

The Claytonian is a unique bed and breakfast inn, open year-round with large, charming rooms, each with its own distinct theme. Along the magnificent Mississippi River, one mile off the Great River Road, which affords one of the most scenic routes in the United States. The village of Clayton is surrounded by many historical sites, recreation areas, antique shops, and a rural warmth not found in other areas. The Claytonian provides a delicious breakfast, complimentary bicycles. Cable TV. A public boat ramp is available.

Hosts: Don and Eileen Christensen
Rooms: 5 (3 PB: 2 SB) $50-65
Full Breakfast
Credit Cards: A, B
Notes: 2, 5, 7, 8, 9, 11, 12, 13

DAVENPORT

Bed & Breakfasts of the Quad City Area Room Availability Cooperative

P.O. Box 3464, Rock Island, IL 61201
(309) 786-3513

Bishop's House Inn. (319) 322-8303. Circa 1871. This large Italianate-style mansion is in

NOTES: Credit cards accepted: A MasterCard; B Visa; C American Express; D Discover; E Diner's Club; F Other; 2 Personal checks accepted; 3 Lunch available; 4 Dinner available; 5 Open all year; 6 Pets welcome;

the heart of Davenport. The inn abounds with gorgeous Victorian detail inside and out. Five guest chambers and one suite, each with private bath are furnished with fine antiques. A full breakfast is served in the formal dining room. The first floor parlors can provide an intimate setting for corporate meetings or retreats, dinners, receptions, and weddings. $65-140.

Fulton's Landing. (319) 322-4069. This large Italianate stone residence has a bird's-eye view of the Mississippi River. In the heart of downtown Davenport, it's only minutes from any Quad City activity. Five bedrooms and a full breakfast wait for visitors. $60-125.

Latimer Bed & Breakfast. (319) 289-5747. This 1905 house has been home to the Latimer family since 1949. There are four warm and cozy bedrooms, with one handicapped accessible. $40.

Varner's Caboose. (319) 381-3652. Stay in a real Rock Island Lines caboose. The caboose is self-contained with bath, shower, and complete kitchen. It sleeps four with a queen-size bed and two single beds in the cupola. A fully prepared country breakfast is left in the caboose for guests' pleasure. $55.

Bishop's House Inn

1527 Brady Street, 52803
(319) 322-8303

Italianate-style mansion, circa 1871. Listed in the National Register of Historical Places, the inn abounds with gorgeous Victorian detail inside and out. Five guest chambers and one suite, each with private bath and antique furnishings await the discerning guest. A full breakfast is served in the formal dining room. Further amenities include the first-floor parlors which provide an intimate setting for dinners, receptions, and weddings.

Hosts: Judy and Tom Callahan
Rooms: 6 (PB) $65-140
Full Breakfast
Credit Cards: A, B
Notes: 2, 5, 7, 9, 12, 15

Fulton's Landing Guest House

1206 East River Drive, 52803
(319) 322-4069

The old Fulton mansion is a large Italianate stone residence built in 1871 by Ambrose Fulton. Listed in the National Register of Historic Places, the home offers a majestic view of the Mississippi River and is only minutes away from all area attractions. Five bedrooms are available for guests. A full breakfast is served in the dining room. Two large porches overlook the river, one on the main floor and the other on the second floor with easy access from all the bedrooms. On Route 67 near downtown Davenport.

Hosts: Pat and Bill Schmidt
Rooms: 5 (PB) $60-125
Full Breakfast
Credit Cards: A, B, C
Notes: 2, 5, 7

Fulton's Landing Guest House

The Woodlands

The Woodlands

P.O. Box 127, Princeton, 52768
(319) 289-4661
e-mail: betswallace@email.msn.com

A secluded woodland escape that can be as private or social as guests wish. The Woodlands bed and breakfast is nestled among pines on 26 acres of forest and meadows in a private wildlife refuge. Guests delight in an elegant breakfast by the swimming pool or by a cozy fireplace while viewing the outdoor wildlife activity. Boating and fishing on the Mississippi River, cross-country skiing, golfing, and hiking are available. A short drive to the Quad City metropolitan area.

Hosts: The Wallace Family
Rooms: 3 (2 PB; 1 SB) $75-125
Full Breakfast
Credit Cards: None
Notes: 2, 3, 4, 5, 8, 9, 10, 11, 12, 13, 14

DECORAH

Montgomery Mansion Bed & Breakfast

812 Maple Avenue, 52101
(319) 382-5088; (800) 892-4955

A fine old brick house built in 1877 on more than three lots, close to downtown, museums, Luther College, city parks, and tennis courts. Swimming, canoeing, and skiing in season. The house is air conditioned. A full breakfast is served to guests in the dining room. While close to downtown, we are in a quiet neighborhood.

Hosts: Bob and Diane Ward
Rooms: 4 (1 PB; 3 SB) $45-55
Full Breakfast
Credit Cards: A, B, D
Notes: 2, 5, 8, 9, 10, 11, 12, 13, 14

DUBUQUE

The Hancock House Bed & Breakfast Inn

1105 Grove Terrace, 52001
(319) 557-8989; FAX (319) 583-0813
www.thehancockhouse.com

Nestled in the bluffs of the mighty Mississippi, the Hancock House offers a panoramic view with old-fashioned elegance. Built in 1891 and restored to its original grandeur, all nine rooms are furnished in period antiques. Private baths, complimentary beverage center, and corporate rates Sunday through Thursday. Private bluffside cottage available.

Hosts: Chuck and Susan Huntley
Rooms: 9 (PB) $75-150
Full Breakfast
Credit Cards: A, B, C, D
Notes: 2, 5, 7, 12, 13, 14

The Hancock House

NOTES: Credit cards accepted: A MasterCard; B Visa; C American Express; D Discover; E Diner's Club; F Other; 2 Personal checks accepted; 3 Lunch available; 4 Dinner available; 5 Open all year; 6 Pets welcome;

The Mandolin Inn

199 Loras Boulevard, 52001
(319) 556-0069; (800) 524-7996
FAX (319) 556-0587

A 1908 Edwardian mansion where the comfort and pleasure of its guests are the primary focus. A gourmet breakfast is served in an oak dining room with an exquisite oil-painted mural while classical music plays softly in the background. For year-round comfort all rooms are provided with queen-size beds, down comforters, and air conditioning. During the summer the veranda is filled with wicker furniture for guests to relax in.

Host: Amy Boyntan
Rooms: 7 (5 PB; 2 SB) $75-135
Full Breakfast
Credit Cards: A, B, C, D
Notes: 2, 5, 7, 8, 9, 12, 13

Bella Vista

The Mandolin Inn

IOWA CITY

Bella Vista Bed & Breakfast

2 Bella Vista Place, 52245
(319) 338-4129

Lovely air-conditioned 1920s home tastefully decorated with antiques and artifacts from travels in Europe and Latin America. Two suites with in-room private baths, a suite with private bath and kitchen, two rooms with shared bath, all with comfortable beds. Guests can relax in the quietness of their room, share the company of other guests in the living room, the front porch, or enjoy the view of the Iowa River from the deck. Guests will enjoy Daissy's helpfulness, hearty breakfasts, and famous coffee. Short distance from downtown and the University of Iowa. One mile south of I-80 at exit 244. Special pricing for extended stays available. Fluent Spanish and some French spoken.

Hostess: Daissy P. Owen
Suites: 3 (PB) $85-95
Rooms: 2 (SB) $55-60
Full Breakfast
Credit Cards: None
Notes: 2, 5, 7, 9, 10, 11, 12

The Golden Haug

517 East Washington Street, 52240
(319) 338-6452

Elegance and whimsy characterize this 1920 house. Guests can retreat to one of four accommodations with in-room private bath or enjoy camaraderie with other guests in the living room. A full breakfast is served family style. Ideal location in downtown Iowa City within a couple of blocks of the University of Iowa, eateries, and shopping. Smoking is permitted outside only.

Hosts: Nila Haug and Dennis Nowotny
Suites: 5(PB) $75-125
Full Breakfast
Credit Cards: None
Notes: 2, 5, 7, 8, 9, 11, 12, 14

7 No smoking; 8 Children welcome; 9 Social drinking allowed; 10 Tennis nearby; 11 Swimming nearby; 12 Golf nearby; 13 Skiing nearby; 14 May be booked through a travel agent; 15 Handicapped accessible.

Haverkamps' Linn Street Homestay

619 North Linn Street, 52245
(319) 337-4363; FAX (319) 354-7057
e-mail: havb-b@soli.inav.net

A large and comfortable 1908 Edwardian-style home filled with antiques and collectibles. Wonderful front porch with old-fashioned swing. Walking distance to University of Iowa campus and the downtown area. Only a short drive to the Amana villages, Kalona, Hoover Museum in West Branch, and Cedar Rapids. One mile south of I-80 at exit 244.

Hosts: Clarence and Dorothy Haverkamp
Rooms: 3 (SB) $45-50
Full Breakfast
Credit Cards: None
Notes: 2, 5, 7, 8, 9, 10, 11, 12, 13

Haverkamps' Linn Street Homestay

KEOTA

Elmhurst

1994 Keokuk Washington Road, 52248
(515) 636-3001

This 1905 Victorian mansion was built with no expense spared by Thomas Singmaster. The family was the world's largest importer of draft horses. The mansion retains much of its original interior grandeur: prismed stained-glass and curved windows, circular solarium, parquet floors, beamed ceilings, Italian marble fireplace mantels, third-floor ballroom, beveled

Elmhurst

plate-glass windows, two grand stairways, leather wall coverings, and more. The house is filled with history and antiques. The house was designed and built by the famous Wetherells. The golf course, a swimming pool, and a nature trail are across the road.

Rooms: 7 (S21/2B) $50
Full Breakfast
Credit Cards: None
Notes: 2, 3, 4, 9, 10, 11, 12

LAKE VIEW

Armstrong House Bed & Breakfast

306 Fifth Street, 51450
(712) 657-2535

An elegantly restored Victorian (circa 1886) built by founding family of Lake View. Inside, the eclectic decor displays a unique combination of Victorian, country, and international furnishings from owner's travels. Breakfast always includes freshly baked pastries and gourmet coffee. A new gift shop on the porch offers items from around the world. Three blocks from Black Hawk Lake and Sauk Rail Trail (for use by hikers, joggers, and bicyclists). Two bicycles are available for guests' use.

Host: Jeanet Henriquez
Rooms: 3 (PB) $57-63
Full or Continental Breakfast
Credit Cards: None
Notes: 2, 7, 8, 9, 10, 11, 12, 13, 14

NOTES: Credit cards accepted: A MasterCard; B Visa; C American Express; D Discover; E Diner's Club; F Other; 2 Personal checks accepted; 3 Lunch available; 4 Dinner available; 5 Open all year; 6 Pets welcome;

MAQUOKETA

Squiers Manor
Bed & Breakfast

418 West Pleasant Street, 52060
(319) 652-6961

Built in 1882, this restored
brick Queen Anne man-
sion features rich,
beautiful woodwork
and period furnish-
ings. Amidst this,
three suites and five
guest rooms provide a
relaxing stay with expected modern comforts,
including in-room telephones, private baths,
Jacuzzis, and TVs. In addition, candlelight
evening dessert and gourmet breakfast are
served.

Hosts: Virl and Kathy Banowetz
Rooms: 8 (PB) $75-185
Full Breakfast
Credit Cards: A, B, C
Notes: 2, 5, 7, 9, 10, 11, 12, 13

MARENGO

Loy's Farm Bed & Breakfast

2077 KK Avenue, 52301
(319) 642-7787

Beautiful modern country home on an active
farm. Farm tours and hunting. Full gourmet
breakfast with homemade products. Exercise
and recreation equipment available. Golf package available. Iowa agriculture ambassadors.
The Tanger outlet, Amana Colonies, Herbert
Hoover Memorial, Kalona Amish, Iowa City,
and Cedar Rapids are nearby. Close to I-80,
exit 216. A rollaway is available at an additional cost. Dinner available upon request.

Hosts: Loy and Robert Walker
Rooms: 3 (1 PB; 2 SB) $60-70
Full Breakfast
Credit Cards: None
Notes: 2, 5, 7, 8, 9, 10, 11, 12, 14

MONTPELIER

Varners' Caboose
Bed & Breakfast

204 East 2nd, P.O. Box 10, 52759
(319) 381-3652

Stay in a real Rock Island Lines caboose. Set
on its own track behind the hosts' house, the
caboose is a self-contained unit, with bath,
shower, and complete kitchen. It sleeps four,
with a queen-size bed and two twins in the
cupola. There are color TV, VCR, central air
and heat, plus plenty of off-street parking. A
fully prepared country breakfast is left in the
caboose kitchen to be enjoyed by guests when-
ever they choose. On Route 22, halfway
between Davenport and Muscatine.

Hosts: Bob and Nancy Varner
Room: 1 (PB) $60
Full Breakfast
Credit Cards: None
Notes: 2, 5, 6, 7, 8, 9

NEW LONDON

Old Brick Bed & Breakfast

2759 Old Highway 34, 52645
(319) 367-5403

This 1860s Italianate-style brick farmhouse,
comfortably furnished with family pieces,

Old Brick

---

7 No smoking; 8 Children welcome; 9 Social drinking allowed; 10 Tennis nearby; 11 Swimming nearby;
12 Golf nearby; 13 Skiing nearby; 14 May be booked through a travel agent; 15 Handicapped accessible.

beckons guests with electric candles in each window. The working grain farm offers an opportunity to view current farming techniques, equipment, and specialty crops. Enjoy peaceful surroundings, walk down a country road, visit area antique shops, or relax in spacious rooms with queen-size beds and private baths. Full breakfast and arrival refreshments are served.

Hosts: Jerry and Caroline Lehman
Rooms: 2 (PB) $55
Full Breakfast
Credit Cards: None
Notes: 2, 4, 5, 7, 8, 10, 11, 12

NEWTON

La Corsette Maison Inn

629 1st Avenue East, 50208
(515) 792-6833

This opulent, Mission-style mansion built in 1909 by Iowa state senator August Bergman maintains the charm of its original oak woodwork, Art Nouveau stained-glass windows, brass light fixtures, and even some original furnishings. Despite the addition of contemporary comforts, the bedchambers' original features have been retained. Down-filled pillows and comforters are available. Enjoy hot spiced wine in front of one of three fireplaces. Pets welcome and children are welcome with prior arrangements.

Host: Kay Owen
Rooms: 7 (PB) $70-185
Full Breakfast
Credit Cards: A, B, C
Notes: 2, 4, 5, 7, 9, 10, 11, 12, 13, 14

La Corsette Maison Inn

PRAIRIE CITY

The Country Connection

The Country Connection Bed & Breakfast

9737 West 93rd Street South, 50228-8306
(515) 994-2023

Guests experience the friendly atmosphere of a working farm community, surrounded by the tranquility of bountiful cropland...away from the hustle and bustle of everyday life. Turn-of-the-century farmhome, period furnishings, walnut woodwork, leaded glass, lace, all blended with privacy, charm, and hospitality; treasures lovingly preserved from six generations. Arise to a hearty country breakfast, served by candlelight, on cheerful sun porch or formal dining room. Complimentary bedtime snack and old-fashioned homemade ice cream are available. Open May through November. Near Walnut Creek Wildlife Refuge and Pella Tulip Time. Twenty miles east of Des Moines.

Hosts: Jim and Alice Foreman
Rooms: 2 (2 SB) $50-60
Full Breakfast
Credit Cards: A, B
Notes: 2, 7, 8, 11, 12

NOTES: Credit cards accepted: A MasterCard; B Visa; C American Express; D Discover; E Diner's Club; F Other; 2 Personal checks accepted; 3 Lunch available; 4 Dinner available; 5 Open all year; 6 Pets welcome;

Kansas

GREAT BEND

Peaceful Acres Bed & Breakfast

Route 5, Box 153, 67530
(316) 793-7527

This sprawling farmhouse has a working windmill, small livestock, chickens, and guineas. Five miles from Great Bend and close to Cheyenne Bottoms and Quivira Wetlands, Fort Larned, Pawnee Rock, Wilson Lake, Lake Kanopolis, and Santa Fe Trail. Enjoy hospitality and the quiet of the country in this farmhouse furnished with some antiques. Homegrown and homemade foods. Full country breakfast is served. Kitchen available for guests' use.

Hosts: Dale and Doris Nitzel
Rooms: 2-3 (SB) $30
Full Breakfast
Credit Cards: None
Notes: 2, 5, 6, 7, 8, 10, 11, 12, 14

PEABODY

Jones Sheep Farm Bed & Breakfast

Rural Route 2, Box 185, 66866
(316) 983-2815

Enjoy a turn-of-the-century home in a pastoral setting. On a working sheep farm "at the end of the road," the house is furnished in 1930s style (no telephone or TV). Quiet and private. A wonderful, historic small town is nearby. The full country breakfast features fresh farm produce. Only one party is booked at a time. One

Jones Sheep Farm

room has a double bed and crib. Additional charge of $20 for extra person in room.

Hosts: Gary and Marilyn Jones
Rooms: 2 (SB) $55
Full Breakfast
Credit Cards: None
Notes: 2, 5, 6, 7, 8, 10, 11, 12

TONGANOXIE

Almeda's Bed & Breakfast Inn

220 South Main Street, 66086
(913) 845-2295

In a picturesque small town which was designated a historic site in 1983, the inn dates back to World War I. Sip a cup of coffee at the stone bar used as a bus stop in 1930. In fact, this room was the inspiration for the play *Bus Stop*. Close driving distance to Kansas City International Airport, Kansas City Country Club Plaza, the Renaissance Festival, Sandstone Theatre, Woodlands racetrack, the National Agriculture Hall of Fame, the University of

Kansas

Kansas, Weston and Snow Creek skiing, Topeka (state capitol), and antique shops. Continental plus breakfast is served.

Hosts: Almeda and Richard Tinberg
Rooms: 7 (PB and SB) $40-65
Continental Breakfast
Credit Cards: None
Notes: 2, 5, 7, 11, 12

ULYSSES

Fort's Cedar View, Inc.

1675 West Patterson Avenue, 67880-8423
(316) 356-2570; e-mail: fort@pld.com
www.kbba.com; www.bedandbreakfast.com

Fort's Cedar View is in the heart of the world's largest natural-gas field. It is on the Santa Fe Trail, eight miles north of famed Wagon Bed Springs, the first source of water after crossing the Cimarron River west of Dodge City, which is 80 miles northeast.

Host: Lynda Fort
Rooms: 5 (2 PB; 3 SB) $45-65
Full Breakfast
Credit Cards: None
Notes: 2, 5, 7, 8, 10, 11, 12

WICHITA

The Castle Inn Riverside

1155 North River Boulevard, 67203
(316) 263-9300; (800) 580-1131
e-mail: lcastle@gte.net
www.castleinnriverside.com

This small luxury inn is a stunning example of Richardsonian Romanesque architecture. Featured in national newspapers and magazines such as *Country Inn* and *Holiday Travel*, the Castle has 14 uniquely appointed guest rooms. Twelve have fireplaces and six have Jacuzzis for two. Minutes away from downtown Wichita, rooms are equipped with TV/VCR, telephones, and data ports especially for the business travelers. A selection of wines and cheeses, homemade desserts and gourmet cof-

The Castle Inn Riverside

fees, and a gourmet breakfast are served daily. Memberships include PAII and ABBA, the later awarded the Castle the prestigious four-crown rating each year since the opening in 1995 by ABBA. Children 10 and older welcome.

Hosts: Terry and Paula Lowry
Rooms: 14 (PB) $125-295
Full Breakfast
Credit Cards: A, B, D
Notes: 2, 5, 7, 9, 10, 12, 14, 15

Inn at the Park

3751 East Douglas, 67218
(316) 652-0500; (800) 258-1951

Elegant Old World charm and comfort in a completely renovated mansion. Twelve distinctive suites, 10 in the main house and 2 in the carriage house. Some of the amenities include fireplaces, whirlpool baths, a private courtyard, a hot tub, and many spacious three-room suites. A preferred hideaway among people looking for a romantic retreat or convenient base of operation for corporate guests. Named one of the top 10 outstanding new inns in the country by *Inn Review* newsletter in 1989, it has been rated "outstanding" by the ABBA for the last five years. Smoking is permitted in designated areas only.

Host: Michelle Hickman
Rooms: 12 (PB) $89-149
Continental Breakfast
Credit Cards: A, B, C, D
Notes: 2, 3, 4, 5, 8, 9, 10, 14

7 No smoking; 8 Children welcome; 9 Social drinking allowed; 10 Tennis nearby; 11 Swimming nearby; 12 Golf nearby; 13 Skiing nearby; 14 May be booked through a travel agent; 15 Handicapped accessible.

Houghton

4

26

45

2

41

41

28

Blaney Park · 2

St. Ignace

75

Mackinac Island

31

Petoskey

Boyne City

Bellaire

23

Leland

Suttons Bay

Glen Arbor

Empire

Elk Rapids

Traverse City

75

131

51

Oscoda

Manistee

27

Harrison

75

Port Austin

25

Port Hope

Ludington 10

Pentwater

10

31

Mt. Pleasant

Alma

Bay City

Saginaw

Port Sanilac

131

Ithaca

Frankenmuth

Muskegon

Ionia

27

Owosso

Flint

89

Grand Haven

198

Lowell

95

75

94

Saugatuck

Holland

Fennville

Dimondale

96

South Haven

Kalamazoo

94

Ann Arbor

Paw Paw

Battle Creek

Brooklyn

23

75

Union Pier

131

Mendon

2

Jonesville

Dundee

Jones

12

New Buffalo

94

31

Pittsford

Michigan

Michigan

Saravilla

ALMA

Saravilla Bed & Breakfast

633 North State Street, 48801-1640
(517) 463-4078; FAX (517) 463-8624
e-mail: ljdarrow@saravilla.com
www.saravilla.com

Enjoy the charm and original features of this 1894, 11,000-square-foot Dutch Colonial home. Guests may enjoy the pool table, the fireplace in the library, and the hot tub in the sunroom. The guest rooms are spacious and quiet; several have fireplaces, and one has a whirlpool tub. A full breakfast is served each morning in the elegant turret dining room. Soaring Eagle Casino is just 20 minutes away.

Hosts: Linda and Jon Darrow
Rooms: 7 (PB) $70-125
Full Breakfast
Credit Cards: A, B, D
Notes: 2, 5, 7, 8, 9, 10, 11, 12, 14

ANN ARBOR

Bed & Breakfast on Campus

921 East Huron, 48104
(734) 994-9100; (734) 741-7527
www.annarbor.org/pages/bbcampus.html

Bed and Breakfast on Campus is housed in a unique contemporary building across the street from the University of Michigan campus and five university theaters. It is within walking distance to the hospital and Ann Arbor's cosmopolitan downtown area with diverse restaurants and theaters. It has a spacious common area and six elegantly furnished guest rooms with private baths and two furnished apartments that may be rented by the week. A full gourmet breakfast is served. Covered parking is provided at the main entrance.

Host: Virginia Mikola
Rooms: 5 (PB) $65-90
Full Breakfast
Credit Cards: A, B, C
Notes: 2, 5, 7, 10, 11, 12

Bed & Breakfast on Campus

NOTES: Credit cards accepted: A MasterCard; B Visa; C American Express; D Discover; E Diner's Club; F Other; 2 Personal checks accepted; 3 Lunch available; 4 Dinner available; 5 Open all year; 6 Pets welcome; 7 No smoking; 8 Children welcome; 9 Social drinking allowed; 10 Tennis nearby; 11 Swimming nearby; 12 Golf nearby; 13 Skiing nearby; 14 May be booked through a travel agent; 15 Handicapped accessible.

The Urban Retreat Bed & Breakfast

2759 Canterbury Road, 48104
(734) 971-8110

This contemporary ranch homestay has provided quiet comfort to business and pleasure travelers since 1986. Minutes from downtown, the Urban Retreat is tucked away on a quiet, tree-lined street, with adjacent parkland offering walking trails. Guest rooms and common areas are lovingly furnished with antiques. Breakfast is served overlooking the gardens. Central air. Resident cats. Inspected and approved. The Urban Retreat welcomes guests from all cultures, races, and lifestyles. Smoking is permitted in designated areas only.

Hosts: Gloria Krys and André Rosalik
Rooms: 2 (1 PB: 1 SB) $60-70
Full Breakfast
Credit Cards: A, B
Notes: 2, 5, 7, 10, 11, 12

BATTLE CREEK

Greencrest Manor

6174 Halbert Road, 49017
(616) 962-8633

To experience Greencrest is to step back in time to a way of life that is rare today. From the moment of entrance through iron gates, guests will be mesmerized. This French Normandy mansion on the highest elevation of St. Mary's Lake is constructed of sandstone, slate, and copper. Formal gardens, fountains, and garden architecture. Chosen by *Country Inns* as one of the "top twelve inns" in North America. Air conditioning, cable TV, and telephones are in all rooms. Continental plus breakfast is served.

Hosts: Kathy and Tom Van Daff
Rooms: 8 (6 PB; 2 SB) $75-200
Continental Breakfast
Credit Cards: A, B, C, E
Notes: 2, 5, 7, 8, 9, 10, 12, 13

BAY CITY

Clements Inn

1712 Center Avenue M-25, 48708
(800) 442-4605; www.laketolake.com/clements/

This 1886 Queen Anne Victorian home features six fireplaces, magnificent woodwork, an oak staircase, amber-colored glass windows, working gas lamps, organ pipes, two claw-foot tubs, and a third-floor ballroom. Each of the six bedrooms includes cable TV, VCR, telephone, a private bath, and air conditioning. Special features include in-room gas fireplaces, in-room whirlpool tubs, and the 1,200-square-foot, Alfred Lord Tennyson Ballroom Suite.

Hosts: Shirley and David Roberts
Rooms: 6 (PB) $70-175
Continental Breakfast
Credit Cards: A, B, C, D
Notes: 2, 5, 7, 9, 10, 11, 12, 13, 14

BELLAIRE

Bellaire Bed & Breakfast

212 Park Street, 49615
(616) 533-6077; (800) 545-0780
e-mail: belbed@aol.com

Stately 1879 home in the northern part of Michigan's Lower Peninsula. The home boasts a wraparound porch which overlooks expansive front grounds with maples that turn to brilliant colors for the Fall Color Tour. Golfers find "the Legend" at Shanty Creek to provide superior golfing enjoyment. During the ski season, Shanty is home to some of the finest skiing in Michigan. Water lovers have their pick of the many pristine lakes and rivers for weekend fun. Continental plus breakfast is served. Children over 12 are welcome.

Hosts: David Schulz and Jim Walker
Rooms: 5 (3 PB; 2 SB) $70-100
Continental Breakfast
Credit Cards: A, B, D
Notes: 2, 5, 7, 9, 10, 11, 12, 13

NOTES: Credit cards accepted: A MasterCard; B Visa; C American Express; D Discover; E Diner's Club; F Other; 2 Personal checks accepted; 3 Lunch available; 4 Dinner available; 5 Open all year; 6 Pets welcome;

BLANEY PARK

Celibeth House Bed & Breakfast

Route 1, Box 58A, Blaney Park Road, 49836
(906) 283-3409

This lovely home is on 86 acres overlooking a small lake. The rooms are spacious and tastefully furnished with antiques. Guests may also use a large living room with fireplace, reading room, enclosed front porch, a large outside deck, and nature trails. Within an hour's drive of most of the scenic attractions in Michigan's Upper Peninsula.

Host: Elsa R. Strom
Rooms: 7 (PB) $60-80
Continental Breakfast
Credit Cards: A, B
Notes: 2, 7, 8, 9

BROOKLYN

The Buffalo Inn

10845 US 12, 49230
(517) 467-6521 (phone/FAX)
www.bbonline.com/mi/buffaloinn

Comfortable, inviting…A uniquely different kind of home with a southwestern charm. Enjoy the full breakfast by the large stone fireplace. Play pinball in the game room where smoking is permitted. Five unique bedrooms

The Buffalo Inn

with private and shared baths, one with fireplace. The inn is along the road known as Antique Alley. The area also offers 54 lakes, numerous golf courses, fine dining, and family attractions. The hostess, Carol Zarr, welcomes guests to the beautiful Irish hills.

Host: Carol Zarr
Rooms: 5 (1 PB; 4 SB) $45-85
Full Breakfast
Credit Cards: A, B
Notes: 2, 5, 8, 9, 11, 12

DIMONDALE

Bannick's Bed & Breakfast

4608 Michigan Road, 48821
(517) 646-0224

This large ranch-style home features attractive decor with stained-glass entrances. Almost three rural acres offer a quiet escape from the fast pace of the workday world. On a main highway (M99) five miles from Lansing and close neighbor to Michigan State University.

Hosts: Pat and Jim Bannick
Rooms: 2 (SB) $25-40
Full Breakfast
Credit Cards: None
Notes: 5, 7, 8, 9, 11, 12, 13

DUNDEE

The Dundee Guest House Bed & Breakfast

522 Tecumseh Street (M 50 at US 23), 48131
(734) 529-5706; (800) 501-4455

Enjoy Monroe County's first bed and breakfast, a 19th-century historic home graced with a beautiful Victorian gazebo and the formal garden. Private baths, air conditioning, family heirlooms, and Continental plus breakfast await guests. Choose from the elegant bridal suite, Loraines Jacuzzi Garden room with its lilac decor, Connie's Carousel room, or Rosemary's

7 No smoking; 8 Children welcome; 9 Social drinking allowed; 10 Tennis nearby; 11 Swimming nearby; 12 Golf nearby; 13 Skiing nearby; 14 May be booked through a travel agent; 15 Handicapped accessible.

room. All this and Cabela's too. Cabela's, the worlds largest outdoors sporting goods store, is just one-half mile away.

Hosts: Karen and Jerry Glover
Rooms: 5 (PB) $65-135
Continental Breakfast
Credit Cards: A, B, D, F
Notes: 2, 5, 7, 8, 9, 10, 12, 14

ELK RAPIDS

Cairn House Bed & Breakfast

8160 Cairn Highway, P.O. Box 858, 49629
(616) 264-8994; e-mail: hperez@cairnhouse.com
www.cairnhouse.com

Elegant Colonial-style home in beautifully landscaped surroundings, 15 miles north of Traverse City. Minutes from Bay. Uniquely decorated rooms. Full breakfast, excellent area for year-round sports, gourmet dining, and shopping. Available for family celebrations and retreats. Children welcome. No smoking or pets. Lots of parking. Off-season rates available from November through April. "Your comfort is my priority."

Hosts: Helen Perez
Rooms: 4 (PB) $70-85
Full Breakfast
Credit Cards: A, B
Notes: 2, 5, 7, 8, 10, 11, 12, 13

Cairn House

EMPIRE

Empire House Bed & Breakfast

11015 LaCore, South, P.O. Box 203, 49630-0203
(616) 326-5524; e-mail: hrfriend@gtii.com

This 19th-century farmhouse, on picturesque acreage, is in the beautiful Sleeping Bear Dunes National Lakeshore area. Four rooms with outside entrances are available for guests. A large screened porch and a separate two-bedroom apartment for weekly use are also on premises. A quiet, homey atmosphere, freshly ground coffee, and a wonderful breakfast. Close to the beaches of Lake Michigan, golf, tennis, hiking trails in the summer and skiing trails in the winter.

Hosts: Rosemary and Harry Friend
Rooms: 4 (1 PB; 3 SB) $60
Apartment: $65
Continental Breakfast
Credit Cards: None
Notes: 2, 10, 11, 12, 13

FENNVILLE

J. Paules Fenn Inn

2254 South 58th Street, 49408
(616) 561-2836 (phone/FAX)

Nestled in the countryside, eight miles from Saugatuck, guests here will find a very traditional bed and breakfast with private and shared baths. The hosts offer large rooms and a wonderful full breakfast every morning, served from 8:00-11:00 A.M. The many decks and flower gardens offer lots of peaceful moments. The inn is just minutes from Holland, Allegan, and South Haven.

Hosts: Paulette J. Clouse and Ewald Males
Rooms: 5 (2 PB: 3 SB) $70-130
Full Breakfast
Credit Cards: A, B, D
Notes: 2, 5, 6, 7, 8, 9, 10, 11, 12, 13, 15

The Kingsley House

626 West Main Street, 49408
(616) 561-6425
www.kingsleyhouse.com

An elegant Victorian inn on the edge of Fennville, near Saugatuck, Holland, and South Haven. The guest rooms are decorated in Victorian elegance. Honeymoon suite with Jacuzzi and fireplace. Beaches, shopping, fine dining, and a playhouse theater nearby. The Allegan State Forest, with miles of nature trails, is enjoyable to explore. Bicycle rides to the lake or winery available. Country lover's delight. Featured in *Innsider* magazine, "Great Lakes Getaway." Chosen one of the top 50 inns in America by *Inn Times*. A Continental plus breakfast is available for those who do not want a full breakfast.

Hosts: Gary and Kari King
Rooms: 8 (PB) $80-165
Full Breakfast
Credit Cards: A, B, C, D
Notes: 2, 4, 5, 7, 9, 10, 11, 12, 13, 14

Avon House

and Cross Roads villages within short driving distances.

Host: Arletta E. Minore
Rooms: 3 (SB) $45
Full Breakfast
Credit Cards: None
Notes: 2, 5, 7, 8, 9, 10, 11, 12, 13

The Kingsley House

FLINT

Avon House Bed & Breakfast

518 Avon Street, 48503
(810) 232-6861

Built in 1893, Avon House is an enchanting Victorian home with spacious rooms, beautiful warm woodwork, and antiques. A comfortable, homey setting for business persons, tourists, and out-of-town guests to enjoy a delicious homemade breakfast served every morning. In Flint's college and cultural area near University of Michigan (Flint) and Mott College. Play-yard for children. Frankenmuth, Birch Run,

FRANKENMUTH

Bavarian Town Bed & Breakfast

206 Beyerlein Street, 48734
(517) 652-8057; e-mail: b+bedb@juno.com

Beautifully decorated rooms in a Cape Cod dwelling just three blocks off of Main Street in the most popular tourist town of Michigan. Quiet residential district. Air conditioning. Bilingual hosts, direct descendants of original German settlers of Frankenmuth, are willing to share hospitality hour and information on Frankenmuth. Full breakfast includes fresh fruit, baked goods, and hot entreés. Private

Bavarian Town

7 No smoking; 8 Children welcome; 9 Social drinking allowed; 10 Tennis nearby; 11 Swimming nearby; 12 Golf nearby; 13 Skiing nearby; 14 May be booked through a travel agent; 15 Handicapped accessible.

toilet and sink. Shared shower. Beautiful yard. Hot tub on outside deck. Sauna in basement.

Hosts: Kathy and Louie Weiss
Rooms: 2 (PB/SB) $70-75
Full Breakfast
Credit Cards: A, B, D
Notes: 2, 5, 7, 8, 9, 10, 11, 12

GLEN ARBOR

Sylvan Inn

6680 Western Avenue, 49636
(213) 334-4333

The Sylvan Inn is a beautifully decorated historic landmark building in the heart of the Sleeping Bear Dunes National Lakeshore. Its easy access to Lake Michigan and other inland lakes makes a stay at the Sylvan Inn a unique experience. Closed March, April, and November. Children over seven welcome.

Hosts: Jenny and Bill Olson
Rooms: 14 (7 PB; 7 SB) $65-130
Continental Breakfast
Credit Cards: A, B
Notes: 2, 7, 9, 10, 11, 12, 13, 14

Sylvan Inn

The White Gull Inn

5926 SW Manitou Trail, 49636
(616) 334-4486; FAX (616) 334-3546

One of Michigan's most scenic areas is home to the White Gull Inn, circa 1900. With the Sleeping Bear Dunes just minutes away and alluring Lake Michigan just one block away, visitors will find no shortage of sightseeing or recreational activities during a stay here. Glen Lake is three miles away. Walk to the area's fine dining and shopping opportunities. The inn's farmhouse setting, country decor, and comfortable guest rooms offer guests a relaxing haven no matter what the season. Each room is decorated with antiques and cable TV. Breakfast consists of a variety of fruit, juices, and home-baked items.

Hosts: Bill and Dotti Thompson
Rooms: 5 (5 SB) $65-75
Continental Breakfast
Credit Cards: A, B, C, D
Notes: 2, 5, 7, 9, 10, 11, 12, 13

GRAND HAVEN

Boyden House Inn Bed & Breakfast

301 South Fifth Street, 49417
(616) 846-3538

Built in 1874, this Victorian-style inn is in the heart of Grand Haven, within walking distance of shopping, restaurants, beach, and the boardwalk. Some rooms have fireplaces and balconies. Two rooms have two-person whirlpool baths. Central air conditioning. Great kitchen and two common rooms are available for guest use. Full homemade breakfast served in the beautiful dining room. Limited handicapped accessibility.

Hosts: Corrie and Berend Snoeyer
Rooms: 7 (PB) $75-100
Suites: 2 (PB) $110-120
Full Breakfast
Credit Cards: A, B, C, D
Notes: 2, 5, 7, 8, 9, 10, 11, 12, 13, 14

Seascape Bed & Breakfast

20009 Breton, Spring Lake, 49456
(616) 842-8409
www.bbonline.com/mi/seascape

On private Lake Michigan beach, scenic lakefront rooms. Relax and enjoy the warm hospi-

NOTES: Credit cards accepted: A MasterCard; B Visa; C American Express; D Discover; E Diner's Club; F Other; 2 Personal checks accepted; 3 Lunch available; 4 Dinner available; 5 Open all year; 6 Pets welcome;

Seascape

tality and cozy "country living" ambiance of this nautical lakeshore home. Full country breakfast served in gathering room with field-stone fireplace or on large wraparound deck. Both offer panoramic views of Grand Haven Harbor. Quiet residential setting. Stroll or cross-country ski through dune preserve. A charming retreat for all seasons.

Host: Susan Meyer
Rooms: 4 (PB) $85-160
Full Breakfast
Credit Cards: A, B
Notes: 2, 5, 7, 9, 10, 11, 12, 13, 14

Village Park Bed & Breakfast

60 West Park Street, Fruitport, 49415-9668
(616) 865-6289; (800) 469-1118
www.bbonline.com/mi/villagepark

Village Park

Overlooking the welcoming waters of Spring Lake and Village Park where guests can picnic, play tennis, or use the pedestrian bike path and boat launch. Spring Lake has access to Lake Michigan. Relaxing common area with fireplace; guests may also relax on the decks or in the hot tub and use the exercise facility with sauna and massage table. Historic setting of mineral springs health resort. Serving the Grand Haven and Muskegon areas. Close to Hoffmaster Park, Gillette Sand Dune Nature Center, and Great Lakes Downs. Weekend packages available.

Hosts: John and Linda Hewett
Rooms: 6 (PB) $60-90
Full and Continental Breakfast
Credit Cards: A, B, D
Notes: 2, 5, 7, 8, 9, 10, 11, 12, 13, 14

HARRISON

Carriage House Inn

1515 Grant Avenue, P.O. Box 130, 48625
(517) 539-1300; FAX (517) 539-5661
e-mail: carhsinn@glccompters.com

The Carriage House Inn is nestled in a pine plantation, overlooking Budd Lake, offering intimate accommodations on 127 acres with hiking trails. Eight guest rooms have private baths, most having whirlpool tubs, cable TVs, VCRs, telephones, coffee makers, refrigerators, and air conditioning. Executive retreat accommodations, private retreats, receptions and training facilities available. Breakfast is provided featuring a wide selections of egg dishes, pancakes, quiches, coffee, tea, juice, and fruit. Gift shop.

Host: Rhonda Hampton
Rooms: 8 (PB) $75-135
Full Breakfast
Credit Cards: A, B, C
Notes: 2, 5, 7, 8, 9, 10, 11, 12, 13, 14, 15

---

7 No smoking; 8 Children welcome; 9 Social drinking allowed; 10 Tennis nearby; 11 Swimming nearby; 12 Golf nearby; 13 Skiing nearby; 14 May be booked through a travel agent; 15 Handicapped accessible.

HOLLAND

Dutch Colonial Inn

560 Central Avenue, 49423
(616) 396-3664; FAX (616) 396-0461
www.laketolake.com/dutchcolonialinn

The award-winning Dutch Colonial Inn, built
in 1928, features elegant decor with 1930s furnishings and lovely heirloom antiques. All
guest rooms have tiled private baths, some with
whirlpool tubs for two, and fireplaces. Honeymoon suites available for that special getaway.
Attractions include excellent shopping, Hope
College, bike paths, ski trails, and Michigan's
finest beaches. Business people welcome; corporate rates available. Air conditioning. Open
year-round with special Christmas touches.
Dutch hospitality at its finest.

Hosts: Bob and Pat Elenbaas
Rooms: 4 (PB) $60-150
Full Breakfast
Credit Cards: A, B, C, D
Notes: 2, 5, 7, 10, 11, 12, 13, 14

Dutch Colonial Inn

North Shore Inn of Holland

686 North Shore Drive, 49424
(616) 394-9050

Views of the blue waters of Lake Macatawa,
gardens of colorful perennials, rich interior
decor, comfortable beds, and a gourmet breakfast are all found at the North Shore Inn of Holland. Three bedrooms offer a choice of lake
views, private or shared baths, balconies, king-
size, queen-size, or double beds. Two and one-
half miles from downtown Holland and Hope
College, the inn is adjacent to 25 miles of bike
paths, and is five miles from Lake Michigan.
Surrounded by two acres; a quiet and peaceful
setting is assured. Children over 12 welcome.

Hosts: Kurt and Beverly Van Crenderen
Rooms: 3 (2 PB; 1 SB) $95-110
Full Breakfast
Credit Cards: None
Notes: 2, 7, 9, 10, 11, 12, 14

HOUGHTON

Charleston House Historic Inn

918 College Avenue, 49931
(800) 482-7404; FAX (906) 482-7068
e-mail: hsullivan@portup.com; www.upbnb.com

The Charleston House Historic Inn, of 1900
Georgian architecture, is listed in the national
register. Double veranda, ceiling fans, wicker
furniture. Ornate woodwork, stained glass windows, library with fireplace, high ceilings, grand
staircase. Comfortable reproduction furnishings,
king-size canopied and twin-size beds. All guest
rooms have private baths, air conditioning, color
cable TV, telephones, in-room coffee/tea service, microwave, refrigerator. Some rooms with
water views, fireplace, and private veranda.
AAA-approved. Smoking limited to garden.
Children 12 and older welcome.

Hosts: John and Helen Sullivan
Rooms: 6 (PB) $98-180
Full Breakfast
Credit Cards: A, B, C
Notes: 2, 5, 7, 9, 10, 11, 12, 13, 14

IONIA

Union Hill Inn Bed & Breakfast

306 Union Street, 48846
(616) 527-0955
e-mail: www.netaddress.com/?n=1
www.home.earthlink.net/~unionhillbb/

Elegant 1868 Italianate-style home that served
as a former station for the underground railroad.

NOTES: Credit cards accepted: A MasterCard; B Visa; C American Express; D Discover; E Diner's Club;
F Other; 2 Personal checks accepted; 3 Lunch available; 4 Dinner available; 5 Open all year; 6 Pets welcome;

The home is beautifully furnished with antiques. Enjoy the living area with fireplace, piano, porcelain village and dolls. Air conditioned. Flower beds surround this home noted for its expansive veranda. Panoramic view overlooking historic city. With all the beauty at Union Hill Inn, the greatest thing you will experience is the love and peace that abide here. Midway between Lansing and Grand Rapids.

Hosts: Tom and Mary Kay Moular
Rooms: 6 (1 PB; 5 SB) $50-95
Full Breakfast
Credit Cards: None
Notes: 2, 5, 7, 8, 10, 11, 12, 14

ITHACA

Chaffins Balmoral Farm Bed 'n Breakfast

1245 West Washington Road, 48847
(517) 875-3410

Turn-of-the-century farmhouse on cash-crop farm. Easily identified by its stone wall and large gambrel-roofed barn. Guests' stay at Balmoral Farm consists of a hot country breakfast featuring homemade blueberry muffins and agricultural information. The remodeled home, furnished with family antiques, had its kitchen featured in *Country Woman*. Central Michigan University and Alma College are nearby. Hiking, bicycling, bowling, and roller skating are

Chaffins Balmoral Farm

available, in addition to antique and gift boutiques. Closed November 15 through April 15.

Host: Sue Chaffin
Rooms: 2 (SB) $50
Full Breakfast
Credit Cards: None
Notes: 2, 10, 11, 12

JONES

Sanctuary at Wildwood

58138 M-40, 49061
(616) 244-5910; (800) 249-5910
FAX (616) 244-9022
e-mail: wildwoodinns@voyager.net
www.rivercountry.com/saw

The Sanctuary at Wildwood, built as a millionaire's estate, has been transformed into a unique nature-orientated bed and breakfast on 95 acres of wooded meadows that abound with wildlife. Walking trails enable guests to enjoy nature all four seasons. Each suite has a fireplace, Jacuzzi, and private bath. Enjoy golfing, canoeing, wineries, and skiing nearby. Full breakfast. Innkeepers enjoy pampering the guests.

Hosts: Dick and Dolly Buerille
Rooms: 11 (PB) $139-179
Full Breakfast
Credit Cards: A, B, C, D, E
Notes: 2, 5, 7, 8, 9, 10, 11, 12, 13, 14, 15

JONESVILLE

The Munro House

202 Maumee, 49250
(517) 849-9292; (800) 320-3792

This 1840 Greek Revival structure was built by George C. Munro, a brigadier general during the Civil War. Visitors can see the secret room used to hide runaway slaves as part of the Underground Railroad. The seven cozy guest rooms, all with private baths, are furnished with period antiques, many with working fireplaces and Jacuzzis. There are five common area rooms, including a library and breakfast

7 No smoking; 8 Children welcome; 9 Social drinking allowed; 10 Tennis nearby; 11 Swimming nearby; 12 Golf nearby; 13 Skiing nearby; 14 May be booked through a travel agent; 15 Handicapped accessible.

The Munro House

room with open hearth fireplace. A full breakfast and evening snack are served.

Host: Joyce A. Yarde
Rooms: 7 (PB) $80-150
Full Breakfast
Credit Cards: A, B, C, D
Notes: 2, 5, 7, 8, 9, 10, 11, 12, 14

KALAMAZOO

Hall House

106 Thompson Street, 49006
(616) 343-2500; (888) 761-2525
FAX (616) 343-1374; www.hallhouse.com

"Experience the Difference" in this 14-room Georgian Revival home in a national historic district. Stay in one of the five beautifully appointed guest rooms—some with fireplaces and Jacuzzis, all with private baths, cable TV/VCRs, air conditioning, and telephones. Full hot breakfast served on weekends. Smoke-free. Near colleges and downtown. Business travelers are welcome.

Hosts: Jerry and Joanne Hofferth
Rooms: 5 (PB) $85-150
Full Breakfast
Credit Cards: A, B, C
Notes: 2, 5, 7, 9, 10, 11, 12, 13, 14

LELAND

Manitou Manor

147 North Manitou Trail, P.O. Box 864, 49654
(616) 256-7712

This century-old farmhouse, nestled among six acres of cherry orchards, makes staying on the Leelanau peninsula a peaceful experience. Manitou Manor is a historical bed and breakfast that boasts private baths and family-style breakfasts. Open year-round. From weddings to quiet getaways, it's a perfect place to celebrate the seasons.

Hosts: The Lambdins
Rooms: 5 (PB) $85-159
Full Breakfast
Credit Cards: A, B, D
Notes: 2, 5, 7, 8, 9, 10, 11, 12, 13

The Riverside Inn

302 River Street, P.O. Box 1135, 49654
(616) 256-9971; (888) 257-0102
FAX (616) 256-2217

Built on the bank of the Leland River, the Riverside Inn is nestled between Lake Leelanau and Lake Michigan. Upstairs, the seven guest rooms are decorated to create the feel and charm of a cozy lake cottage. Downstairs, the newly remodeled lobby bar and dining room offer a casual atmosphere, innovative menus, and a wonderful list of world-class wine, featuring the local vineyards. The beautiful waterfront views and casual fine dining make the Riverside Inn one of the most romantic places to stay and to dine in Leelanau County.

Hosts: Barb and Kate Vilter
Rooms: 7 (4 PB; 3 SB) $55-80
Continental Breakfast
Credit Cards: A, B, C, E
Notes: 4, 7, 10, 11, 12, 13

NOTES: Credit cards accepted: A MasterCard; B Visa; C American Express; D Discover; E Diner's Club; F Other; 2 Personal checks accepted; 3 Lunch available; 4 Dinner available; 5 Open all year; 6 Pets welcome;

LOWELL

McGee Homestead
Bed & Breakfast

2534 Alden Nash Northeast, 49331
(616) 897-8142

Surrounded by orchards, this 1880s brick farm-house stands on five acres and has a barn filled with petting animals. The guest area of the bed and breakfast has its own entrance, living room with fireplace, parlor, and small kitchen. Four spacious guest rooms are individually deco-rated with antiques and all have private baths. A big country breakfast is served. A golf course is next door and Grand Rapids is 20 minutes away. The largest antique mall in Michigan is five miles away.

Hosts: Bill and Ardie Barber
Rooms: 4 (PB) $42-62
Full Breakfast
Credit Cards: A, B, C, D
Notes: 2, 7, 8, 9, 10, 11,12, 13

McGee Homestead

LUDINGTON

Doll House Historical Inn
Bed & Breakfast

709 East Ludington Avenue, 49431
(231) 843-2286; (800) 275-4616
e-mail: 2172doll@public.wscc.net

This 1900 American classic Victorian home maintains a reputation for warmth and wel-come due to the hospitality of 10-year vetern innkeepers. The best part of the morning is a hearty breakfast freshly prepared with plenty

of hot coffee and good conversation. Spring and fall are great times to enjoy a murder mys-tery weekend. New this year, enjoy a combina-tion jeep ride over sand dunes, lodging, and dinner for two. May be booked through a travel agent during the winter.

Hosts: Barb and Joe Gerovac
Rooms: 7 (PB) $70-110
Full Breakfast
Credit Cards: A, B
Notes: 2, 7, 9, 10, 11, 12, 13

The Inn at Ludington

701 East Ludington Avenue, 49431
(616) 845-7055

Make your own history! The Inn at Ludington has had its share of historical residents, from Hall of Famers to hometown heroes, but no one is more important than the guests who are there right now. Create your own memories while soothing oneself in an old-fashioned tub filled with bubbles, relax before a crackling fire, or cuddling in a lace-covered canopied bed. Awake to sunshine and the smell of blueberry muffins baking. All the delights of this beach-front community are nearby. Beach, shops, restaurants, and crosslake car ferry within walking distance. AAA-approved.

Host: Diane and David Nemitz
Rooms: 6 (PB) $75-100
Full Breakfast
Credit Cards: A, B, C
Notes: 2, 5, 7, 9, 10, 11, 12, 13, 14

The Lamplighter

602 East Ludington Avenue, 49431
(616) 843-9792; (800) 301-9792
www.laketolake.com/lamplighter

Unique centennial home in town is only min-utes from beautiful, sandy Lake Michigan beaches, the car ferry to Wisconsin, and one of Michigan's most beautiful state parks. Fine antiques, original paintings and lithographs, queen-size beds, and private baths create a unique ambiance of elegance, comfort, and

7 No smoking; 8 Children welcome; 9 Social drinking allowed; 10 Tennis nearby; 11 Swimming nearby; 12 Golf nearby; 13 Skiing nearby; 14 May be booked through a travel agent; 15 Handicapped accessible.

convenience. A whirlpool for two is the ideal setting for a romantic getaway. Gourmet breakfasts are served in the formal dining room or outdoors in the gazebo. Murder mystery weekend packages available. Smoke free.

Hosts: Judy and Heinz Bertram
Rooms: 5 (PB) $75-135
Full Breakfast
Credit Cards: A, B, C, D
Notes: 2, 5, 7, 9, 10, 11, 12, 13, 14

Snyder's Shoreline Inn

903 West Ludington Avenue, P.O. Box 667, 49431-0667
(616) 845-1261; FAX (616) 843-4441
e-mail: sharon@snydersshoreinn.com
www.snydersshoreinn.com

The inn ranks among the finest in western Michigan with its tremendous views of Lake Michigan and Ludington's active deep-water working harbor. Sleep comfortably in pleasant guest rooms individually decorated with a charm that reflects the owner's personal touch—stenciled walls, pieced quilts, antiques. Enjoy lake-view rooms with patios or private covered balconies, and in-room whirlpool tubs. Complimentary Continental breakfast served in coffee room. Honeymoon suites and luxury barrier-free handicapped rooms. Heated outdoor pool and spa. Packages and off-season rates. Smoke free. Pet free. Reservations a must. AAA.

Hosts: Angie Snyder-Adams
Rooms: 44 (PB) $65-289
Continental Breakfast
Credit Cards: A, B, C
Notes: 7, 10, 11, 12, 15

MACKINAC ISLAND

Cloghaun

P.O. Box 203, 49757
(906) 847-3885; (888) 442-5929
www.cloghaun.com

This lovely Victorian furnished home, built in 1884, has been preserved by descendants of the

Cloghaun

original owners and represents the elegance and ambiance of a bygone era. Cloghaun offers guests a tranquil, romantic interlude with serenity and charm. Each guest room is individually decorated with antiques from the late 1800s and evokes a feeling of casual elegance. Ideally located on Market Street and close to shops, restaurants, and ferry lines. Experience your dream getaway at Cloghaun. Continental plus breakfast and afternoon tea included.

Hosts: Marti and Paul Carey
Rooms: 11 (9 PB; 2 SB) $90-140
Continental Breakfast
Credit Cards: None
Notes: 2, 7, 8, 9, 10, 11, 12, 14

MANISTEE

1879 E. E. Douville House

111 Pine Street, 49660
(616) 723-8654

This Victorian home, completed with lumber from nearby forests, features ornate pine woodwork hand-carved by area craftsmen. Interior wooden shutters on windows, a winding staircase, and elaborate archways with pocket doors are also original to the house. Antiques and collectibles fill the home. Ceiling fans in every room. Manistee Victorian Village, riverwalk to Lake Michigan, and historic buildings are nearby.

NOTES: Credit cards accepted: A MasterCard; B Visa; C American Express; D Discover; E Diner's Club; F Other; 2 Personal checks accepted; 3 Lunch available; 4 Dinner available; 5 Open all year; 6 Pets welcome;

1879 E. E. Douville House

Hosts: Barbara and Bill Johnson
Rooms: 2 (SB) $55-65
Continental Breakfast
Credit Cards: None
Notes: 2, 5, 7, 9, 10, 11, 12, 13

MANISTIQUE

Royal Rose Bed & Breakfast

230 Arbutus Avenue, 49854
(906) 341-4886; e-mail: gsablack@up.net

Experience the elegant, but relaxed atmosphere of this newly remodeled 1903 home. Guest rooms have queen-size beds and are uniquely decorated. Enjoy the sunroom where guests can read or socialize by the fireplace or view the spectacular sights of Lake Michigan. Savor the full breakfast served in the formal dining room or out on the large deck. Within walking distance to shopping, dining, movies, the marina, and the boardwalk.

Hosts: Gilbert and Rosemary Sablack
Rooms: 4 (4 SB) $65-85
Full Breakfast
Credit Cards: A, B, D
Notes: 2, 7, 10, 11, 12

MENDON

Mendon Country Inn

440 West Main Street, P.O. Box 98, 49072
(616) 496-8132; (800) 304-3366

FAX (616) 496-8403
e-mail: wildwoodinns@voyager.net
www.rivercountry.com/mci

The historic Wakeman House, now known as the Mendon Country Inn, was originally built in 1843 and rebuilt out of brick in 1873 by Adams Wakeman. Eight-foot windows, high ceilings, and spacious rooms complement the walnut spiral staircase in the lobby. There are numerous antique shops, a local Amish settlement, flea markets, golf, and wineries nearby. There are bicycles for two and canoes available at the inn. Hosts endeavor to provide guests with the comforts of home, the friendliness of small-town life, a great Continental plus breakfast, nine Jacuzzi suites with fireplaces, and a truly enjoyable stay. Smoking not permitted in public areas.

Hosts: Dick and Dolly Buerkle
Rooms: 18 (PB) $50-159
Continental Breakfast
Credit Cards: A, B, C, D
Notes: 2, 5, 8, 9, 10, 11, 12, 13, 14, 15

Mendon Country Inn

MOUNT PLEASANT

Country Chalet Bed & Breakfast

723 South Meridian Road, 48858
(517) 772-9259

The Country Chalet is a comfortable Bavarian-style home atop a hill surrounded by rolling wooded farmland, 25 acres of pastures, and woods and ponds that are playgrounds to wild animals and birds. Guests in the three upper-level bedrooms share a living/dining room with fireplace. For those who love to watch good college competition, Central

7 No smoking; 8 Children welcome; 9 Social drinking allowed; 10 Tennis nearby; 11 Swimming nearby;
12 Golf nearby; 13 Skiing nearby; 14 May be booked through a travel agent; 15 Handicapped accessible.

Michigan University is less than a 10-minute drive from the chalet.

Hosts: Ron and Carolyn Lutz
Rooms: 3 (SB) $55-69
Full Breakfast
Credit Cards: None
Notes: 2, 5, 7, 8, 9, 12

MUSKEGON

Port City Victorian Inn

1259 Lakeshore Drive, 49441
(616) 759-0205; (800) 274-3574
e-mail: pcvicinn@gte.com
www.bbonline.com/mi/portcity

An 1877 romantic Victorian getaway on the bluffs of Muskegon Lake. Just minutes from Lake Michigan beaches, state parks, downtown theaters, sports arena, and restaurants. Five-bedroom home featuring suites with lake views and private double-whirlpool baths. One room decorated with a masculine nautical look with a private bath. Other rooms are elegantly decorated with the flair of the Victorian era. The main floor is all common area for guests' enjoyment. All rooms are provided with air conditioning, cable TV, telephone jacks/computer modem ready, and desks. Fax available.

Port City Victorian Inn

Hosts: Frederick and Barbara Schossau
Rooms: 5 (3 PB; 2 SB) $75-125
Full Breakfast
Credit Cards: A, B, C, D
Notes: 2, 5, 7, 8, 9, 10, 11, 12, 13, 14

NEW BUFFALO

Sans Souci Euro Inn

19265 South Lakeside Road, 49117
(616) 756-3141; FAX (616) 756-5511
e-mail: sans-souci@worldnetatt.net
www.sans-souci.com

Sans Souci (without a care) is far removed from the hustle of everyday life. Inside the gates, guests will find silence and serenity. Lakeside cottages, honeymoon suites, vacation homes with whirlpools and fireplaces. Enjoy a 50-acre nature retreat with private lake and beach (fishing, swimming) and wondrous wildlife. Bird watchers' paradise—spring and fall migration stopover. Fine dining, art/antiques, wineries, golf courses nearby. Family reunions, small seminars welcome. AAA-approved. Chicago is 70 miles away.

Host: Angie Siewert (owner)
Rooms: 9 (PB) $115-195
Full Breakfast
Credit Cards: A, B, C, D
Notes: 2, 5, 8, 9, 10, 11, 12, 13, 14, 15

OWOSSO

R&R Farm-Ranch

308 East Hibbard Road, 48867
(517) 723-3232; (517) 723-2553

A newly remodeled farmhouse from the early 1900s, the Rossman's ranch sits on 150 acres overlooking the Maple River Valley. The large circular drive and white board fences lead to stables of horses and cattle. Guests may use the family parlor, game room, and fireplace or stroll about the gardens and pastures along the river. Breakfast is served in the dining room or outside on the deck. Central air conditioning. Cross-country skiing nearby.

Hosts: Carl and Jeanne Rossman
Rooms: 3 (SB) $45-55
Continental Breakfast
Credit Cards: None
Notes: 2, 5, 6, 7, 8, 10, 12, 13

PENTWATER

Pentwater Inn

180 East Lowell, Box 98, 49449
(616) 869-5909

Lovely 1868 Victorian Inn with English and
American antiques in beautifully appointed
rooms. Charter boats, marinas, international
shopping, the beach on Lake Michigan, and
good food and drink all within a few minutes'
walk. At the inn, enjoy complimentary drinks
and snacks each evening at 6:00 p.m. and a
breakfast to remember. Cable TV, or relax on
one of the decks. Fishing, cross-country skiing,
and golf are nearby. Jacuzzi suite.

Hosts: Donna and Quintus Renshaw
Rooms: 5 (PB) $75-125
Full Breakfast
Credit Cards: A, B
Notes: 2, 5, 7, 8, 9, 10, 11, 12, 13

Pentwater Inn

PETOSKEY

Montgomery Place Bed & Breakfast

618 East Lake Street, 49770
(616) 347-1338

Montgomery Place is a magnificently preserved Victorian home sitting on a hillside in
Petoskey, overlooking Lake Michigan's Little
Traverse Bay from its 80-foot grand veranda.
Close to shops, galleries, and all vacation activities, Montgomery Place features four large,
comfortable rooms, private baths, a full
gourmet breakfast, and afternoon wine and
snacks.

Hosts: Ruth Bellissimo and Diane Gillette
Rooms: 4 (PB) $95-135
Full Breakfast
Credit Cards: A, B, D
Notes: 2, 5, 7, 9, 10, 11, 12, 13, 14

Terrace Inn

Terrace Inn

1549 Glendale, P.O. Box 266, 49770
(800) 530-9898; FAX (616) 347-2407
e-mail: terracei@freeway.net
www.freeway.net/terracei

In the heart of Victorian Bay View, a fairy-tale
village of over 425 cottages adjacent to
Petoskey. Unique turn-of-the-century country-
inn charm. A private Lake Michigan beach,
tennis courts, and hiking/cross-country ski
trails are steps away. Golf, ski, murder mystery
and many other specialty packages offered.
Dine outdoors on the porch or in the beautiful
dining room. Excellent for romantic getaways.
Complimentary use of bicycles. With 43 guest
rooms, a perfect spot for retreats or conferences. Open year-round. Limited handicapped
accessibility.

7 No smoking; 8 Children welcome; 9 Social drinking allowed; 10 Tennis nearby; 11 Swimming nearby;
12 Golf nearby; 13 Skiing nearby; 14 May be booked through a travel agent; 15 Handicapped accessible.

Hosts: Tom and Denise Erhart
Rooms: 43 (PB) $49-149
Continental Breakfast
Credit Cards: A, B, C
Notes: 2, 4, 5, 7, 8, 9, 10, 11, 12, 13, 14, 15

PITTSFORD

The Rocking Horse Inn

8652 North Street, 49271
(517) 523-3826

Relax and enjoy the quiet comfort of this Brick
Italianates' lovely wraparound porch. Evening
refreshments are served and a full breakfast in
the morning. Minutes from Hillsdale College,
golf, and antiquing. Michigan Speedway is
about 30 minutes away. Corporate rates.

Hosts: Phil and Mary Ann Meredith
Rooms: 3 (PB) $60-75
Full Breakfast
Credit Cards: A, B
Notes: 2, 5, 7, 11, 12

PORT AUSTIN

Lake Street Manor
Bed & Breakfast

8569 Lake Street, 48467
(517) 738-7720

This brick Victorian, circa 1875, has a fenced
in garden back yard, pavilion with picnic
tables, chairs, and a brick barbecue for guests'
enjoyment. TV/VCR with movies in all rooms.
Hot tub in bay room, sitting room to play cards
and read. One double bed in all rooms, two
persons per room. Kitchen open to guests. Special weekday rates. Two-night minimal reservations on Memorial through Labor Day
weekends. Bikes for guests to use. Open April
through November.

Hosts: Carolyn Greenwood and dog Libby
Rooms: 5 (3 PB; 2 SB) $65-75
Continental Breakfast
Credit Cards: A, B, D
Notes: 2, 9, 10, 11, 12, 13

PORT HOPE

The Stafford House

4489 Main Street, 48468
(517) 428-4554

With delicious full buffet-style breakfasts,
afternoon refreshments, or special dinner packages, guests enjoy staying in this 1886 country
Victorian home. There are also many amenities
to leave guests with lasting memories. From
spectacular sunrises to moonlit nights they
enjoy golf, charter fishing, scenic lighthouses,
antiquing, lakeshore parks, sandy beaches, and
much, much more.

Hosts: Greg and Kathy Gephart
Rooms: 4 (PB) $65-85
Full Breakfast
Credit Cards: A, B
Notes: 2, 4, 5, 7, 8, 11, 12, 13, 14

PORT SANILAC

Raymond House Inn

111 South Ridge Street, M-25, 48469
(810) 622-8800; (800) 622-7229
FAX (810) 622-8485
www.bbonline.com/mi/raymond

Luxury and comfort, 500 feet from Lake
Huron harbor. Seven spacious bed chambers
with warm period furnishings, private baths,
and central air. Old-fashioned parlor. Harbor
Light Gift and Art Gallery on site. Fitness and
"pamper" studio. Collection of original
boudoir dolls. Built in 1872. Listed in register
of historical sites. Original Victoriana is preserved: gingerbread façade, white icicle trim,
classic moldings, and hand-crocheted trims.
Highest quality rating. Nearby are lighthouse,
marina, beach, swimming, restaurants, sunken
wrecks, museum, barn theater, golf, tennis, and
antiques.

Hosts: The Bobofchaks
Rooms: 7 (5 PB; 2 SB) $65-115
Full Breakfast
Credit Cards: A, B, D
Notes: 2, 5, 7, 9, 10, 11, 12, 14

NOTES: Credit cards accepted: A MasterCard; B Visa; C American Express; D Discover; E Diner's Club;
F Other; 2 Personal checks accepted; 3 Lunch available; 4 Dinner available; 5 Open all year; 6 Pets welcome;

SAGINAW

Montague Inn

1581 South Washington Avenue, 48601
(517) 752-3939; FAX (517) 752-3159
www.montagueinn.com

This restored Georgian mansion is surrounded by spacious lawns with flower and herb gardens. Summer evenings may be spent under the trees watching the wildlife. Enjoy winter evenings curled up in front of the roaring fire in the library. Fine cuisine is offered for lunch and dinner Tuesday through Saturday in the dining room overlooking the grounds. The inn is minutes from historic Frankenmuth and the outlets at Birch Run.

Rooms: 18 (16 PB; 2 SB)
Continental Breakfast
Credit Cards: A, B, C
Notes: 2, 3, 4, 5, 7, 8, 9, 10, 11, 12, 13, 15

ST. IGNACE

The Colonial House Inn

90 North State Street, 49781
(906) 643-6900

In the heart, and wrapped in the history, of downtown St. Ignace, the Colonial House Inn is a delightful Victorian-style home overlooking the Mackinac Straits. Six rooms, individually named, are furnished in Victorian style, providing a peaceful oasis. The wraparound veranda and second-floor balcony are wonderful places to sit, relax, observe, and enjoy the beauty of the Straits area including Mackinac Island, minutes away by ferry.

Host: Elizabeth Brown
Rooms: 6 (PB) $59-99
Full Breakfast
Credit Cards: A, B, D
Notes: 2, 7, 9, 10, 11, 12

SAUGATUCK

Beechwood Manor Bed & Breakfast

736 Pleasant Street, 49453
(616) 857-1587; FAX (616) 857-3909

Historic restored treasure on the hill. Built in 1870s as a private home for a diplomat. Listed in the national register. The finest accommodations and hospitality, heirloom furnishings. Covered veranda with rockers, the perfect relaxing setting. A waterfront cottage available. All travelers welcome. Inquire about accommodations for children. Just blocks from the heart of town. Four minutes' drive to Lake Michigan beach.

Hosts: James and Sherron Lemons
Rooms: 5 (PB) $125-225
Full and Continental Breakfast
Credit Cards: A, B
Notes: 5, 7, 8, 9, 10, 11, 12, 13, 14

Maplewood Hotel

428 Butler Street, P.O. Box 1059, 49453
(616) 857-1771; (800) 650-9790
FAX (616) 857-1773

Adjacent to the village green in the heart of downtown Saugatuck, the Maplewood Hotel is steps from shopping and restaurants. Elegant rooms with private baths, air conditioning, TVs, and telephones; some with fireplaces and Jacuzzis. Gourmet breakfast is included. Enjoy the deck with a heated lap pool or the common room with a wood-burning fireplace. Conference facilities, fax, and copier are available. Rated excellent by the American Bed and Breakfast Association.

Host: Catherine L. Simon
Rooms: 15 (PB) $100-185
Full Breakfast
Credit Cards: A, B, C
Notes: 2, 5, 7, 8, 9, 10, 11, 12, 13, 14, 15

7 No smoking; 8 Children welcome; 9 Social drinking allowed; 10 Tennis nearby; 11 Swimming nearby; 12 Golf nearby; 13 Skiing nearby; 14 May be booked through a travel agent; 15 Handicapped accessible.

The Park House Bed & Breakfast and Cottages

888 Holland Street, 49453
(616) 857-4535; (800) 321-4535
FAX (616) 857-1065
e-mail: parkhouse@softhouse.com

Saugatuck's oldest residence (circa 1857), Susan B. Anthony once slept here and now guests can too. Full breakfast, air conditioning, close to town, beach, and cross-country trails. Three bedrooms for two, one family suite, two Jacuzzi suites, and two cottages feature fireplaces. Some offer TV/VCR, telephone, breakfast in bed. Handicapped accessible. Winter brings murder mysteries and progressive dinner packages. Inquire about hosts' bed and breakfast in Mexico.

Hosts: Joe and Lynda Petty; Dan Osborn
Rooms: 8 (PB) $95-165
Full Breakfast
Credit Cards: A, B, C, D
Notes: 2, 5, 7, 8, 9, 10, 11, 12, 13, 14, 15

Rosemont Inn

83 Lakeshore Drive, P.O. Box 214, 49453
(616) 857-2637; (800) 721-2637
www.rosemontinn.com

This country inn on Lake Michigan, selected as "One of the Midwest's Top Ten Romantic Retreats" by the *Chicago Sun Times*, offers lake-view rooms with gas fireplaces and

Rosemont Inn

Jacuzzi suites. Other areas include a lakeside gathering room to view spectacular sunsets and a poolside great room, both with fireplaces. Enjoy the lake-viewing gazebo, complimentary bicycles, large custom-designed indoor whirlpool/sauna. Outdoor heated swimming pool. Waterfall garden. Full buffet breakfast and evening hors d'oeuvres. The inn is fully air conditioned. Direct beach access at doorstep.

Hosts: The Sajdak Family
Rooms: 14 (PB) $95-255
Full Breakfast
Credit Cards: A, B, C, D
Notes: 2, 5, 7, 9, 10, 11, 12, 13, 14, 15

Sherwood Forest

Sherwood Forest Bed & Breakfast

938 Center Street, P.O. Box 315, 49453
(800) 838-1246

This beautiful Victorian-style house is surrounded by woods. Guest rooms are decorated with antiques and traditional furnishings. Two suites are available with Jacuzzi and fireplace. Another has a large mural, along with a fireplace. The bed and breakfast has central air conditioning, a heated swimming pool, and a wraparound porch. The eastern shore of Lake Michigan and a public beach are a half-block away. The charming shops and restaurants of Saugatuck are just two miles away.

Hosts: Keith and Susan Charak
Rooms: 4 (PB) $85-165
Continental Breakfast

NOTES: Credit cards accepted: A MasterCard; B Visa; C American Express; D Discover; E Diner's Club; F Other; 2 Personal checks accepted; 3 Lunch available; 4 Dinner available; 5 Open all year; 6 Pets welcome;

Credit Cards: A, B, D, E
Notes: 2, 5, 7, 9, 10, 11, 12, 13, 14

Twin Gables Country Inn

900 Lake Street, P.O. Box 881, 49453
(800) 231-2185; FAX (616) 857-3482
e-mail: relax@twingablesinn.com
www.twingablesinn.com

Enjoy personalized service at this historic bed
and breakfast. This pleasant, romantic inn, is
just a short walk to the village center, while
still being in a country-like setting on 1.25
rolling acres. Relax on the porch, delight in the
sunset over Lake Kalamazoo. Fourteen rooms
with private bath and central air, several with
fireplaces, plus three cottages with kitchens.
Gourmet breakfasts served in a spacious common room. Enjoy the hot tub, fireplace, gardens, and summer pool.

Hosts: Bob Lawrence and Susan Schwaderer
Rooms: 14 (PB) $75-150
Continental Breakfast
Credit Cards: A, B, C, D
Notes: 2, 5, 7, 8, 9, 10, 11, 12, 13, 14, 15

Twin Oaks Inn

227 Griffith Street, P.O. Box 867, 49453
(616) 857-1600

Built in 1860, this totally renovated inn offers
old English warmth and charm along with all
modern amenities. Queen- or king-size beds
and private baths. Air conditioning, along with
cable TV, VCRs, and a library of more than
700 films, assures a wonderful stay no matter
what the weather. Common areas with fireplace and outdoor hot tub, along with antiques
throughout, guarantee a memorable escape.
Homemade breakfast. Cottage with sleeping
loft and private hot tub.

Hosts: Nancy and Jerry Horney
Rooms: 6 (PB) $65-125
Cottage: 1
Full and Continental Breakfast
Credit Cards: A, B, D
Notes: 2, 5, 7, 8, 9, 10, 11, 12, 13, 14

SAUGATUCK (DOUGLAS)

J. Paules Fenn Inn

2254 South 58th Street, Fennville, 49408
(616) 561-2836 (phone/FAX)

Nestled in the countryside, eight miles from
Saugatuck, guests here will find a very traditional bed and breakfast with private and
shared baths. The hosts offer large rooms and a
wonderful full breakfast every morning, served
from 8:00-11:00 A.M. The many decks and
flower gardens offer lots of peaceful moments.
The inn is just minutes from Holland, Allegan,
and South Haven.

Hosts: Paulette J. Clouse and Ewald Males
Rooms: 5 (2 PB: 3 SB) $70-130
Full Breakfast
Credit Cards: A, B, D
Notes: 2, 5, 6, 7, 8, 9, 10, 11, 12, 13, 15

SOUTH HAVEN

A Country Place Bed & Breakfast

79 North Shore Drive North, 49090
(616) 637-5523
e-mail: acountryplace@cybersol.com
www.csi-net.net/acountryplace

Experience gracious hospitality at this lovingly
restored 1860s Greek
Revival. The English
country theme evi-
dent throughout is
created by beautiful
florals and antique
treasures collected dur-
ing the hosts' stay in England. A "sin"sational
breakfast is served by the fireside or on the
deck overlooking the garden, spacious lawn,
and gazebo, all surrounded by six acres of
peaceful woodland. Lake Michigan beach
access one-half block away. Complimentary
refreshments are available.

Hosts: Art and Lee Niffenegger
Rooms: 5 (PB) $75-125

7 No smoking; 8 Children welcome; 9 Social drinking allowed; 10 Tennis nearby; 11 Swimming nearby;
12 Golf nearby; 13 Skiing nearby; 14 May be booked through a travel agent; 15 Handicapped accessible.

Full Breakfast
Credit Cards: A, B, C, D
Notes: 2, 7, 9, 10, 11, 12, 14

Seymour House Bed & Breakfast

1248 Blue Star Highway, 49090
(616) 227-3918
www.seymourhouse.com

On 11 acres of beautiful countryside, one-half mile from Lake Michigan and minutes to Saugatuck and South Haven. This Italianate-style 1862 mansion has original pocket doors and intricate carved woodwork. Some guest rooms with fireplace and Jacuzzi. Two-bedroom guest log cabin also available. Close to sandy beaches, wineries, three golf courses, antique shops, orchards, and restaurants. Enjoy the best of both worlds—close to activities in the area, yet in minutes return to the peaceful and tranquil setting of the Seymour House. Children are welcome in the cabin.

Hosts: Tom and Gwen Paton
Rooms: 5 (PB) $80-145
Full Breakfast
Credit Cards: A, B
Notes: 2, 5, 7, 9, 11, 12, 13, 14

Seymour House

Yelton Manor Bed & Breakfast

140 North Shore Drive, 49090
(616) 637-5220
www.yeltonmanor.com

Elegant, gracious Victorian mansions on the sunset shore of Lake Michigan. Seventeen gorgeous rooms, all with private bath, some with Jacuzzi and fireplace. Panoramic lake views, prize-winning gardens, two salons with fireplaces, cozy wing chairs, floral carpets, four-

Yelton Manor

poster beds, and a pampering staff set the tone for relaxation and romance. Guests will never want to leave after enjoying the wonderful breakfasts, day-long treats, and evening hors d'oeuvres.

Hosts: Elaine and Rob
Rooms: 17 (PB) $90-265
Full Breakfast
Credit Cards: A, B, C
Notes: 2, 5, 7, 9, 10, 11, 12, 13

SUTTONS BAY

Open Windows Bed & Breakfast

613 St. Mary's Avenue, P.O. Box 698, 49682
(231) 271-4300; (800) 520-3722
e-mail: openwindows@centuryinter.net
www.leelanau.com/openwindows

A charming century-old home with lovely gardens and front porch for viewing the bay. This warm, inviting home is decorated with guests' comfort in mind. Enjoy the hearty homemade

Open Windows

NOTES: Credit cards accepted: A MasterCard; B Visa; C American Express; D Discover; E Diner's Club; F Other; 2 Personal checks accepted; 3 Lunch available; 4 Dinner available; 5 Open all year; 6 Pets welcome;

breakfasts and the friendly atmosphere. The village with its beaches, unique shops, and fine restaurants is just a short walk away, or ride the bikes and explore the surrounding countryside. Fireplace, beach fires and picnics, sunsets on Lake Michigan. Fifteen miles from Traverse City. Special weekend packages.

Hosts: Don and Norma Blumenschine
Rooms: 3 (PB) $105-140
Full Breakfast
Credit Cards: None
Notes: 2, 3, 4, 5, 7, 10, 11, 12, 13, 14

TRAVERSE CITY

Bowers Harbor Bed & Breakfast

13972 Peninsula Drive, 49686
(616) 223-7869
www.pentel.net/~verbanic

Private sandy beach, West Bay sunsets, and all the fun of Traverse City are found at this bed and breakfast on Old Mission Peninsula. Three lovely bedrooms available, all with private baths and brass beds. Enjoy the beautiful sunsets from the wraparound stone front porch or from the beach. Bowers Harbor is close to restaurants and wineries. Rates include a full breakfast. No smoking is permitted inside the bed and breakfast.

Hosts: Gary and Mary Ann Verbanic
Rooms: 3 (PB) $110-140
Full Breakfast
Credit Cards: None
Notes: 2, 5, 7, 9, 10, 11, 12, 13

Cherry Knoll Farm Bed & Breakfast

2856 Hammond Road East, 49685
(517) 436-3529

On 115 acres of working farmland this Victorian farm house was built in 1863. Five bedrooms. TV, air conditioning. Ski and snow mobiling available in winter. Cherry picking during the summer. Ten miles from Traverse City. Golf courses, skiing, skating, swimming.

Hosts: Jim and Joan Demlow
Rooms: 4 (4 S3B) $65
Full Breakfast
Credit Cards: A, B, D, E
Notes: 2, 5, 7, 8, 9, 10, 11, 12, 13

Linden Lea on Long Lake

279 South Long Lake Road, 49684
(231) 943-9182; e-mail: lindenlea@aol.com

Enchanting spot on a crystal-clear lake reminiscent of *On Golden Pond*. Lakeside bedrooms have window seats and queen-size beds. Antiques and treasures throughout the home. Relax by the fire and listen for loons. Peaceful sandy private beach with rowboat and paddleboat. Incredible breakfasts. Central air conditioning. Spectacular sunsets. "Guests tell us we are one of the best!"

Hosts: Jim and Vicky McDonnell
Rooms: 2 (PB) $85-110
Full Breakfast
Credit Cards: None
Notes: 2, 5, 7, 8, 9, 10, 11, 12, 13, 14

UNION PIER

The Inn at Union Pier

9708 Berrien Street, P.O. Box 222, 49129
(616) 469-4700
www.innatunionpier.com

Only 90 minutes from Chicago and 200 steps to the beach, the inn caters to both weekend getaways and weekday corporate retreats. Choose from 16 guest rooms, many featuring Swedish fireplaces and porches or balconies, and two luxurious whirlpool suites. Unwind in the outdoor hot tub or sauna, or enjoy Michigan wines and popcorn in the great room. "Harbor Country" offers diverse dining, antiquing, and wineries, and year-round outdoor activities from biking to cross-country skiing.

Hosts: Joyce Erickson Pitts and Mark Pitts
Rooms: 16 (PB) $135-205
Full Breakfast
Credit Cards: A, B, D
Notes: 2, 5, 7, 9, 10, 11, 12, 13

7 No smoking; 8 Children welcome; 9 Social drinking allowed; 10 Tennis nearby; 11 Swimming nearby; 12 Golf nearby; 13 Skiing nearby; 14 May be booked through a travel agent; 15 Handicapped accessible.

Crookston

Lake
Kabetogama

Lutsen • Grand Marais

Nevis
• Park Rapids
• Cross Lake
• New York Mills
Duluth
Fergus Falls
Batle Lake
Alexandria
• Morris
Annandale •
Brooklyn Center
Stillwater
Minneapolis • St. Paul
• Chaska Hastings • Afton
Red Wing • Lake City
Kenyon • • Wabasha
Winona
Sherburn
Houston •

Minnesota

Minnesota

Afton House Inn

AFTON

Afton House Inn

3291 South St. Croix Trail, 55001
(651) 436-8883; FAX (651) 436-6859
e-mail: info@aftonhouseinn.com

All of the charm of a historic country inn. Each room is unique in decor, with an antique ambiance, along with the modern conveniences of a private bath and TV. Deluxe rooms feature whirlpool tubs and outdoor balconies overlooking the St. Croix River. Treat yourself to an evening or weekend away. Whether you are planning a honeymoon night, a winter ski weekend, or summer getaway…The historic Afton House Inn is worth remembering.

Hosts: Gordy and Kathy Jarvis
Rooms: 15 (PB) $60-140
Continental Breakfast
Credit Cards: A, B, C, D
Notes: 2, 3, 4, 5, 7, 8, 9, 10, 11, 12, 13, 14, 15

Afton's Mulberry Pond Bed & Breakfast

3786 River Road, 55001
(651) 436-8086

Tucked in the woods overlooking the beautiful St. Croix River, Mulberry Pond is the perfect place to get away from it all. Furnished in a charming blend of contemporary and antique, it features private baths, whirlpools, private beach, free overnight boat docking, Continental breakfast.

Hosts: Nick and Elaine Mucciacciaro, owners
Rooms: 2 (PB) $95
Continental Breakfast
Credit Cards: A, B
Notes: 2, 5, 7, 11, 13, 14

ALEXANDRIA

Cedar Rose Inn

422 Seventh Avenue West, 56308
(320) 762-8430; (888) 203-5333

From the wild blooming roses in the summer, to the warm crackling fire in the winter, the Cedar Rose Inn offers year-round comfort for anyone away from home. In the "silk stocking" historic district near downtown Alexandria,

Cedar Rose Inn

NOTES: Credit cards accepted: A MasterCard; B Visa; C American Express; D Discover; E Diner's Club; F Other; 2 Personal checks accepted; 3 Lunch available; 4 Dinner available; 5 Open all year; 6 Pets welcome; 7 No smoking; 8 Children welcome; 9 Social drinking allowed; 10 Tennis nearby; 11 Swimming nearby; 12 Golf nearby; 13 Skiing nearby; 14 May be booked through a travel agent; 15 Handicapped accessible.

guests can easily access the many shops and recreational activities in this quaint city of lakes. The inn was built in 1903 and retains the beautiful original structure providing a romantic escape into history.

Hosts: Aggie and Florian Ledermann
Rooms: 4 (PB) $75-125
Full Breakfast
Credit Cards: A, B, C, D
Notes: 2, 5, 7, 9, 10, 11, 12, 13, 14

ANNANDALE

Thayer's Historic Bed & Breakfast

Highway 55–60 West Elm Street, P.O. Box 246, 55302
(320) 274-8222; (800) 944-6595
FAX (320) 274-5051
www.bbonline.com/mn/thayer

A unique, casually elegant, gracious inn notable for comfort and good conversation was built in 1895 and is in the national historic register. Authentic antiques, private baths, claw-foot tubs, air conditioning, hot tub, sauna, liquor lounge, gourmet dining, fireplaces, whirlpools, murder mystery dinners, and customized packages featuring satin sheets and breakfast in bed. Owner is a psychic and readings are by appoint-

Thayer's

ment. Location has easy access to Minneapolis and St. Cloud on Highway 55.

Host: Sharon Gammell
Rooms: 11 (PB) $48.50-147
Full or Continental Breakfast
Credit Cards: A, B, C, D
Notes: 2, 3, 4, 5, 6, 9, 10, 11, 12, 13, 14

BROOKLYN CENTER

Inn on the Farm

6150 Summit Drive North, 55430
(800) 428-8382; www.innonthefarm.com

The Inn on the Farm at Earle Brown Heritage Center offers a bed and breakfast experience guests will never forget. Housed in a cluster of historic farm buildings, the inn is on the grounds of a beautifully restored Victorian gentlemen's country estate, just 10 minutes from the heart of downtown Minneapolis. The Inn on the Farm is on the edge of the Green, the estate's beautifully landscaped central mall. In summer, guests will enjoy the shaded walking paths which lead them across the Green's extensive lawns.

Rooms: 10 (PB) $110-140
Full Breakfast
Credit Cards: A, B, C, D, E
Notes: 5, 7, 10, 11, 12, 15

CHASKA

Bluff Creek Inn

1161 Bluff Creek Drive, 55318
(612) 445-2735

Country inn (circa 1860) has country charm in Minnesota River valley. Thirty minutes to downtown Minneapolis. Various rooms, whirlpool, fireplace. One of top 10 Midwest inns (*Chicago Tribune*). Minutes to Mall of America, Landscape Arboretum, Chanhassen Dinner Theatre, Renaissance Festival, casino, horse races. Nearby walking/biking/ski trails.

NOTES: Credit cards accepted: A MasterCard; B Visa; C American Express; D Discover; E Diner's Club; F Other; 2 Personal checks accepted; 3 Lunch available; 4 Dinner available; 5 Open all year; 6 Pets welcome;

Bluff Creek Inn

Bountiful three-course breakfast, hors d'oeuvres. Children over 12 welcome. No pets. No smoking.

Hosts: Maida and Jim Eggen
Rooms: 5 (PB) $85-175
Full Breakfast
Credit Cards: A, B
Notes: 2, 5, 7, 9, 11, 12

CROOKSTON

Elm Street Inn

422 Elm Street, 56716
(218) 281-2343
e-mail:legal@beltrami.means.net

Lovingly restored 1910 home with antiques, hardwood floors, stained-glass windows. Pri-

Elm Street Inn

vate baths. Wicker-filled sun porch. Old-fashioned beds with quilts. Memorable candlelight breakfast. Indoor community pool next door. Excellent bird watching. Near the University of Minnesota campus. No pets. Smoke-free.

Hosts: John and Sheryl Winters
Rooms: 4 (PB) $55-65
Full Breakfast
Credit Cards: A, B, C, D
Notes: 2, 5, 7, 9, 10, 11, 12, 14

CROSS LAKE

Birch Hill Inne Bed & Breakfast

P.O. Box 468, 56442
(218) 692-4857; e-mail: stay@birchhillinne.com
www.birchhillinne.com

Five guest rooms, private baths, two with Jacuzzi tubs. Private wildflower gardens, hiking and cross-country ski trails. Antique furnishings. Sumptuous Continental breakfast. Spacious screened porch. Pine-paneled breakfast room with fireplace. Canoe, paddle boat and bicycles available. Tennis, bike path, golf nearby. On the beautiful Whitefish chain of lakes. Twenty-three miles north of Brainerd. Open year-round. No smoking. No pets. No accommodations for children.

Hosts: Steve and Heidi Engen
Rooms: 5 (PB) $72-80
Continental Breakfast
Credit Cards: A, B, C
Notes: 2, 5, 7, 9, 10, 11, 12, 13

Manhattan Beach Lodge

County Road 66, P.O. Box 719, 56442
(218) 692-3381; (800) 399-4360
FAX (218) 692-2774
e-mail: mblodge@crosslake.net
www.mblodge.com

When the Manhattan Beach Lodge was built in 1929, it brought a touch of civilization to Minnesota's lake country wilderness. The same is still true today as visitors watch an eagle soar overhead or the sunset over the 14 lakes of the Whitefish chain. The lodge provides casual

7 No smoking; 8 Children welcome; 9 Social drinking allowed; 10 Tennis nearby; 11 Swimming nearby; 12 Golf nearby; 13 Skiing nearby; 14 May be booked through a travel agent; 15 Handicapped accessible.

Manhattan Beach Lodge

elegance in lodging and dining and a wealth of activities, such as hiking, biking, boating, fishing, golf, skiing, snowshoeing, and more. The Lodge is rustic where guests expect it to be and wonderfully restored with all the conveniences when guests want it to be.

Hosts: Mary and John Zesbaugh
Rooms: 18 (PB) $69-169
Continental Breakfast
Credit Cards: A, B, C, D
Notes: 2, 3, 4, 5, 7, 8, 9, 10, 11, 12, 13, 14, 15

DULUTH

Olcott House Bed & Breakfast Inn

2316 East First Street, 55812
(800) 715-1339; www.visitduluth.com/olcotthouse

Historic 1904 Georgian Colonial mansion offering over 10,000 square feet of elegant living. Tastefully decorated romantic suites with working fireplaces and private baths. Carriage house is perfect for honeymoons and special occasions. Library, music room, grand porch, lake views. Smoke free. Candlelight breakfasts, antiques, gift certificates. Midweek discounts. AAA-approved. Children 12 and older welcome.

Hosts: Barb and Don Trueman
Rooms: 6 (PB) $85-149
Full Breakfast
Credit Cards: A, B, D
Notes: 2, 5, 7, 9, 10, 11, 12, 13, 14

Pj's Bed & Breakfast

5757 Berquist Road, 55804
(218) 525-2508; e-mail: pjsbb@cpinternet.com
www.cp.duluth.mn.us/pjsbb

"The Inn with the Superior View." Each of five rooms offers a queen-size bed, private bath, and elegantly furnished in different themes: Heavenly Hideaway, Captain's Cove, Rose's Retreat, Country Corner, and Sweetheart Safari. Spacious seating area with corner fireplace and large deck with breathtaking view. Large specialized breakfast awaits guests while enjoying the grandeur of the Northland.

Hosts: Phil and Jan Hanson (Micheal and Sarah)
Rooms: 5 (PB) $85-125
Full Breakfast
Credit Cards: None
Notes: 2, 5, 7, 9, 11, 12, 13

Spinnaker Inn Bed & Breakfast

5427 North Shore Scenic Drive, 55804-2939
(218) 525-2838; (800) 525-2838
www.cp.duluth.mn.us/~spinninn

Quiet, relaxing lodging overlooking Lake Superior. Large yet cozy guest rooms with beautiful view of lake. Nautical decor throughout. Large lakeside deck, cable TV, stone fireplace in dining room. Hearty breakfast. Near antique, collectible, and gift shops. Close to cross-country ski areas. Extended stay discounts. A visit to Duluth and the North Shore of Lake Superior is a "must" vacation. Lake Superior is the largest freshwater lake in the world by surface area.

Hosts: Clare Carpenter and Dan Whalen
Rooms: 2 (2 SB) $75-90
Full Breakfast
Credit Cards: A, B, D
Notes: 2, 5, 7, 12, 13

NOTES: Credit cards accepted: A MasterCard; B Visa; C American Express; D Discover; E Diner's Club; F Other; 2 Personal checks accepted; 3 Lunch available; 4 Dinner available; 5 Open all year; 6 Pets welcome;

FERGUS FALLS _____

Bergerud Bs
(Bed, Breakfast, & Bakery)

Route 5, Box 61, 56537
(218) 736-4720; (800) 557-4720

Enjoy a night of restful tranquility at a century
farm setting in a home built in 1895 by the
owner's grandfather. The house has been modernized, but the original structure remains much
the same. Excellent bird watching, nearby
waterfowl production area, and an occasional
deer wanders through the yard. Fifteen-minute
drive to antique shops, historical museum,
shopping, fishing, boating, and swimming.
Awaken to the smell of flavored coffee and a
sumptuous breakfast of your choice.

Hosts: James and Sylvia Bergerud
Rooms: 3 (1 PB; 2 SB) $45-75
Full Breakfast
Credit Cards: None
Notes: 2, 5, 7

GRAND MARAIS _____

Old Shore
Beach Bed & Breakfast

1434 Old Shore Road, 55604
(218) 387-9707; (888) 387-9707
FAX (218) 387-9811
e-mail: visit@oldshorebeach.com

Old Shore Beach Bed and Breakfast sits along a
pebble beach on the shore of Lake Superior.
This newly built lakeshore home began welcoming guests in 1997. Four guest rooms have private baths, queen- or king-size beds, in-room
seating areas, and many views of Lake Superior.
The grand cobblestone fireplace and its comfortable living room welcome all visitors. Full
breakfast is served in the lake-view dining room.
A large deck and lakeside seating, sauna, rental
of mountain bikes and snowshoes, cozy terry-
cloth robes and slippers in each room contribute
to relaxation. Picnic-style lunch available.

Host: Paulette Anholm
Rooms: 4 (PB) $95-115
Full Breakfast
Credit Cards: A, B
Notes: 2, 5, 7, 11, 12, 13

Pincushion Mountain

Pincushion Mountain
Bed & Breakfast

968 Gunflint Trail, 55604
(218) 387-1276; (800) 542-1226
e-mail: pincushion@boreal.org
www.pincushionbb.com

Three miles north of Grand Marais. Secluded
on forested ridge offering views of Lake Superior 1,000 feet below. Newer inn (circa 1986)
decorated in country fashion. Private baths, full
breakfast, sauna, beamed common area with
fireplace and deck. Vast network of hiking,
biking, cross-country skiing, and snowshoeing
trails maintained to doorstep. BWCA canoe
entry close by.

Hosts: Scott and Mary Beattie
Rooms 4 (PB) $90-105
Full Breakfast
Credit Cards: A, B
Notes: 2, 3, 5, 7, 9, 10, 11, 12, 13, 14

HASTINGS _____

Thorwood Historic Inns

315 Pine Street, 55033
(651) 437-3297; (888) 846-7966
FAX (651) 437-4129; e-mail: mrthorwood@aol.com
www.thorwoodinn.com

Be pampered with privacy at these two national
register inns, lovingly restored to feature 15

7 No smoking; 8 Children welcome; 9 Social drinking allowed; 10 Tennis nearby; 11 Swimming nearby;
12 Golf nearby; 13 Skiing nearby; 14 May be booked through a travel agent; 15 Handicapped accessible.

unique, luxurious suites with fireplaces, whirlpools, or both, or a magnificent steam shower. Enjoy a three-course breakfast and an optional dinner in the privacy of own suite, served to guests' schedule. These 1880 inns are close to quaint downtown on the banks of the Mississippi. Antiquing, biking, nature center, winery, St. Croix River nearby.

Hosts: Pam and Dick Thorsen
Rooms: 15 (PB) $97-257
Full Breakfast
Credit Cards: A, B, C, D
Notes: 2, 4, 5, 7, 9, 10, 11, 12, 13, 14

HOUSTON

Addie's Attic Bed & Breakfast

117 South Jackson Street, P.O. Box 677, 55943
(507) 896-3010; FAX (507) 896-4010

This beautiful turn-of-the-century home, circa 1903, has a cozy front parlor with curved glass window. Games, TV, and player piano available. Guest rooms are decorated and furnished with attic finds. Hearty country breakfast served in dining room. Near hiking, biking, cross-country skiing trails, canoeing, and antique shops. Weekday rates.

Hosts: Fred and Marilyn Huhn
Rooms: 3 (3 SB) $40-50
Full Breakfast
Credit Cards: None
Notes: 2, 7, 9, 10, 11, 12, 13

KENYON

Grandfather's Woods

3640-450th Street. 55946
(507) 789-6414

Charming 1860s fifth-generation working farmstead showcases family antiques and memorabilia used to distinctively decorate three cozy guest rooms, one with fireplace. A large inviting guest area consists of parlor, hearthside dining room (fruit and treats always available), sitting porches. Several garden

swings and small pond are tucked into the colorful cottage garden. Guests hike or cross-country ski through 65 acres of wooded trails. The Percheron draft horse team provides hay- or sleighrides.

Hosts: Judy and George Langemo
Rooms: 3 (2 PB; 1 SB) $60-70
Full and Continental Breakfast
Credit Cards: None
Notes: 2, 3, 4, 5, 7, 8, 11, 12, 13

LAKE CITY

Victorian Bed & Breakfast

620 South High Street, 55041-1757
(651) 345-2167; (888) 345-2167

Built in 1896, this Stick-style Victorian overlooks beautiful Lake Pepin, which is part of the Hiawatha Valley of the Mississippi River. Noted for its scenic bluffs and high concentration of eagles, swans, and waterfowl, Lake Pepin can be seen from every room. Original stained-glass windows and carved butternut woodwork are outstanding features of this house. The adjacent guest house features rooms with whirlpools and fireplaces as well as lake views.

Hosts: Bernie and Ione Link
Rooms: 5 (PB) $65-135
Full Breakfast
Credit Cards: None
Notes: 2, 5, 7, 9, 10, 11, 12, 13

Victorian

LAKE KABETOGAMA

Bunt's Kabinns

12497 Burma Road, 56669
(218) 875-2691; (888) 741-1020
FAX (218) 875-3008

Two private cabins and a four-room inn near the Canadian border and Voyageurs National Park, on the shores of Lake Kabetogama. The small inn is in a converted school and church building. Private baths, full kitchens, fireplaces, whirlpool, Jacuzzis, saunas, many decks, beach, dock, satellite, color TVs, VCRs, and washers and dryers. Truly three touches of class in the midst of the wilderness.

Host: Bob Buntrock
Rooms: 6 (PB) $60-180
Continental Breakfast
Credit Cards: A, B, C, D
Notes: 2, 3, 4, 5, 8, 9, 10, 11, 12, 13, 14, 15

LUTSEN

Lindgren's Bed & Breakfast

5552 County Road 35, P.O. Box 56, 55612-0056
(218) 663-7450

A 1920s log home in Superior National Forest on walkable shoreline of Lake Superior. Massive stone fireplaces, Finnish sauna, whirlpool, baby grand piano, TVs, VCR, and CD player. A hearty Northwoods breakfast is served. In center of area known for skiing, golf, stream

Lindgren's

and lake fishing, skyride, mountain biking, snowmobiling, horseback riding, alpine slide, kayaking, fall colors, Superior Hiking Trail, Boundary Waters Canoe Area entry point, and state parks. Spacious manicured grounds. One-half mile off scenic Highway 61 on the Lake Superior Circle Tour. AAA-approved. Children 12 and older welcome.

Host: Shirley Lindgren
Rooms: 4 (PB) $85-125
Full Breakfast
Credit Cards: A, B
Notes: 2, 3, 5, 7, 9, 10, 11, 12, 13, 14

MINNEAPOLIS

Evelo's Bed & Breakfast

2301 Bryant Avenue South, 55405
(612) 374-9656

This 1897 house is in the Lowry Hill East neighborhood and has a well-preserved Victorian interior. The three guest rooms are on the third floor, each furnished in period furniture. The entire first floor is done in original dark oak millwork. A small refrigerator, coffee maker, telephone, fax, and TV are available for guest use. Air conditioned. The bed and breakfast is within walking distance of downtown, Lake of the Isles, Upton shopping area, Walker Art Center, Guthrie Theater, and the Minneapolis Institute of Arts. Established in 1979. Cross-country skiing nearby.

Hosts: David and Sheryl Evelo
Rooms: 3 (SB) $60
Continental Breakfast
Credit Cards: A, B, C, D, E
Notes: 2, 5, 7, 9, 10, 11, 12, 13

Nan's Bed & Breakfast

2304 Fremont Avenue South, 55405
(612) 377-5118; (800) 214-5118
e-mail: zosel@mn.mcad.edu

Comfortable urban 1890s Victorian family home offering guest rooms furnished with antiques. Friendly, outgoing hosts will help

7 No smoking; 8 Children welcome; 9 Social drinking allowed; 10 Tennis nearby; 11 Swimming nearby; 12 Golf nearby; 13 Skiing nearby; 14 May be booked through a travel agent; 15 Handicapped accessible.

guests find their way around town. Near downtown, lakes, theaters, galleries, restaurants, and shopping. One block from buses. Smoking permitted in designated areas only.

Hosts: Nan and Jim Zosel
Rooms: 3 (SB) $55-60
Full Breakfast
Credit Cards: A, B, C, E
Notes: 2, 5, 8, 11, 12

MONTICELLO

The Rand House

One Old Territorial Road, 55362
(612) 295-6037; e-mail: randhouse@aol.com
www.randhouse.com

An elegant three-story Queen Anne mansion, the Rand House is listed in the National Register of Historic Places as one of the last remaining Victorian country estates of its kind in the greater Twin Cities metro area. Set on three secluded acres, the Rand House offers extensive grounds, Victorian gardens, fountain ponds, all just 40 minutes from downtown Minneapolis. Guests will enjoy the winter parlor with its massive stone fireplace, the sunny solarium, drawing room, library and formal dining room—all furnished in period antiques and oriental carpets. Candlelight breakfasts are special, too, with linen, china, silver, flowers, and the Rand House's unique gourmet specialities.

Hosts: Duffy and Merrill Busch
Rooms: 4 (PB) $90-145
Full Breakfast
Credit Cards: A, B
Notes: 2, 5, 7, 10, 11, 12, 13, 14

The Rand House

MORRIS

The American House

410 East Third Street, 56267
(320) 589-4054

Victorian home decorated with antiques and country charm. Ride the tandem bike on scenic trails. Within walking distance of area restaurants and shops. One block from the University of Minnesota-Morris campus.

Host: Karen Berget
Rooms: 3 (SB) $40-60
Full Breakfast
Credit Cards: A, B
Notes: 2, 5, 7, 8, 9, 10, 11, 12, 14

NEVIS

The Park Street Inn

Route 3, Box 554, 56467-9704
(218) 652-4500; (800) 797-1778

This 1912 home is richly furnished with antiques, stained glass, carved oak woodwork, and a Mission-style fireplace. Suite features a double whirlpool and a sunroom that overlooks Lake Belle Taine. The new Grotto has a huge whirlpool and king-size bed. City park and beach across the street. Heartland Trail one block away for hiking, bicycling, and snowmobiling. Close to restaurants, antique and gift shops, golfing, and horseback riding. Older children welcome. Pets by arrangement.

Hosts: Irene and Len Hall
Rooms: 4 (PB) $70-125
Full Breakfast
Credit Cards: A, B
Notes: 2, 5, 9, 11, 12, 13, 14

NEW YORK MILLS

Whistle Stop Inn
Bed & Breakfast

Route 1, Box 85, 56567
(218) 385-2223; (800) 328-6315

NOTES: Credit cards accepted: A MasterCard; B Visa; C American Express; D Discover; E Diner's Club; F Other; 2 Personal checks accepted; 3 Lunch available; 4 Dinner available; 5 Open all year; 6 Pets welcome;

Travel Back in Time...Early 1900s Pullman dining car, now your private "Palace Car." Featuring double whirlpool, air conditioning, TV/VCR, microwave and refrigerator, mahogany paneling and floral carpeting throughout. Also "Roaring Twenties" caboose with whirlpool, queen-size Murphy bed and refrigerator. A 1903 Victorian home with three guest rooms, all with private baths, antiques, and railroad memorabilia in every nook and cranny.

Rooms: 5 (PB) $49-125
Credit Cards: A, B, C, D
Notes: 2, 5, 7, 9, 12, 13, 14

PARK RAPIDS

Dickson Viking Hus Bed & Breakfast

202 East Fourth Street, 56470
(218) 732-8089; (888) 899-7292

"Aunt Helen" invites guests to this charming contemporary home with vaulted ceiling and fireplace in the living room that features a watercolor exhibit. Big breakfast. Bicycle or snowmobile the Heartland Trail. Visit Itasca Park and the source of the Mississippi or cross-country ski. Unique shop and restaurant attractions. State inspected.

Host: Helen K. Dickson
Rooms: 3 (1 PB; 2 SB) $42-60
Full Breakfast
Credit Cards: A, B
Notes: 2, 5, 7, 10, 12, 13

RED WING

The Red Wing Blackbird

722 West Fifth Street, 55066
(651) 388-2292; FAX (651) 388-0304
e-mail: blakbird@pressenter.com
www.pressenter.com/~blakbird/

The Red Wing Blackbird is a fine example of Queen Anne architecture and was built in 1880. A charming three-season porch was added recently. The home with its beautifully

crafted woodwork, fireplaces, and Victorian charm has been lovingly maintained since its construction. The Petter Dass Room is a spacious room and has an adjoining sitting area with a king-size bed, private, double, whirlpool bath and shower. The Signe Room has a Norwegian hand-tooled queen-size bed and private bath with shower.

Rooms: 2 (PB) $90-135
Full Breakfast
Credit Cards: A, B
Notes: 2, 5, 8, 9, 10, 11, 12, 13

ST. PAUL

Chatsworth Bed & Breakfast

984 Ashland Avenue, 55104
(612) 227-4288; FAX (612) 225-8217

Take refuge from the hustle and bustle of daily life at the spacious 1902 Victorian inn in a beautiful and serene wooded setting. Whether guests seek a convenient haven for business travel or a destination for a romantic getaway, they enjoy the lovely gardens and experience the warm and comfortable elegance of Chatsworth. Three blocks from the many excellent restaurants and unique shops on Grand Avenue. Also in the vicinity are numerous colleges and churches. Only minutes away from the Chatsworth is the Twin Cities' international airport, the Mall of America, and the downtown areas of both St. Paul and Minneapolis.

Chatsworth

Room: 5 (3 PB; 2 SB) $80-130
Full Breakfast
Credit Cards: A, B, C, D
Notes: 2, 4, 5, 7, 9, 10, 11, 12, 13, 14

The Garden Gate Bed & Breakfast

925 Goodrich Avenue, 55105-3127
(612) 227-8430; (800) 967-2703

A garden of delights awaits guests at this Victorian duplex in the Victoria crossings neighborhood of St. Paul. Easy access to either St. Paul or Minneapolis, business center, airport, state capitol, shops, restaurants, coffee shops. Choice of four rooms with two shared baths.

Hosts: Mary and Miles Conway
Rooms: 4 (2 SB) $65-75
Continental Breakfast
Credit Cards: A, B, C, D
Notes: 2, 5, 7, 8, 9, 10, 11, 12, 13

The Garden Gate

SHERBURN

Four Columns Inn

668 140th Street, 56171
(507) 764-8861

Built in 1884 as a stagecoach stop, this lovingly remodeled Greek Revival inn welcomes travelers. Four antique-filled guest bedrooms, claw-foot tubs, and working fireplaces wel-

Four Columns Inn

come guests. A library, circular stairway, living room with a grand piano, and a solarium with a redwood hot tub make a stay here memorable. A hideaway bridal suite with access to a roof deck with a super view of the countryside is perfect for honeymooners. There is also a romantic getaway Victorian gazebo. Near lakes, antiques, amusement park, and live theater. Two miles north of I-90 on Highway 4, between Chicago and the Black Hills. Call for brochure. AAA three-diamond-rated.

Hosts: Norman and Pennie Kittleson
Rooms: 4 (3 PB; 1 SB) $65-75
Full Breakfast
Credit Cards: None
Notes: 2, 5, 7, 8, 10, 11, 12, 13, 14

STILLWATER

Aurora Staples Inn

303 North Fourth Street, 55082
(651) 351-1187

Lovely Queen Anne Victorian home in a historic rivertown. Built by a lumber baron for his daughter. Includes formal gardens, air conditioning, whirlpools, and fireplaces. Furnished and decorated appropriate to the Victorian era. Guests are served a full breakfast. Close to antique shops, book stores, and wonderful restaurants.

Hosts: Carol Hendrickson and Jenny Roesler
Rooms: 5 (PB) $105-150
Full Breakfast
Credit Cards: A, B, C
Notes: 2, 5, 7, 9, 12, 13, 14

NOTES: Credit cards accepted: A MasterCard; B Visa; C American Express; D Discover; E Diner's Club; F Other; 2 Personal checks accepted; 3 Lunch available; 4 Dinner available; 5 Open all year; 6 Pets welcome;

The Elephant Walk Inc.

801West Pine Street, 55082
(651) 430-0359; (888) 430-0359
www.elephantwalkbb.com

A unique getaway—each room reflects a country. Gourmet breakfast, basket of homemade crackers, cheese, and bottle of champagne or wine to start guests' stay. All rooms have gas fireplaces, double whirlpools, queen-size beds—balconies and a rooftop garden suite make guests' stay unforgettable.

Hosts: Rita Graybill and Mike Robinson
Rooms: 4 (PB) $119-239
Full Breakfast
Credit Cards: A, B, D, E
Notes: 2, 5, 7, 9, 10, 11, 12, 13

James Mulvey Residence Inn

622 West Churchill Street, 55082
(612) 430-8008; FAX (612) 430-2801
www.contn/bb

This is an enchanting place. Built in 1878 by lumberman James A. Mulvey, the Italianate residence and stone carriage house grace the most visited historic rivertown in the upper Midwest. Exclusively for guests are the grand parlor, formal dining room, Victorian sun porch, and seven fabulously decorated guest rooms filled with exquisite art and antiques. Four-course breakfast, double whirlpools, mountain bikes, fireplaces, and air conditioning. Grace-filled service from innkeepers who care.

Hosts: Jill and Truett Lawson
Rooms: 7 (PB) $99-199
Full Breakfast
Credit Cards: A, B, C, D
Notes: 2, 5, 7, 9, 10, 11, 12, 13, 14

The Rivertown Inn

306 West Olive Street, 55082
(651) 430-2955; (800) 562-3632
FAX (651) 430-0034; e-mail: rivertn@aol.com
www.rivertowninn.com

Beautifully restored 1882 three-story lumberman's mansion. Eight charming guest rooms

individually decorated with fine Victorian antiques; all with private baths, five with double whirlpools and fireplaces. Four blocks from historic Main Street. Award-winning full breakfast. Stillwater's first bed and breakfast, celebrating 16 years of outstanding service. Open year-round, midweek discounts.

Hosts: Chuck and Judy Dougherty
Rooms: 8 (PB) $79-179
Full Breakfast
Credit Cards: A, B, C, D
Notes: 2, 5, 7, 9, 10, 11, 12, 13, 14

WABASHA

Eagles on the River Bed & Breakfast

1000 Marina Drive, P.O. Box 185, 55981
(651) 565-3509; (800) 684-6813
e-mail: sandy@EaglesOnTheRiver
www.EaglesOnTheRiver.com

Mississippi River views from Wabasha's landmark contemporary bed and breakfast. Marina one-half block away. Whirlpool, romantic fireplace, sauna, full breakfast, TV, VCR, private baths. Game room has pool table, darts, board games, refrigerator, and microwave. Mall of America is 90 minutes away. Nearby are kayak, canoe, bike, cross-country and downhill ski, boat, and pontoon rentals. Eagle watching. State parks and hiking. Six area golf courses. Honeymooners love the privacy. Patio area. River mile marker 759.4.

Rooms: 2 (PB) $109-159
Full Breakfast
Credit Cards: A, B, C, D
Notes: 2, 5, 7, 9, 10, 11, 12, 13, 14

Eagles on the River

7 No smoking; 8 Children welcome; 9 Social drinking allowed; 10 Tennis nearby; 11 Swimming nearby; 12 Golf nearby; 13 Skiing nearby; 14 May be booked through a travel agent; 15 Handicapped accessible.

WINONA

Carriage House Bed & Breakfast

420 Main Street, 55987
(507) 452-8256; FAX (507) 452-0939
www.chbb.com

The Carriage House Bed and Breakfast is in the center of Winona, a historic town on the mighty Mississippi River. All of the beautifully decorated rooms have private baths and two rooms have gas-fired fireplaces and Jacuzzi whirlpool baths. Built in 1870, the Carriage House features a four-season porch, tandem bicycles, and a wonderful breakfast. Hosts' 1929 Model A Ford is available for special occasions. Continental plus breakfast served.

Hosts: Deb and Don Salyards
Rooms: 4 (PB) $80-150
Continental Breakfast
Credit Cards: A, B, C, D
Notes: 2, 5, 7, 9, 10, 11, 12, 13

Carriage House

Missouri

Borgman's

ARROW ROCK

Borgman's Bed & Breakfast

706 Van Buren, 65320
(660) 837-3350

The hosts invite guests to experience the historic town of Arrow Rock in the warmth of the century-old home. Choose one of four spacious guest rooms that share three baths, and relax in the sitting room or on the porch. Wind up the old Victrola for a song, choose a game or puzzle, browse through a book, or just sit for a spell and listen to the sounds of Arrow Rock. In the morning guests will enjoy a family-style breakfast of freshly baked bread, juice or fruit, coffee, and tea.

Hosts: Kathy and Helen Borgman
Rooms: 4 (S3B) $55-60
Continental Breakfast
Credit Cards: None
Notes: 2, 5, 7, 8

BONNE TERRE

Victorian Veranda Bed & Breakfast

207 East School Street, 63628
(573) 358-1134; (800) 343-1134

Elegant 1880 Victorian mansion overlooking the town Bicentennial Park. Choose from four romantic guest rooms, all with own private baths. Three have thermal massage baths for two. Guests may relax in the parlor or cozy up to the fireplace in the gathering room. The aroma of freshly ground coffee and variety of home-baked goodies will guide the guest to the large dining room for a candlelight breakfast. "So come enjoy the porch swing on this large wrap-around veranda and escape to a quiet getaway."

Hosts: Galen and Karen Forney
Rooms: 4 (PB) $70-90
Full Breakfast
Credit Cards: A, B, D
Notes: 2, 5, 7, 8, 9, 10, 11, 12, 14

BRANSON

The Barger House Bed & Breakfast

621 Lakeshore Drive, 65616
(417) 335-2134; (800) 266-2134

On Lake Taneycomo in the beautiful Ozark Mountains, the Barger House is a charming version of an 18th-century Colonial home. A deck with a hot tub and large pool provides a

Missouri

beautiful view of the lake and downtown Branson. Trout fishing off the private boat dock. Delicious breakfast served in the dining room or on the deck. Wedding and honeymoon packages available.

Host: Ralph Barger
Rooms: 3 (PB) $75-95
Full Breakfast
Credit Cards: A, B, D
Notes: 2, 3, 4, 5, 8, 9, 10, 11, 12, 14

Branson Hotel

Branson Hotel Bed & Breakfast

214 West Main Street, 65616
(417) 335-6104

Historic hotel established 1903. Local landmark. Restored for bed and breakfast in 1992. Perfectly located for all attractions. Walk to shops, antiques, cafés. Lake Toneycomo is three blocks away. Eight guest rooms beautifully furnished with antiques and reproductions. Cable TV and telephones. Central air. Two king-size bedrooms—the Honeymoon Suite and Celebration Suite on the first floor. Six queen-size bedrooms on the second floor. Inquire about accommodations for children.

Rooms: 8 (PB) $85-105
Full Breakfast
Credit Cards: A, B
Notes: 7, 9, 10, 11, 12, 14

Branson House Bed & Breakfast Inn

120 North 4th Street, 65616
(417) 334-0959

Surrounded by rock walls of native fieldstone, old oak trees, and country flower gardens, the Branson House sits on a hillside of downtown Branson overlooking the historical town and bluffs of Lake Taneycomo. Built in 1923, the architecture of this spacious home is unique to the area and remains Branson's grandest old home. AAA three-diamond, Mobil Travel Guide recommended, approved by and member of Bed and Breakfast Inns of Missouri. Close to all attractions.

Rooms: 6 (PB) $65-90
Full Breakfast
Credit Cards: A, B, C
Notes: 2, 7, 9, 10, 11, 12, 14

Cameron's Crag

P.O. Box 295, Point Lookout, 65615
(800) 933-8529

Perched high on a bluff overlooking Lake Taneycomo and Branson, Cameron's Crag offers three guest suites featuring spectacular scenery, a hearty breakfast, and easy access to area attractions. All suites have private entrances, king-size beds, hot tubs, private baths, and cable TV/VCR. One suite has full kitchen, whirlpool, and hot tub.

Cameron's Crag

NOTES: Credit cards accepted: A MasterCard; B Visa; C American Express; D Discover; E Diner's Club; F Other; 2 Personal checks accepted; 3 Lunch available; 4 Dinner available; 5 Open all year; 6 Pets welcome; 7 No smoking; 8 Children welcome; 9 Social drinking allowed; 10 Tennis nearby; 11 Swimming nearby; 12 Golf nearby; 13 Skiing nearby; 14 May be booked through a travel agent; 15 Handicapped accessible.

Hosts: Kay and Glen Cameron
Rooms: 3 (PB) $85-105
Full Breakfast
Credit Cards: A, B, C, D
Notes: 2, 5, 7, 8, 9, 10, 11, 12, 14

Josie's Peaceful Getaway

Indian Point, HCR. 1, Box 1104, 65616
(417) 338-2978; (800) 289-4125
www.bbonline.com/mo/josies

A pristine, gorgeous lakefront view awaits guests at Josie's on famous Table Rock Lake. Sunsets and moonlit nights lace the sky. Contemporary design with cathedral ceilings and a 15-foot-high stone fireplace. Victorian touches include stained glass, china dishes, crystal goblets, candlelight, and fresh flowers. Experience cozy wood-burning fireplaces, lavish Jacuzzi spas, or a secluded picnic lunch in the gazebo. Air conditioned. Celebrate honeymoons/ anniversaries in style. Five minutes to marina and Silver Dollar City. Eight miles to the music shows in Branson. Inquire about accommodations for children. Continental breakfast served Wednesdays and Thursdays.

Hosts: Bill and JoAnne Coats
Rooms: 2 (PB) $60-110
Suite: 1
Full and Continental Breakfast
Credit Cards: A, B, C, D
Notes: 2, 5, 7, 9, 11, 12, 14

Red Bud Cove
Bed & Breakfast Suites

162 Lakewood Drive (Lake Road 65-48,
County Road 65-180), Hollister, 65672
(800) 677-5525

On beautiful Table Rock Lake and just 15 minutes from Branson. Spend the evening in comfort in a spacious suite with lakefront patio and deck. Eight suites with private entrances have living rooms (some with fireplaces), bedrooms with king- or queen-size beds, bathrooms (some with spas), fully equipped kitchenettes and dining areas, air conditioning, TV, and telephone. Full breakfast is served in the main

Red Bud Cove

dining room. Outdoor hot tub, rental boats, and dock space are available for guests' added enjoyment.

Rooms: 8 (PB) $85-105
Full Breakfast
Credit Cards: A, B
Notes: 7, 9, 10, 11, 12, 14

CAMERON

Cook's Country Cottage

7880 Northeast Bacon Road, 64429
(816) 632-1776

This country estate, nestled in 40 acres of hardwood timber, offers a serene getaway spot. A private lake, walking trails, water garden, fountains, and a host of wildlife and songbirds entertain and delight guests as they enjoy the peaceful atmosphere. Private entrances and baths assure guests of their privacy while they

Cook's Country Cottage

choose to relax in beautiful rooms furnished in country decor. Shopping and tours to local historical sites including Missouri's largest Amish settlement are available. Warm baked cookies and fresh flowers awaiting guests in their rooms make them feel like "coming home."

Hosts: Don and Loura Cook
Rooms: 2 (PB) $50-75
Full Breakfast
Credit Cards: None
Notes: 2, 3, 4, 5, 7, 10, 11, 12, 13

DIXON

Rock Eddy Bluff Farm

HCR 62, Box 241, 65459
(573) 759-6081; (800) 335-5921
www.rockeddy.com

Plan an escape to the hills! This rural inn is a nature-lover's dream. Perched atop an Ozark river bluff it provides two scenic guest rooms. They feature unpretentious, old-time furnishings, comfortable, antique, queen-size beds, and a spectacular view of the river valley. Turkey Ridge Cottage is popular with groups of two to six people. Or step back in time at secluded Line Camp, where modern contraptions are prohibited. Canoes are provided for guests. Explore the river, fish, or swim. Just relax or hike the wooded hills. Accompany hosts in an Amish horse-drawn wagon.

Hosts: Kathy and Tom Corey
Rooms: 4 (1 PB; 3 SB) $65-95
Full Breakfast
Credit Cards: A, B, D
Notes: 2, 5, 6, 8, 9, 11, 12

FORDLAND

Red Oak Inn

1046 Red Oak Road, 65652
(417) 767-2444

A true country bed and breakfast. A 1940s barn converted to a three-story inn with five guest rooms with private baths. Several sitting rooms and side porches for guests to use. Breakfast served in a lovely sun room or by the fireplace. Close to Branson, Bass Pro, Laura Ingalls Wilder Home, and many more attractions.

Hosts: Carol and Larry Alberty
Rooms: 5 (PB) $70-85
Full Breakfast
Credit Cards: None
Notes: 2, 3, 7, 12

FULTON

Romancing the Past Victorian Inn

830 Court Street, 65251
(573) 592-1996
e-mail: innkeeper@sockets.net
www.romancingthepast.com

Victorian enchantment; spacious lawn and serene gardens enfold 1860s home in graceful old neighborhood. Grand hall with magnificent arch and staircase. Elegantly appointed rooms with period adornments. Luxurious private baths. Lavish antiques, bed drapings, and floral throughout. Enjoy excellent food, hot tub, and many amenities to pamper guests. Walk to many fascinating amusements including antique and gift shops, restaurants, museums, parks. Inspected and approved by Bed and Breakfast Inn of Missouri. Featured in *Mid-West Living*, May.

Romancing the Past Victorian Inn

---

7 No smoking; 8 Children welcome; 9 Social drinking allowed; 10 Tennis nearby; 11 Swimming nearby; 12 Golf nearby; 13 Skiing nearby; 14 May be booked through a travel agent; 15 Handicapped accessible.

Hosts: Jim and Renee Yeager
Rooms: 3 (PB) $80-120
Full Breakfast
Credit Cards: A, B, C, D
Notes: 2, 5, 7, 8, 9, 10, 11, 12, 15

HANNIBAL

Fifth Street Mansion
Bed & Breakfast Inn

213 South Fifth Street, 63401
(573) 221-0445; (800) 874-5661
www.hanmo.com/fifthstreetmansion

This Italianate mansion, built in 1858, is one of
the remnants of "Millionaires' Row," an
impressive block of grand homes built and
owned by some of Hannibal's wealthiest and
most influential citizens. The interior features
unique fireplaces, stained glass, and original
chandeliers, with large rooms featuring
antiques and period decor. Whether seeking a
romantic hideaway or a homelike setting on
business trips, guests will find Fifth Street
Mansion offers a blend of Victorian charm and
contemporary comforts with plenty of old-
fashioned hospitality.

Hosts: Mike and Donalene Andreotti
Rooms: 7 (PB) $75-90
Full Breakfast
Credit Cards: A, B, C, D
Notes: 2, 5, 7, 8, 9, 10, 12, 14

Fifth Street Mansion

INDEPENDENCE

Woodstock Inn
Bed & Breakfast

1212 West Lexington Street, 64050
(816) 833-2233; (800) 276-5202
FAX (816) 461-7226
www.independence-missouri.com

Nestled within Independence's famous historical district, the Woodstock Inn Bed and Breakfast is just a short stroll away from all the sites
one comes to Independence to see. Eleven
warm and inviting rooms, each with a distinct
personality and private bath, some with
thermo-massage tubs and fireplace. And after a
restful night's sleep, wake up to a piping-hot
cup of coffee and take a seat at the long oak
dining table. Tempt one's palate with the
house's specialty, gourmet Belgian waffles
topped with powdered sugar and smothered
with specialty syrups or fresh fruit sauce. The
full breakfast is exactly what is needed to start
off a wonderful day of sightseeing. Inquire
about accommodations for children.

Hosts: Todd and Patricia Justice
Rooms: 11 (PB) $65-139
Full Breakfast
Credit Cards: A, B, C, D
Notes: 2, 5, 7, 12, 14, 15

KANSAS CITY

Bed & Breakfast Kansas City

P.O. Box 14781, Lenexa, KS 66285
(913) 888-3636

Thirty Victorian turn-of-the-century or contemporary homes and inns for great getaways.
Accommodations near Country Club Plaza,
Kansas City, Independence, or adjacent historic towns. All sizes of beds and all with private bath, all serve full breakfast. Some with
fireplace, Jacuzzi, pool, or hot tub. Accommodations also available in the country. Two
accommodations are handicapped accessible.

NOTES: Credit cards accepted: A MasterCard; B Visa; C American Express; D Discover; E Diner's Club;
F Other; 2 Personal checks accepted; 3 Lunch available; 4 Dinner available; 5 Open all year; 6 Pets welcome;

Agent: Edwina Monroe
Accommodations: (PB) $60-160
Full Breakfast
Credit Cards: None
Notes: 2, 5, 7

The Doanleigh Inn

The Doanleigh Inn

217 East 37th Street, 64111
(816) 753-2667; FAX (816) 531-5185
www.doanleigh.com

In the heart of the city, the Doanleigh Inn stands between the famed Country Club Plaza and Hallmark Crown Center. Lovely European and American antiques enhance the Georgian architecture of the inn. Wine and hors d'oeuvres await guests each evening and a full gourmet breakfast is served each morning. Fireplaces and Jacuzzis provide the ultimate in relaxation. Other amenities include afternoon cookies, daily newspapers, free local calls and faxes, and in-room computer modem access.

Hosts: Cynthia Brogdon and Terry Maturo
Rooms: 5 (PB) $105-160
Full Breakfast
Credit Cards: A, B, C, D
Notes: 2, 5, 7, 9, 10, 14

Pridewell

600 West 50th Street, 64112
(816) 931-1642

A fine Tudor residence in a residential area on the site of the Civil War battle of Westport. Near the Nelson Art Gallery, University of Missouri-Kansas City, Missouri Repertory Theatre, and Rockhurst College. Adjacent to Country Club Plaza shopping district, including several four-star restaurants, public transportation, public tennis courts, and park.

Hosts: Edwin and Louann White
Rooms: 2 (1 PB; 1 SB) $80-85
Full Breakfast
Credit Cards: None
Notes: 2, 5, 7, 8, 9, 14

OZARK

Smokey Hollow Lake Bed & Breakfast

880 Cash Spring Road, 65721
(417) 485-0286; (800) 485-0286

A country retreat nestled in 180 acres of Ozarks hills and hollows. Fishing lake, canoe, and paddle boat for guests' enjoyment. Current accommodations include private loft with whirlpool for two, queen-size bed, kitchen, and living area. Country decor. Breakfast delivered from main house. Planning to open rooms in main log lodge in the near future.

Hosts: Brenda and Richard Bilyeu
Rooms: 1 (PB) $75-90
Full and Continental Breakfast
Credit Cards: None
Notes: 2, 5, 7, 8, 14

ROCHEPORT

School House Bed & Breakfast Inn

504 Third Street, 65279
(573) 698-2022; www.schoolhousebandb.com

This historic three-story brick building was once a school house. Now luxuriously appointed as a country inn, it features 13-foot-high ceilings, custom-made plantation shutters, beautiful antiques, and two suites with private spa. Each room is accented with a few reminders of the inn's simple past like the large

7 No smoking; 8 Children welcome; 9 Social drinking allowed; 10 Tennis nearby; 11 Swimming nearby; 12 Golf nearby; 13 Skiing nearby; 14 May be booked through a travel agent; 15 Handicapped accessible.

framed prints of the famous *Dick and Jane Primer*. The basement houses an antique book shop. Within walking distance are cafés, a winery, galleries, antique shops, and a 200-mile-long hiking and biking trail.

Hosts: Vicki and John Ott; Penny Province
Rooms: 10 (PB) $85-175
Full Breakfast
Credit Cards: A, B
Notes: 2, 5, 7, 8, 9, 10, 11, 12, 14, 15

Boone's Lick Trail Inn

SAGINAW

Lakeside Cottages

P.O. Box 99, 64864
(417) 781-9230

We are just three miles from Joplin, on 40 acres, with two cottages overlooking a five-acre lake. Boats and fishing are free for guests. Cottages include fireplace, Jacuzzi for two, queen-size feather bed, TV, VCR, stereo, fully equipped kitchen, and propane barbecue grill. The inn specializes in honeymoons and anniversaries. A real romantic getaway for two.

Hosts: Breeze and "C.J." (Clyde Jeffries)
Rooms: 2 (PB) $114-129
Continental Breakfast
Credit Cards: A, B
Notes: 5, 7, 9

ST. CHARLES

Boone's Lick Trail Inn

1000 South Main Street, 63301
(636) 947-7000; FAX (636) 946-2637
www.booneslick.com

The Boone's Lick Trail Inn is named for the road blazed by the sons of Daniel Boone for transporting salt. The inn, circa 1840, is now the southern anchor of the St. Charles National Historic District, a delightful 10-block area filled with historic buildings, cobblestone streets, gas lamps, and more than 100 shops, boutiques, and restaurants. At the doorstep, lie the historic 230-mile hiking and biking Katy Trail State Park,

Casino St. Charles, Lewis and Clark Center, a certified site on the Lewis and Clark Trail, Missouri's first state capitol, and Frenchtown, with the St. Rose Philippine Duchesne Shrine. Closed Christmas Day and Easter Saturday.

Hosts: V'Anne and Paul Mydler
Rooms: 5 (PB) $95-175
Full Breakfast
Credit Cards: A, B, C, D, E
Notes: 2, 7, 8, 9, 10, 11, 12, 14, 15

STE. GENEVIEVE

The Creole House

339 St. Mary's Road, 63670
(573) 883-7171; (800) 275-6041
FAX (573) 883-7831; e-mail: creolehs@brick.net

French Creole-style house on two and one-half acres in city limits of Missouri's oldest town. Amenities include spacious rooms and suites, jacuzzi bathtubs, private baths, sitting rooms, fireplaces, indoor heated swimming pool. King- and queen-size beds, TVs in rooms, breezy galerie with rockers for relaxing, full gourmet breakfast. Restaurants, shops, and French Colonial homes are a short walk away. Golf, hiking, and marina nearby. Open year-round. "Hospitality is our only business." Member PAII. Smoking permitted on galerie only. Children five and older welcome.

Hosts: Royce and Marge Wilhauk
Rooms: 4 (PB) $85-135
Full Breakfast
Credit Cards: A, B, D
Notes: 2, 5, 9, 10, 11, 12, 14

NOTES: Credit cards accepted: A MasterCard; B Visa; C American Express; D Discover; E Diner's Club; F Other; 2 Personal checks accepted; 3 Lunch available; 4 Dinner available; 5 Open all year; 6 Pets welcome;

Inn St. Gemme Beauvais

78 North Main, 63670
(314) 883-5744; (800) 818-5744

This magnificent structure has been redecorated and updated recently. It boasts of being the oldest continuously operated inn in Missouri and is in the historic district. Each room has a unique theme and most are two-room suites. A three-course breakfast is served in the elegant Victorian living room, and all historic buildings are within walking distance. High tea and hors d'oeuvres are served daily. Two-person Jacuzzis, fireplaces. AAA- and Mobil-approved.

Host: Janet Joggerst
Rooms: 9 (PB) $89-199
Full Breakfast
Credit Cards: A, B, C, D
Notes: 2, 5, 7, 8, 9, 10, 11, 12

ST. LOUIS

Lafayette House
Bed & Breakfast

2156 Lafayette Avenue, 63104-2543
(314) 772-4429; (800) 641-8965
FAX (314) 664-8965
www.bbonline.com/mo/lafayette/

The Lafayette House has expanded and the hosts would like to welcome guests to their new addition. Two historically significant homes are only minutes from downtown St. Louis. Attend a baseball or football game, shop

Lafayette House

at historic Union Station, visit the Gateway Arch, science center, zoo, or simply stroll through lovely Lafayette Square Park. For the business guests, there are a fax, in-room telephones, and flexible breakfast hours. AAA-inspected and -approved. Resident cats.

Hosts: Nancy Hammersmith and Annalise Millet
Rooms: 11 (8 PB; 3 SB) $65-150
Full Breakfast
Credit Cards: A, B, C, D, E
Notes: 2, 5, 7, 9, 12, 14

Napoleon's Retreat

Napoleon's Retreat
Bed & Breakfast

1815 Lafayette Avenue, 63104
(314) 772-6979; (800) 700-9980

Built in 1880 in historic Lafayette Square, recently chosen as one of America's "Prettiest Painted Places," this elegant, fully restored French Second Empire Victorian offers stunning accommodations in an exquisite, yet comfortable, setting. Furnished with fine antiques and artwork, all air-conditioned guest rooms feature private baths, cable TV, and private telephones. The Carriage House suite features a kitchen as well as balcony overlooking the garden courtyard, while another room boasts a gas fireplace and oversize whirlpool bath. A two-minute walk to several restaurants, Napoleon's Retreat is just one and one-half miles from downtown St. Louis, including the convention center, sports stadiums, and the arch.

7 No smoking; 8 Children welcome; 9 Social drinking allowed; 10 Tennis nearby; 11 Swimming nearby; 12 Golf nearby; 13 Skiing nearby; 14 May be booked through a travel agent; 15 Handicapped accessible.

Hosts: Michael Lance and Jeff Archuleta
Rooms: 5 (PB) $80-150
Full Breakfast
Credit Cards: A, B, C, D, E
Notes: 2, 5, 7, 9, 12, 14

The Winter House

The Winter House

3522 Arsenal Street, 63118
(314) 664-4399
e-mail: kmwinter@swbell.net

Nine-room Victorian built in 1897 features pressed-tin ceiling in lower bedroom, a suite with TV, and the Rose Room with king-size bed on second floor. Live piano music complimentary at breakfast with advance notice. Fruit, candy, and fresh flowers are provided in bedrooms. Nearby attractions include a Victorian walking park in the national register and the Missouri Botanical Garden. Within six miles are the Gateway Arch, Busch Stadium, St. Louis Science Center, Trans World Dome, zoo, symphony, and Union Station. Walk to fine dining. Reservations required. Additional fee of $20 for one-night stays.

Host: Kendall Winter
Rooms: 2 (PB) $90-110
Suite: 1 (PB) $105
Full Breakfast
Credit Cards: A, B, C, D, E, F
Notes: 2, 5, 7, 8, 9, 10, 14

SPRINGFIELD

The Mansion at Elfindale

1701 South Fort, 65807
(417) 831-7242

The Mansion at Elfindale is a charming completely restored Victorian home that is now a bed and breakfast inn. Each of the 13 bedroom suites is decorated and furnished with antiques of the era and has a private bath. Delicious full buffet breakfast is served daily. Although noted for elegance and serenity, the Mansion is just minutes from Bass Pro shop, the art museum, Hammons Hall for Performing Arts, Landers Theatre, and Stained Glass Theatre, and more. Learn more about the would-be resident Shah of Iran from the Mansion History Book, available for sale. The Mansion hosts many retreats and conferences. Open year-round. No smoking or alcohol allowed on premises. Children 12 and older are welcome.

Rooms: 13 (PB) $75-125
Full Breakfast
Credit Cards: A, B, C, D
Notes: 2, 5, 7, 15

Virginia Rose Bed & Breakfast

317 East Glenwood, 65807
(417) 883-0693; (800) 345-1412
e-mail: vrosebb@mocom.net

This two-story farmhouse built in 1906 offers a country atmosphere and hospitality right in

Virginia Rose

town. On a tree-covered acre, the home is complete with red barn, rockers on the porch, lovely period furnishings, and quilts on queen-size beds. Guests can relax in the parlor as they read or watch TV. Hearty homemade breakfasts are served with freshly baked muffins or biscuits on Virginia Rose dishes that have been lovingly collected for years. Approved member of Bed and Breakfast Inns of Missouri.

Hosts: Jackie and Virginia Buck
Rooms: 5 (PB) $50-100
Full Breakfast
Credit Cards: A, B, C, D
Notes: 2, 5, 7, 8, 10, 11, 12, 14

Walnut Street Inn

Walnut Street Inn

900 East Walnut Street, 65806
(417) 864-6346; (800) 593-6346

This award-winning 1894 Queen Anne Victorian inn, in the historic district, invites guests to escape. Friendly innkeepers, flickering fireplaces, European antiques, four-poster beds, feather comforters, Jacuzzis, skylights, and Victorian flower gardens abound. Walk to performing arts centers, theaters, cafés, boutiques, and antique shops. Near Bass Pro Shops Outdoor World, Branson music shows, with the glorious Ozark Mountains at the back door.

Hosts: Gary and Paula Blankenship
Rooms: 12 (PB) $84-159
Full Breakfast
Credit Cards: A, B, C, D, E, F
Notes: 2, 5, 7, 8, 9, 10, 11, 12, 14

WARRENSBURG

Cedarcroft Farm & Cottage

431 Southeast County Road Y, 64093-8316
(660) 747-5728; (800) 368-4944
e-mail: infoad@cedarcroft.com
www.cedarcroft.com

Cedarcroft Farm offers old-fashioned country hospitality, country quiet, and more-than-you-can-eat country cooking on an 1867 family farm listed in the National Register of Historic Places. Guests may explore the 80 acres of secluded woods, meadows, and streams, and savor a full country breakfast. Hosts are Civil War re-enactors who demonstrate 1860s soldiers' life. Home of Old Star Fertilizer, as featured on CNN. New secluded cottage has all romantic amenities.

Hosts: Sandra and Bill Wayne
Suite: 1 (PB) $75-90
Cottage: (PB) $160-200
Full Breakfast
Credit Cards: A, B, C, D
Notes: 2, 4, 5, 7, 8, 9, 11, 12, 14

Cedarcroft Farm

7 No smoking; 8 Children welcome; 9 Social drinking allowed; 10 Tennis nearby; 11 Swimming nearby; 12 Golf nearby; 13 Skiing nearby; 14 May be booked through a travel agent; 15 Handicapped accessible.

WASHINGTON

Washington House Bed & Breakfast

100 West Front Street, 63090
(314) 742-4360

Washington House, built circa 1837, is in a national historic district. This authentically restored inn on the Missouri River features river views, canopied beds, antiques, and full breakfast. Washington House is in the heart of Missouri's wine country, only 45 minutes west of St. Louis.

Hosts: Terry and Sue Black
Rooms: 2 (PB) $75
Full Breakfast
Credit Cards: A, B
Notes: 2, 5, 7, 8, 9, 10, 11, 12, 13

Washington House

WESTON

Benner House Bed & Breakfast

645 Main Street, 64098
(816) 640-2616

Victorian home built in 1898, listed in the national register. A pleasant walk from downtown historic district of Weston with museums, antique shops, galleries, wineries, fine restaurants, and specialty shops. Perfect setting for a wedding, honeymoon, anniversary, or just a very special time away. Private baths, hot tub on back deck, swimming pool. Full breakfast.

Hosts: John and Julie Pasley
Rooms: 4 (PB) $90-100
Full Breakfast
Credit Cards: A, B, C, D
Notes: 2, 5, 7, 9, 11, 12, 13, 14

NOTES: Credit cards accepted: A MasterCard; B Visa; C American Express; D Discover; E Diner's Club;
F Other; 2 Personal checks accepted; 3 Lunch available; 4 Dinner available; 5 Open all year; 6 Pets welcome;

Nebraska

BEATRICE

Carriage House Bed & Breakfast

25478 South 23rd Road, 68310
(402) 228-0356

Step back in time as you step in our front door. Guests can relax in the beautiful Victorian guest parlor with fireplace, admire the inn, decorated throughout with period antiques, or tour the 1887 barn and enjoy petting and hand-feeding the llamas. The bed and breakfast is on 10 acres east of town and offers peace and quiet with a beautiful "sunset" view overlooking Beatrice which guests can enjoy from the gazebo or large wraparound porch.

Hosts: David and Lorraine Bigley
Rooms: 6 (1 PB; 5 SB) $55-75
Full Breakfast
Credit Cards: A, B
Notes: 5, 6, 7, 9, 10, 11, 12

CRETE

The Parson's House

638 Forest Avenue, 68333-2935
(402) 826-2634

Enjoy warm hospitality in a restored four-square home built at the turn of the century in a quiet neighborhood near Doane College and its beautiful campus. Furnished with much antique furniture and a modern whirlpool bathtub. A full breakfast is served in the formal dining room.

Host: Sandy Richardson
Rooms: 2 (SB) $45
Full Breakfast
Credit Cards: None
Notes: 2, 5, 7, 10, 11, 12

DIXON

The George's

57759-874 Road, 68732-3024
(402) 584-2625; e-mail: DixonMom@aol.com

Spacious, air-conditioned farmhouse 35 miles west of Sioux City, Iowa. Enjoy country hospitality, hearty breakfasts, hiking, bird watching, and hunting during pheasant season. Table games, relaxing with a book, local fairs and celebrations. Many recreational activities within easy driving distance. Quiet and relaxing setting. Pets welcome by prior arrangement.

Host: Mrs. Marie George
Rooms: 6 (6 SB) $40-45
Full Breakfast
Credit Cards: None
Notes: 2, 7, 8, 9, 10, 11, 12

FUNK

Uncle Sam's Hilltop Lodge

Rural Route 1, Box 110, 68940
(308) 995-5568 (evenings)
(308) 995-2204 (answering machine)
e-mail: samsLodge@hotmail.com

Uncle Sam says "we want you for our guest." Only five minutes from I-80. This spacious 1979 solar home is built into Nebraska's sandhills. All four levels are ground-level with an indoor sand pile and game room. Two rooms are available, a brass queen-size bed with private

---

7 No smoking; 8 Children welcome; 9 Social drinking allowed; 10 Tennis nearby; 11 Swimming nearby; 12 Golf nearby; 13 Skiing nearby; 14 May be booked through a travel agent; 15 Handicapped accessible.

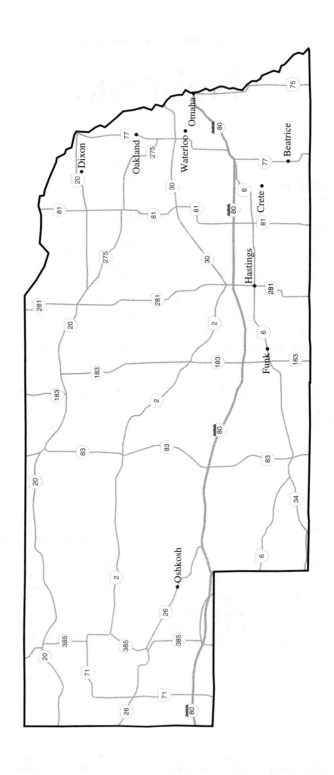

Nebraska

bath, and an antique four-poster full-size bed with a shared bath and a sunken tub for two. Relax by the fireplaces or tour the nearby Pioneer Village, Cabela's, Morris Cookbooks, Phelps Country Museum, and the Great Platte River Road Archway Monument or see the Sandhill Cranes. The white ones have been on our land. Start the day with a hearty country breakfast served in the formal dining room and end with a complimentary bedtime snack.

Hosts: Sam and Sharon Schrock
Rooms: 2 (1 PB; 1 SB) $40-60
Full Breakfast
Credit Cards: None
Notes: 2, 5, 6, 7, 8, 10, 11, 12

HASTINGS

Grandma's Victorian Inn Bed & Breakfast

1826 West Third Street, 68901
(402) 462-2013

Built circa 1886, this Victorian home has an open staircase and outstanding woodwork. For guests' comfort, each room has a private bath. Antique furniture is exhibited in the home with an accent on rocking chairs and a queen-size bed is in each room. Breakfast is served in the dining room; breakfast in bed can be arranged at additional charge. Return to the memories of yore and "whispers of yesterday." Children over 12 are welcome.

Manager/Innkeeper: Tim Sassman
Rooms: 5 (PB) $60
Full Breakfast
Credit Cards: A, B, D
Notes: 5, 7, 10, 11, 12, 15

OAKLAND

Benson Bed & Breakfast

402 North Oakland Avenue, 68045-1135
(402) 685-6051; e-mail: sanderson@genesisnet.net
www.bbonline.com/ne/benson/

Benson

Downtown brick landmark, built in 1905, beautifully renovated by the Andersons into a cozy retreat for a weary traveler. Relax in the Garden room overlooking the Main Street of a quiet ethnic Swedish community. Decorated with family antiques, guests will feel right at home. Large whirlpool bath and TV on the bathroom wall adds to the special effect. The food is great and served at a time to meet guests' schedule. Bed and Breakfast is on the second floor. Children over 12 welcome.

Hosts: Stan and Norma Anderson
Rooms: 3 (3 SB) $50-60
Full Breakfast
Credit Cards: D
Notes: 2, 5, 7, 10, 11, 12, 14

OMAHA

The Offutt House

140 North 39th Street, 68131
(402) 553-0951

This comfortable mansion, built in 1894, is in the section of large homes built around the same time by Omaha's most wealthy residents. Rooms are comfortably spacious and furnished with antiques. Some feature fireplaces. The house is near downtown Omaha and the historic Old Market area, which offers many beautiful shops and excellent restaurants. Full breakfast offered. Reservations requested.

NOTES: Credit cards accepted: A MasterCard; B Visa; C American Express; D Discover; E Diner's Club; F Other; 2 Personal checks accepted; 3 Lunch available; 4 Dinner available; 5 Open all year; 6 Pets welcome; 7 No smoking; 8 Children welcome; 9 Social drinking allowed; 10 Tennis nearby; 11 Swimming nearby; 12 Golf nearby; 13 Skiing nearby; 14 May be booked through a travel agent; 15 Handicapped accessible.

The Offutt House

Hosts: Janet and Paul Koenig
Rooms: 6 (PB) $65-105
Full Breakfast
Credit Cards: A, B, C, D
Notes: 2, 5, 6, 7, 8, 9, 10, 11, 12

OSHKOSH

Locust Tree Bed & Breakfast

400 West Fifth, 69154
(308) 772-3530
www.rimstarintl.com/loc00001.htm

Enjoy small town hospitality in a contemporary family home. The large brick home is graced with majestic spruce and locust trees. Fenced, spacious back yard and large parking lot are available. All rooms are air conditioned. Enjoy the spa and terry-cloth robes. Easy access to Ash Hollow State Park and Museum, Oregon and Mormon Trails, Pony Express route, and Lake McConaughy.

Hosts: Pete and Ardena Regier
Rooms: 2 (PB) $45-75
Continental Breakfast
Credit Cards: None
Notes: 2, 5, 7, 8, 10, 11, 12, 14

WATERLOO

The J.C. Robinson House

102 Lincoln Avenue, 68069-0190
(402) 779-2704; (800) 779-2705

This wonderful bed and breakfast was built in 1905 and is in the national historic register. The 21-room mansion retains its original appointments including hardwood floors, carved paneling, stained and leaded glass, tiled fireplaces, and pocket doors. Antique furnishings, including an extensive clock collection dating from 1735, create an atmosphere of relaxation and rest. The house invites guests to step back in time to an earlier, gracious era.

Hosts: Bill and Linda Clark
Rooms: 4 (1 PB; 3 SB) $50-80
Full and Continental Breakfast
Credit Cards: None
Notes: 2, 5, 7, 9, 11, 12, 14

The J.C. Robinson House

NOTES: Credit cards accepted: A MasterCard; B Visa; C American Express; D Discover; E Diner's Club; F Other; 2 Personal checks accepted; 3 Lunch available; 4 Dinner available; 5 Open all year; 6 Pets welcome;

North Dakota

DICKINSON

Hartfiel Inn

509 Third Avenue West, 58601
(701) 225-6710; FAX (701) 225-1184

The Hartfiel Inn was originally built in 1908. Decorating of the inn was inspired by travels to Europe. Every room holds many cultural surprises. Special features include candlelight breakfast in the formal dining room or on the terrace. Large private back yard with waterfall and garden. Large fireplace and formal library. Private hot tub room. The inn is designed to spoil the most discriminating of tastes. Close to many tourist sites.

Hosts: Rick and Quita Hartfiel
Rooms: 4 (PB) $59-89
Full Breakfast
Credit Cards: A, B
Notes: 2, 5, 6, 8, 9, 10, 11, 12, 14

LUVERNE

Volden Farm Bed & Breakfast

11943 County Road 26, 58056
(701) 769-2275; FAX (603) 696-5946
e-mail: voldenfarm_bb@broadvu.com
www.broadvu.com/voldenfarm

"Come find yourself on the prairie." A retreat in the real sense of the word. Peace, quiet, beauty, good books, art, nature, and animals join with home comforts, good food, great coffee, and conversation for an ideal stay on the Volden farm. Four guest rooms available with shared and private baths. Separate house avail-

Volden Farm

able for privacy with balcony, feather bed, and more. Inquire about accommodations for pets. Outdoor smoking permitted. Snowshoeing is also nearby.

Hosts: Jim and JoAnne Wold
Rooms: 4 (1 PB; 3 SB) $60-95
Full Breakfast
Credit Cards: None
Notes: 2, 3, 4, 5, 7, 8, 9, 10, 11, 12, 13, 14

MCCLUSKY

Midstate Bed & Breakfast

980 Highway 200 Northeast, 58463-9281
(701) 363-2520 (phone/FAX); (888) 434-2520
www.bbonline.com/nd/midstate

An easy location to find! This 1980s home is on a working farm at mile marker 232 on Highway 200, the highway known to be the most economical passage through the northern U.S. Guests enter through a plant-filled atrium to a private lower level that also includes guests' own TV lounge. In an area of abundant upland game, waterfowl, and deer. Guests are allowed hunting privilege on over 4,000 acres.

7 No smoking; 8 Children welcome; 9 Social drinking allowed; 10 Tennis nearby; 11 Swimming nearby; 12 Golf nearby; 13 Skiing nearby; 14 May be booked through a travel agent; 15 Handicapped accessible.

North Dakota

Air conditioning. Close to the Lewis and Clark Trail and the Lewis and Clark Interpretive Center at Washburn. Elegance and excellence in hospitality, yet economical. Inquire about accommodations for pets.

Hosts: Grace and Allen Faul
Rooms: 4 (1 PB; 3 SB) $35
Full Breakfast
Credit Cards: None
Notes: 2, 3, 4, 7, 8, 9, 10, 11

NOTES: Credit cards accepted: A MasterCard; B Visa; C American Express; D Discover; E Diner's Club; F Other; 2 Personal checks accepted; 3 Lunch available; 4 Dinner available; 5 Open all year; 6 Pets welcome; 7 No smoking; 8 Children welcome; 9 Social drinking allowed; 10 Tennis nearby; 11 Swimming nearby; 12 Golf nearby; 13 Skiing nearby; 14 May be booked through a travel agent; 15 Handicapped accessible.

Ohio

Ohio

AKRON

Portage House
Bed & Breakfast

601 Copley Road, 44320
(330) 535-1952; e-mail: portagehse@aol.com

This gracious Tudor home, nestled in a park-like setting, dates back to 1917. A stone wall at the corner of the street served as the western boundary of the United States in 1785. Jeanne, and her late husband, Harry, who was a physics professor at nearby University of Akron, opened the bed and breakfast in 1982. Jeanne and her daughter, Carol, continue to operate the bed and breakfast, residing in the third-floor apartment. When bread is in the oven, get set for a taste treat!

Hosts: Jeanne and Carol Pinnick
Rooms: 4 (1 PB; 3 SB) $50
Full Breakfast
Credit Cards: None
Notes: 2, 5, 6, 7, 8, 9, 12

BEACH CITY

Herb Nest Bed & Breakfast

13642 Navarre Road Southwest, 44608
(330) 756-0094

Two guest rooms await guests in this 100-year-old home. A complimentary Continental breakfast is served at guests' request. Large bedroom has a deck with private entrance, antique double bed. Victorian antiques and country reproductions furnish the home. Relax on the porch, deck, flagstone patio, or herb ter-race. During cooler times, guests may want to spend the evening in the family room, where a warm fire will be burning. Celebration arrangements, birthdays, anniversaries, honeymoons, reunions can be done at an additional fee. Gift certificates available.

Hosts: Walt and Sue Helline
Rooms: 2 (1 SB) $45-55
Continental Breakfast
Credit Cards: None
Notes: 2, 5, 7, 8, 10, 11, 12

BELLVILLE

The Frederick Fitting House

72 Fitting Avenue, 44813-1043
(419) 886-2863

An 1863 Victorian home in a quaint country village between Columbus and Cleveland. Near Mohican and Malabar Farm State Parks, downhill and cross-country skiing, bike trail, canoeing, and Kenyon College. Gourmet breakfast served in the formal dining room, or

garden gazebo. Closed Thanksgiving and Christmas.

Host: Barbara Lomax
Rooms: 3 (PB) $69-79
Full Breakfast
Credit Cards: None
Notes: 2, 7, 10, 11, 12, 13

BERLIN

The Oaks Inn

4752 US 62, P.O. Box 421, 44610
(330) 893-3061; (800) 246-2504

Hometown lodging within walking distance to all Berlin shops and eateries. Featuring four attractively decorated country/Victorian rooms including two master suites. The master lofted suite is unique with skylights, whirlpool/shower and a private sitting room, very romantic. All rooms have private baths, entrances, air conditioning, cable TV, are smoke-free and exceptionally clean. An in-room Continental breakfast is provided. Located in Berlin, 500 feet north of State Route 39 on US 62, next to Dutch Country Kitchen Restaurant.

Rooms: 3 (PB) $55-95
Continental Breakfast
Credit Cards: A, B, D
Notes: 2, 5, 7, 8, 10, 12, 14

CHILLICOTHE

Chillicothe Bed & Breakfast

202 South Paint Street, 45601
(740) 772-6848; (877) 484-4510
e-mail: jack@bright.net
www.bestinns.net/usa/oh/chil/html

Chillicothe Bed and Breakfast, a 14-room brick, Italianate-style historic home, is centrally located on one of the principal streets of Ohio's first capital. The house was built in 1864 by the owner of Chillicothe's first paper mill. It is beautifully decorated with art, antiques, and

Chillicothe

collectibles, and has an extensive art and theater library. The hosts are Katie and Jack Sullivan. Katie is involved with local Civic Theater and Jack is an artist with a studio on the grounds.

Hosts: Katie and Jack Sullivan
Rooms: 4 (1-1/2 PB; 3 SB) $50-60
Full Breakfast
Credit Cards: A, B, C
Notes: 2, 5, 7, 8, 9

The Greenhouse Bed & Breakfast

47 East Fifth Street, 45601
(740) 775-5313

Built in 1894, this elegant Queen Anne-style home is listed in the National Register of Historic Places. It has leaded- and stained-glass doors and windows, parquet floors, cherry-

The Greenhouse

NOTES: Credit cards accepted: A MasterCard; B Visa; C American Express; D Discover; E Diner's Club; F Other; 2 Personal checks accepted; 3 Lunch available; 4 Dinner available; 5 Open all year; 6 Pets welcome;

beamed ceilings, eight fireplaces, and a large wraparound porch and patio—where smoking is permitted. The four spacious guest rooms, all with private baths, are quiet, comfortable, air conditioned, have cable TV and are furnished with period antiques. Breakfast is served in the formal cherry dining room. Located in the historic district within walking distance of historical museums, antique and specialty shops, restaurants, the Majestic Theatre, the Pump House Art Gallery, and a short drive to Adena, Tecumseh, Hopewell Culture, and Chillicothe Paints Professional Baseball. AAA three-diamond-rating.

Hosts: Tom and Dee Shoemaker
Rooms: 4 (PB) $60-80
Full Breakfast
Credit Cards: A, B, C
Notes: 2, 5, 7, 8, 9, 10, 11, 12, 13

CINCINNATI

The Victoria Inn of Hyde Park

3567 Shaw Avenue, 45208
(513) 321-3567; (888) 422-4629
FAX (513) 321-3147

The Victoria Inn of Hyde Park is an elegant and comfortable bed and breakfast in the heart of Cincinnati's most charming neighborhood. The inn received a *Better Homes & Gardens* award for outstanding renovation. Perfect for business or romantic getaway. Fifteen minutes from downtown, Riverfront Stadium, the zoo,

The Victoria Inn of Hyde Park

and numerous local universities. The only bed and breakfast in the area that supplies private telephones, a fax, copier, and in-ground swimming pool. Voted Best B&B, *Cincinnati* magazine, October 1993.

Hosts: Tom Possert and Debra Moore
Rooms: 4 (PB) $99-169
Full Breakfast
Credit Cards: A, B, C
Notes: 2, 5, 7, 10, 11, 12

CINCINNATI/HIGGINSPORT

Ohio River House Bed & Breakfast

101 Brown Street, P.O. Box 188, 45131
(937) 375-4395; FAX (937) 375-4394
e-mail: FDSINC@bright.net
www.ohioriverhouse.com

Thirty-five miles east of Cincinnati on scenic US 52, the antique-filled Ohio River House offers a truly outstanding view while capturing the ambiance of years past. The hosts offer very large rooms with an adjacent antique shop and gallery for guests' browsing pleasure. Come, enjoy a full family-style breakfast in the brick-floored kitchen as well as evening snacks at either the river's edge, in the comfort of the parlor, or in the spacious living room, which is boldly decorated in a manner reminiscent of an old paddle-wheel riverboat.

Hosts: Andy and Judy Lloyd
Rooms: 5 (3 PB; 2 SB) $65-100
Full Breakfast
Credit Cards: A, B
Notes: 2, 5, 6, 7, 8, 9, 10, 11, 12

CLEVELAND

Crest Bed & Breakfast

1489 Crest Road, 44121
(216) 382-5801
e-mail: iu305@cleveland.freenet.edu

A two-room bed and breakfast on a residential street. Comfortable antique-filled living and sunroom. Located on a bus line, near many cultural activities and major medical facilities. Two rooms share a bath. Maximum three persons sharing a bath. Continental plus breakfast including fresh-baked pastries and fresh fruit. Hosts very knowledgeable about Cleveland.

Rooms: 3 (1 PB; 2 SB) $75-95
Continental Breakfast
Credit Cards: None
Notes: 2, 5, 7, 8, 10

Private Lodgings, Inc. A-1

P.O. Box 18557, 44118
(216) 321-3213; FAX (216) 321-8707
e-mail: privatlodg@aol.com
www.en.com/privlodg

A variety of accommodations including bed and breakfast lodgings, homeshare for longer stays, or short-term rentals in houses and apartments in the greater Cleveland area. Near the Cleveland Clinic, Case Western Reserve University, major museums and galleries, metro park system, downtown Cleveland business district, and Lake Erie. No credit cards. President: Jean Stanley. $45-125.

Cleveland Heights. Eastside location adjacent to CWRU, museums, hospital, and other attractions. Bed and breakfast in gracious homes; easy access to downtown. Weekly and monthly rates available. $55-84.

Croft. Wonderful red farmhouse just south of downtown in suburban location. Close to I-77. Two antique-filled guest rooms on the second floor share a bathroom. Full breakfast. $65-75.

Downtown Cleveland. Historic brownstone. Four-story property in national historic register with four guest rooms on two floors. Easy access to downtown and University Circle. Wonderful antiques. Large Continental breakfast served. $65-110.

Geauga County. Wonderful horse farm 30 minutes from downtown Cleveland. Wood-

burning fireplace and in-ground swimming pool (in season). Four guest rooms with private baths. Full breakfast. $85-100.

Oberlin. Two miles from Oberlin College, 45 minutes to downtown Cleveland. The hosts share their home with two well-behaved black labs. Beautiful new home with terrific guest suites. Full breakfast. $75-85.

Ohio City. Historic Cleveland neighborhood with access to downtown. Gracious hosts with charming antiques. Full breakfast. $75.

Shaker Heights. Beautiful eastside location. Rapid transit access to downtown and airport. Nightly, weekly, and monthly rates available.

Shaker Square. Historic neighborhood on rapid transit line to downtown and airport. Five minute car/bus ride to University Circle and Cleveland Clinic. Walk to shops and restaurants. The gracious hosts offer two guest rooms, each with private bath. Full breakfast. $65-85.

University Circle. Terrific Cleveland Heights property overlooking University Circle. Two large guest rooms. Walk to museums and CWRU. Continental breakfast. $65-85.

Western Suburbs 1. Olmstead Falls adjacent to metropark. Close to NASA and airport. Walking trails nearby. Beautiful home. Full breakfast. $65-75.

COLUMBUS

Henderson House Bed & Breakfast

1544 Atcheson Street, 43203
(614) 258-3463

A Georgian 19th-century home once the farmhouse of Ohio governor and president Rutherford B. Hayes with an attached coach house

---

suite with private entrance, kitchen, telephone, and cable TV. On five acres in the heart of the city with off-street parking, five minutes from airport, downtown business district, convention center, OSU, restaurants, shopping malls, and less than a mile from major highways. Also, perfect for small business meetings, retreats, and social functions. Three rooms share one bath. A Continental plus breakfast served.

Host: Lee Henderson-Johnson
Rooms: 4 (1 PB; 3 S1B) $70-85
Full Breakfast
Credit Cards: None
Notes: 2, 5, 7, 9, 10, 11, 12, 15

Lansing Street

The House of the Seven Goebels

4975 Hayden Run Road, 43221
(614) 761-9595; e-mail: 7goebels@compuserve.com

On two acres along a meandering stream, the House of the Seven Goebels bed and breakfast is an authentic reproduction of a 1780 Connecticut River Valley farmhouse. It is convenient to both I-270 and northwest Columbus. Large rooms include private baths, fireplaces, and queen-size canopied beds. Antiques, piano, and semi-grand concert harp in front parlor. Close to antique stores, Ohio State University, downtown Columbus. Relax on the stone patio or play a game of croquet.

Hosts: Pat and Frank Goebel
Rooms: 2 (PB) $75
Full Breakfast
Credit Cards: A, B
Notes: 2, 5, 7, 10

Lansing Street Bed & Breakfast

180 Lansing Street, 43206
(614) 444-8488; (800) 383-7839
e-mail: basicsmom@aol.com

Lansing Street Bed and Breakfast is in the heart of German Village, a popular historic area adjacent to downtown. The village is famous for restored homes with slate roofs, wrought-iron gates, and secluded courtyards. Quaint shops and great restaurants along cob-blestone streets add to the charm of the village. This large home is tastefully furnished and is decorated with carefully selected artwork. The great room, with brick fireplace, overlooks the courtyard with birds, wind chimes, and fountains. Two spacious suites have all the desired amenities, including private baths. Creative gourmet breakfasts are served each morning by a hostess who loves to cook.

Host: Marcia A. Barck
Rooms: 2 (PB) $80
Full Breakfast
Credit Cards: A
Notes: 2, 5, 7, 8, 9, 10

Shamrock Bed & Breakfast

5657 Sunbury Road, Gaharina, 43230-1147
(614) 337-9849; e-mail: shamrockbb@juno.com

The Shamrock is a brick split-level ranch on over an acre of professionally landscaped grounds with perennial beds, roses, grape arbor, and flowering bushes. Guests enjoy the entire first floor, fireplace, Florida room, and

Shamrock

7 No smoking; 8 Children welcome; 9 Social drinking allowed; 10 Tennis nearby; 11 Swimming nearby; 12 Golf nearby; 13 Skiing nearby; 14 May be booked through a travel agent; 15 Handicapped accessible.

patio with gas grill. All rooms are furnished with original art and antiques. Large library. CDs and videos are available. Easy freeway access to most attractions and close to airport and Easton. Large traditional Irish breakfast. Generally handicapped accessible. Smoking permitted in designated areas only.

Host: Tom McLaughlin
Rooms: 2 (PB) $60
Full Breakfast
Credit Cards: None
Notes: 2, 3, 5, 7, 8, 10, 11, 12, 13, 15

DANVILLE

The White Oak Inn

The White Oak Inn

29683 Walhonding Road, 43014
(740) 599-6107

This turn-of-the-century farmhouse in a rolling, wooded countryside features antiques and natural oak woodwork. Guests read, play board games, or socialize in the common room with a fireplace, or relax on the 50-foot-long front porch. An outdoor enthusiast's haven. Three rooms have fireplaces. Near the world's largest Amish population and historic Roscoe Village.

Hosts: Yvonne and Ian Martin
Rooms: 10 (PB) $70-140
Full Breakfast
Credit Cards: A, B, C, D
Notes: 2, 4, 5, 7, 9, 10, 11, 12, 13, 14

DEERSVILLE

Mulberry Lane

224 West Main Street, 44693
(740) 922-0425

Built in 1830, restored in 1989, and tastefully furnished with antiques and period pieces, Mulberry Lane is a great getaway. Peaceful Little Deersville lies between two large lakes where guests can go fishing and boating. Country auctions, antique shops, glass factories, the birthplaces of Clark Gable and General George Armstrong Custer, early Moravian settlements, and Amish country are all within reach. If guests don't feel like touring, they are welcome to relax on the porch swing with a good book. Freshly baked muffins are always served with Dick and Ferrel's breakfasts in their country kitchen.

Hosts: Dick and Ferrel Zeimer
Rooms: 3 (1 PB; 2 SB) $60-70
Full Breakfast
Credit Cards: None
Notes: 2, 5, 7, 9, 11

DE GRAFF

Rollicking Hills Bed & Breakfast

1 Rollicking Hills, 43318
(937) 585-5161

Indian, pioneer, and glacial history abound on the Rollicking Hills 160-acre farm. Explore the nature trails and 20 acres of woods while walking a llama or riding a horse. The five-acre farm pond is well-stocked with large-mouth

Rollicking Hills

NOTES: Credit cards accepted: A MasterCard; B Visa; C American Express; D Discover; E Diner's Club; F Other; 2 Personal checks accepted; 3 Lunch available; 4 Dinner available; 5 Open all year; 6 Pets welcome;

bass and blue gill waiting for first-time or experienced anglers. Canoes, rowboat, and paddle boat are at the dock. Cool off by taking a dip in the in-ground swimming pool. Learn what all can be done with llama fiber.

Hosts: Susie and Bob Smithers
Rooms: 1 (PB) $65
Full Breakfast
Credit Cards: None
Notes: 2, 5, 7, 8, 11

DELLROY (ATWOOD LAKE REGION)

Whispering Pines

Whispering Pines Bed & Breakfast

P.O. Box 340, 44620
(330) 735-2824; FAX (330) 735-7006
www.bbonline.com/oh/whispering/

Come to this 1880 Victorian home overlooking Atwood Lake. Filled with elegant antiques of the period, each guest room has a breathtaking view of the lake and a private bath. Two rooms have a wood-burning fireplace. The Honeymoon Suite features a two-person Jacuzzi, balcony, king-size bed, and wood-burning fireplace. Central air. Brick courtyard and gardens. A scrumptious breakfast served on the enclosed porch makes this a perfect romantic getaway. Pontoon with deluxe scating is available for rental. Golf, boating, nature, and relaxation.

Hosts: Bill and Linda Horn
Rooms: 5 (PB) $90-140
Honeymoon Suite: $175
Full Breakfast
Credit Cards: A, B, C, D
Notes: 2, 5, 7, 9, 10, 11, 12, 14

FREDERICKTOWN

Heartland Country Resort

2994 Township Road 190, 43019
(800) 230-7030

The Heartland Country Resort is a beautifully remodeled, spacious 1878 farmhouse and a new secluded log home, both with scenic views of rolling fields, pastures, and woods. There is a variety of things to do, including horseback riding on wooded trails with streams and hills or riding in one of the arenas. Guests can go swimming in the heated pool in the summer, go skiing in the winter, play pool in the large recreation room, or just relax on the comfortable screened porch or deck. A new meeting facility with lots of oak, a fireplace, and wonderful views is now available. Continental plus breakfast served. Lunch and dinner available by prior arrangement. Inquire about pets. Smoking permitted only on the porches.

Host: Dorene Henschen
Rooms: 6 (PB) $80-175
Continental Breakfast
Credit Cards: A, B, D
Notes: 2, 5, 8, 9, 11, 12, 13, 14, 15

Heartland Country Resort

7 No smoking; 8 Children welcome; 9 Social drinking allowed; 10 Tennis nearby; 11 Swimming nearby; 12 Golf nearby; 13 Skiing nearby; 14 May be booked through a travel agent; 15 Handicapped accessible.

GEORGETOWN

Bailey House Bed & Breakfast

112 North Water Street, 45121-1332
(937) 378-3087; (937) 378-6237

The Bailey House is a Greek Revival brick home built in 1830. The spacious rooms have Federal-style mantels, woodwork, and original ash flooring. Guest rooms have antique beds, chests of drawers, and washstands. Bailey House offers small-town friendliness, a restful setting in a historic area, and a full breakfast to start the day. U. S. Grant home and school, art gallery, and antique shops are within walking distance. Boating, fishing, hiking are available nearby. No smoking in the guest rooms.

Hosts: Nancy Purdy and Jane Sininger
Rooms: 4 (SB) $55
Full Breakfast
Credit Cards: None
Notes: 2, 5, 8, 9, 10, 12

HANOVERTON

The Spread Eagle Tavern

10150 Plymouth Street, P.O. Box 277, 44423
(330) 223-1583

The Spread Eagle Tavern is an artfully restored Federal-style three-story historic brick inn that features a gourmet restaurant, a unique rathskeller, seven dining rooms, and five guest rooms for overnight lodging. All rooms are tastefully decorated with antiques that give insight into Ohio's canal-period history. Listed in the National Register of Historic Places. Quiet, romantic, and unique.

Hosts: Peter and Jean Johnson
Rooms: 5 (PB) $100-200
Continental Breakfast
Credit Cards: A, B, D
Notes: 3, 4, 5, 7, 8, 9, 12

HIRAM

The Lily Ponds

The Lily Ponds

6720 Route 82, 44234
(330) 569-3222; (800) 325-5087
FAX (330) 569-3223

This spacious, lovely, antique-filled home in a quiet country setting is surrounded by woods and ponds. Five-minute walk to Hiram College campus; 15-minute drive to SeaWorld, Geauga Lake, and Aurora Farms and Outlet Center; 45 minutes to Cleveland, Akron, and Youngstown. Charming guest rooms with private baths. Central air conditioning. Cross-country skis and skiing on property. Eight miles from Ohio Turnpike, exit 193.

Host: Marilane Spencer
Rooms: 3 (PB) $55-85
Full Breakfast
Credit Cards: A, B
Notes: 2, 5, 6, 7, 8, 9, 10, 11, 12, 13, 14

HUBBARD

Julia's Bed & Breakfast

6219 West Liberty Street, 44425
(330) 534-1342 (phone/FAX); (888) 758-5427
e-mail: wwwjuliasb&b.com

I-80 East or West to 193 North to Route 304 East. Historic property. Whirlpools in all bed-

NOTES: Credit cards accepted: A MasterCard; B Visa; C American Express; D Discover; E Diner's Club; F Other; 2 Personal checks accepted; 3 Lunch available; 4 Dinner available; 5 Open all year; 6 Pets welcome;

rooms, private baths/showers. Rehearsal dinners, garden or indoor wedding facilities, catering honeymoon nights, reception facilities, meeting space, reunions. On golf course.

Rooms: 6 (PB) $99-250
Full Breakfast
Credit Cards: A, B, D
Notes: 5, 7, 11, 12, 15

HURON

Captain Montague's Bed & Breakfast

229 Center Street, 44839
(419) 433-4756; (800) 276-4756
e-mail: judytann@aol.com
www.innsandouts.com/inns/p208270.html

The Captain's is that perfect romantic retreat in a stately southern Colonial manor that radiates Victorian charm. Experience a bygone era of lace, luster, and love. Nestled in the heart of vacationland on the shores of Lake Erie, the Captain's is within minutes of golf courses, estuaries, boating, and shopping. Cedar Point

Captain Montague's

and the Lake Erie islands are nearby. Enjoy the in-ground swimming pool and impeccable gardens. The Captain's is truly in the heart of Ohio. Minimum weekend stay is two nights, Memorial Day through Labor Day. Continental plus breakfast. Showcased in *Midwest Living*, August 1995.

Hosts: Judy and Mike Tann
Rooms: 7 (PB) $85-150
Continental Breakfast
Credit Cards: A, B, D
Notes: 2, 5, 7, 9, 10, 11, 12, 14

JACKSON

My Thyme Bed & Breakfast

14701 State Route 93, 45640
(740) 286-6067

My Thyme is an elegant bed and breakfast inn set in a gracious turn-of-the-century home in Jackson. In the rolling foothills of southern Ohio, My Thyme offers year-round lodging and relaxation—a peaceful haven away from home.

Hosts: Patty Elliott and Kris Miller
Rooms: 4 (4 SB) $65
Full Breakfast
Credit Cards: A, B
Notes: 2, 5, 7, 10, 11, 12

LAURELVILLE

Painted Valley Farm Bed & Breakfast

17232 Curtis Road, 43135
(888) 887-4446
www.hockinghills.com/paintedvalley

This newly built log home, on a 150-acre horse farm in the Hocking Hills Region, was specifically designed to ensure guests country privacy with a touch of pampering. Guests are encouraged to make themselves at home in the two spacious guest rooms, each with a queen-size bed and full private inclusive bath. Candlelight breakfasts. Hot tub with terry-cloth robes and beach towels provided. Wraparound porches

7 No smoking; 8 Children welcome; 9 Social drinking allowed; 10 Tennis nearby; 11 Swimming nearby; 12 Golf nearby; 13 Skiing nearby; 14 May be booked through a travel agent; 15 Handicapped accessible.

Painted Valley Farm

and large deck for relaxing. Turndown service. Call for family and extended rates. Children over six welcome. Canoeing, horseback riding, and rock climbing are nearby.

Hosts: Larry and Luanne Guffey
Rooms: 2 (PB) $65
Full Breakfast
Credit Cards: None
Notes: 2, 5, 7, 9, 11, 12, 14

LEBANON

Burl Manor Bed & Breakfast

230 South Mechanic Street, 45036
(513) 934-0400; (800) 450-0401
FAX (513) 934-0402; e-mail: jor@your-net.com
www.lebanon-ohio.com/burlmanor.html

In historic Lebanon, the Burl Manor was built in the mid 1800s by William H. P. Denney, the editor and publisher of Ohio's oldest weekly newspaper. This historical Italian home reflects days of the past with the spacious parlor and formal dining room. It also features a unique sunroom in the center-court staircase. The bedrooms are decorated with turn-of-the-century decor. Each queen-size bedroom has a private bath. Enjoy time indoors with a game room or bumper pool, board games, TV, VCR with a film library. Outdoor activities include an in-ground swimming pool, volleyball, and croquet. A golf center with tennis is just a block away.

Hosts: Liz and Jay Jorling
Rooms: 4 (PB) $80
Full Breakfast
Credit Cards: A, B
Notes: 2, 5, 7, 8, 10, 11, 12

LOGAN

The Inn At Cedar Falls

21190 State Route 374, 43138
(740) 385-7489; (800) 65-FALLS
FAX (740) 385-0820
www.innatcedarfalls.com

Settled on 60 acres surrounded by Hocking Hills State Parks, the Inn features the harmony of nature and the simple joys of earth's beauty. Relax in a setting formed during the ice age. Mammoth rock formations, caves, and waterfalls share their breathtaking beauty. The Inn offers antique-furnished rooms and renovated, fully equipped, and secluded 19th-century log cabins. Dining awaits guests in 1840s log houses where they can watch gourmet meals being prepared in the open kitchen. Smoking permitted in designated areas only.

Host: Ellen Grinsfelder
Rooms: 15 (PB) $65-230
Full Breakfast
Credit Cards: A, B
Notes: 2, 3, 4, 5, 8, 9, 11, 12, 14, 15

MARION

Olde Towne Manor

245 St. James Street, 43302
(740) 382-2402; (800) 341-6163
FAX (740) 387-1490

This elegant stone home is on a beautiful acre of land on a quiet street in Marion's historic

Olde Towne Manor

NOTES: Credit cards accepted: A MasterCard; B Visa; C American Express; D Discover; E Diner's Club; F Other; 2 Personal checks accepted; 3 Lunch available; 4 Dinner available; 5 Open all year; 6 Pets welcome;

district. Enjoy a quiet setting in the gazebo or relax while reading a book from the library. A leisurely stroll will take guests to the home of President Warren G. Harding and the Harding Memorial. Guests can unwind in the hot tub or sauna or enjoy a glass of local wine in the pub while shooting a game of pool.

Hosts: Steve and Marsha Adams
Rooms: 4 (PB) $55-65
Continental Breakfast
Credit Cards: A, B, C
Notes: 2, 5, 9, 10

MESOPOTAMIA

Old Stone House Bed & Breakfast

8505 Route 534, Box 177, 44439
(440) 693-4186

"Evoke your fondest memories in this setting from the past." Welcome to this 200-year-old sandstone home on 20 acres amidst historical Mesopotamia and its Amish. The intrigue of history and the nostalgia of country await guests. Laced with romance, but intimate; serene and restful. Retreat to therapeutic whirlpools with sensual aromatherapy. Forty-one miles east of Cleveland; 30-minute drive from Sea World; factory outlets; wineries; covered bridges; Lake Erie. Amish dinner and/or buggy ride; gift certificates available.

Host: Darcy Miller
Rooms: 3 (PB) $95
Full Breakfast
Credit Cards: None
Notes: 2, 5, 7, 8, 9, 11, 12, 13, 14

Old Stone House

MILLERSBURG

Fields of Home Guest House

7278 County Road 201, 44654
(330) 674-7152
www.bbonline.com/oh/fieldsofhome

Log cabin bed and breakfast four miles northwest of Berlin, in the heart of the world's largest Amish community, surrounded by the rolling hills and fields farmed with horses. Spacious rooms include private baths with whirlpool tubs, telephones, clock radios with CD players, some with fireplaces and kitchenettes. Breakfast includes fruit, muffins, rolls, cereals, juice, tea, and coffee. Relax on the front porch rockers or take a stroll around the fish pond and perennial gardens.

Hosts: Mervin and Ruth Yoder
Rooms: 5 (PB) $65-125
Continental Breakfast
Credit Cards: A, B, D
Notes: 2, 5, 7, 8, 12, 14, 15

OXFORD

The Duck Pond

6391 Morning Sun Road, State Road 732 North
P.O. Box 407, 45056 (mailing)
(513) 523-8914

An 1863 Civil War farmhouse on five and one-half acres. Furnished in country antiques and collectibles. Full country-style breakfast, including such specialties as Hawaiian French toast, German pancakes, and breakfast casseroles. Three miles north of Miami University, two miles south of Hueston Woods State Park with golf, nature trails, boating, swimming, and fishing. Enjoy antiquing in several nearby towns. Certified and approved by Ohio Bed and Breakfast Association. Closed Christmas.

Host: Marge Pendleton
Rooms: 4 (2 PB; 2 SB) $67-75
Full Breakfast
Credit Cards: None
Notes: 2, 7, 10, 11, 12

7 No smoking; 8 Children welcome; 9 Social drinking allowed; 10 Tennis nearby; 11 Swimming nearby; 12 Golf nearby; 13 Skiing nearby; 14 May be booked through a travel agent; 15 Handicapped accessible.

PAINESVILLE

Rider's Inn Bed & Breakfast

792 Mentor Avenue, 44077
(440) 354-8200; (440) 942-2742
FAX (440) 350-9385

This historic stagecoach inn built in 1812 is one mile west of downtown Painesville on Route 20. Choose from 10 guest rooms, each with private bath, air conditioning, king- or queen-size beds, and fine antique furnishings that are for sale. Area attractions include Lake Erie College, Fairport Harbor, Grand River Winery, Indian Museum, golf, tennis, horseback riding, water sports, and Amish country tours. Full breakfast in bed available. A full service restaurant and separate English pub offer additional meals and a Sunday stagecoach brunch. Facilities for meetings and social functions are also available. Inquire about accommodations for pets. Restaurant is handicapped accessible.

Hosts: Elaine Crane and Gary Herman
Rooms: 10 (8 PB; 2 SB) $75-99
Full Breakfast
Credit Cards: A, B, C, D
Notes: 2, 3, 4, 5, 7, 8, 9, 10, 11, 12, 13, 14

Rider's Inn

POLAND (YOUNGSTOWN)

Inn at the Green

500 South Main Street, 44514
(330) 757-4688

A classically proportioned Victorian townhouse on the south end of the green in pre-

Inn at the Green

served Connecticut Western Reserve village. Featuring beautiful large moldings, 12-foot ceilings, five lovely working Italian marble fireplaces, interior-shuttered windows, the original poplar floors, and a relaxing patio garden. Children over seven are welcome.

Hosts: Ginny and Steve Meloy
Rooms: 4 (PB) $55-60
Continental Breakfast
Credit Cards: A, B, D
Notes: 2, 5, 9, 10, 11, 12, 14

POMEROY

Holly Hill Inn

114 Butternut Avenue, 45769
(614) 992-5657

The Holly Hill Inn, built in 1836, is nestled among the hills along the beautiful Ohio River. It offers a peaceful atmosphere of holly trees, ivy-covered stone walls, and flower gardens. Enjoy a breathtaking river view, antiques, and period furnishings throughout, four working fireplaces, and tranquil outdoor sitting areas. Breakfast can range from a down-home country-style menu to a delicious health-conscious meal. Air conditioned and smoke free.

Hosts: George and Mary Stewart
Rooms: 4 (4 SB) $59-79
Full Breakfast
Credit Cards: A, B
Notes: 2, 5, 7, 8, 10, 11, 12

NOTES: Credit cards accepted: A MasterCard; B Visa; C American Express; D Discover; E Diner's Club; F Other; 2 Personal checks accepted; 3 Lunch available; 4 Dinner available; 5 Open all year; 6 Pets welcome;

PORT CLINTON

The Five Bells Inn

2766 Sand Road, 43452
(888) 734-1555; www.5Bellsinn.com

Spectacular sunsets and access to sandy Lake Erie beach enhance the stay at this beautiful 1907 Dutch Colonial inn. King- and queen-size suites with private baths, TV/VCR, and air conditioning. Sumptuous breakfast in the dining room or outside decks. Hot tub, lagoon with row/paddle boat. Family cottage also available. Close to shopping, restaurants, ferries to other islands, hiking, and nature trails.

Hosts: Eileen and Jerry Jarc and Family
Rooms: 7 (PB) $89-139
Full Breakfast
Credit Cards: A, B
Notes: 2, 7, 8, 9, 10, 11, 12, 14

PUT-IN-BAY

Trenton Guest House

511 Trenton Avenue, P.O. Box 607, 43456
(419) 285-2306; www.trenton.put-in-bay.com

Enjoy the tranquility of Put-in-Bay's finest bed and breakfast, on a three-acre wooded lot overlooking the Heineman Winery Vineyards, featuring a large front porch, bright cheery breakfast room, and three comfortable guest rooms, each with its own king-size bed and private bath, just one-half mile from town.

Trenton Guest House

Hosts: Michael and Susan Byrnes
Rooms: 3 (PB) $80-130
Continental Breakfast
Credit Cards: A, B
Notes: 2, 7, 9, 11

RAVENNA

Rocking Horse Inn

248 West Riddle Avenue, 44266
(330) 297-5720; (800) 457-0439

This Victorian home is 128 years. It sits on land that was part of the western reserve. After a sheriff sale, the home was completed by Quincy Cook, the owner of the mill which still exists today. It was purchased by Immaculate Conception Church and used as a convent for more than 30 years. Purchasing the home in 1991, Jim and Carolyn have filled it with antiques and opened it as a bed and breakfast.

Hosts: James and Carolyn Leffler
Rooms: 4 (PB) $55-85
Continental Breakfast
Credit Cards: D
Notes: 2, 5, 7, 9, 12

RIPLEY

Misty River Bed & Breakfast

206 North Front Street, 45167
(937) 392-1556 (phone/FAX)

Each of the guest rooms in this charming riverfront home has its own private bath. The decor is a comfortable mix of country and antique, with a wood-burning fireplace in the living room and a big front porch where guests can relax and enjoy the river boats and the gorgeous sunsets. In the morning, guests will be served a delicious home-cooked breakfast, including Dotty's wonderful yeast cinnamon rolls. Ulysses S. Grant boarded here when he was 16. Ripley is also famous for its involvement in the Underground Railroad. Smoking permitted outside on the porch only.

7 No smoking; 8 Children welcome; 9 Social drinking allowed; 10 Tennis nearby; 11 Swimming nearby; 12 Golf nearby; 13 Skiing nearby; 14 May be booked through a travel agent; 15 Handicapped accessible.

Hosts: Dorothy Prevost and Lanny Warren
Rooms: 2 (PB) $75
Full Breakfast
Credit Cards: None
Notes: 2, 5, 7, 9, 14

ROCKBRIDGE

Glenlaurel: A Scottish Country Inn & Cottages

14940 Mount Olive Road, 43149-9736
(740) 385-4070; (800) 809-7378
FAX (740) 385-9669
www.glenlaurelinn.com

Glenlaurel, a Scottish country inn with wooded cottages, has been labeled the premier romantic getaway in the Midwest. The 130-acre estate offers walking trails, rock cliffs, and waterfalls. The Manor House, which overlooks Camusfearna Gorge, has two guest rooms and two guest suites. Each room offers a lavish two-person whirlpool tub in the bathroom, gas log fireplace in the bedroom, and private balcony. Four wooded cottages are a 10-minute walk from the Manor House. They offer kitchenette, living room, bedroom, gas log fireplace, screened porch, and hot tub on a private deck overlooking the gorge. Dinner in one of the two dining rooms is available by reservation. The estate is totally smoke free.

Host: Michael Daniels
Rooms: 2 (PB) $120-250
Suites: 2 (PB)
Cottages: 4
Full Breakfast
Credit Cards: A, B, C, D
Notes: 2, 3, 5, 7, 9, 11, 12, 14, 15

SANDUSKY

The Big Oak Bed & Breakfast

2501 South Campbell Street, 44870
(419) 627-0329

An 1879 Victorian farmhouse, furnished with antiques and family heirlooms. Enjoy the 14 large rooms, especially the great room with Franklin stove. The hosts enjoy gardening, card games, and travel. Guests are encouraged to enjoy the patio, terrace, many small gardens, and large porch with gazebo. Visit Cedar Point and local museums. Cruise Lake Erie to Put-in-Bay and Kelley's Island. Visit Edison's birthplace. Golfing, swimming, shopping, dining, and entertainment nearby. Continental plus breakfast included in rates. Air conditioned.

Hosts: Jim and Jeanne Ryan
Rooms: 4 (1 PB; 3 SB) $45-90
Continental Breakfast
Credit Cards: None
Notes: 2, 5, 7, 8, 11, 12

1890 Queen Anne

1890 Queen Anne Bed & Breakfast

714 Wayne Street, 44870-3507
(419) 626-0391; FAX (419) 626-3064

Enjoy the ambiance and luxury of sharing this gorgeous Victorian home with Dr. Bob and Wendy Kromer. Three large rooms with king-size beds and private bath await guests' visit. Continental plus breakfast served in lovely screened porch overlooking the flagstone patio and water fountain. Well-manicured floral gardens and lawn add natural beauty. Close to Cedar Point and ferries to Lake Erie Islands. Air conditioning, TV, VCR, off-street parking.

Host: Dr. Robert and Wendy Kromer
Rooms: 3 (PB) $115-135
Continental Breakfast
Credit Cards: A, B, D
Notes: 2, 5, 7

NOTES: Credit cards accepted: A MasterCard; B Visa; C American Express; D Discover; E Diner's Club; F Other; 2 Personal checks accepted; 3 Lunch available; 4 Dinner available; 5 Open all year; 6 Pets welcome;

The Red Gables

The Red Gables
Bed & Breakfast

421 Wayne Street, 44870
(419) 625-1189
www.bbonline.com/oh/redgables/

Circa 1907 Tudor Revival in the Old Plat District. The great room, where breakfast is served, features a massive fireplace, large bay window, and plenty of oak woodwork. The style is eclectic, from oriental artifacts in the great room to flowered chintz in the bedroom. Slipcovers, curtains, and comforters have been made by the innkeeper, a semiretired theatrical costume maker. Guests have access to a refrigerator and coffee maker. Air conditioned. Inquire about accommodations for children. Four blocks from Sandusky Bay. Guests have said, "It's like going to Grandma's house."

Host: Jo Ellen Cuthbertson
Rooms: 4 (2 PB; 2 SB) $75-100
Continental Breakfast
Credit Cards: A, B
Notes: 2, 5, 7, 9, 10, 11, 12

Wagner's 1844 Inn

230 East Washington Street, 44870
(419) 626-1726
e-mail: wagnersinn@sanduskyohio
www.lrbcg.com/wagnersinn

Elegantly restored, antique-filled Victorian home. Built in 1844 and listed in the National Register of Historic Places. Features a Victorian parlor with antique Steinway piano, living room with wood-burning fireplace, billiard room, screened porch, and enclosed courtyard. Air conditioning. In downtown Sandusky within walking distance of parks, historic buildings, antique shops, museums, and ferries to Cedar Point and Lake Erie islands. Inquire about accommodations for pets. Limited accessibility for handicapped.

Hosts: Walt and Barb Wagner
Rooms: 3 (PB) $60-100
Continental Breakfast
Credit Cards: A, B, D
Notes: 5, 7, 9, 10, 11, 12

SOUTH BLOOMINGVILLE

Steep Woods

24830 State Route 56, 43152
(614) 332-6084; (800) 900-2954

Hillside log home with two guest rooms, shared bath, full breakfast. Nearby is the Hocking State Park with its famous recessed caves, waterfalls, and unusual rock formations. New at Steep Woods is an authentic railroad caboose! Fully equipped, can sleep five. Continental breakfast is provided. Open year-round.

Steep Woods

7 No smoking; 8 Children welcome; 9 Social drinking allowed; 10 Tennis nearby; 11 Swimming nearby; 12 Golf nearby; 13 Skiing nearby; 14 May be booked through a travel agent; 15 Handicapped accessible.

Hosts: Barbara and Brad Holt
Rooms: 2 (SB) $40
Full and Continental Breakfast
Credit Cards: B
Notes: 2, 5, 7, 8, 9, 11

SUGAR GROVE

Hickory Bend Bed & Breakfast

7541 Dupler Road Southeast, 43155
(740) 746-8381

Twin Creek Country

Hickory Bend Bed and Breakfast is on 10 acres of woods in the Hocking Hills of southeastern Ohio. "It is so quiet out here," Pat says, "we take a chair out to the road on Sundays and watch the car go by." The approach road often offers guests a sight of deer grazing or a flock of wild turkey feeding on the hillside. The bird feeder invites, among other species, cardinals, chickadees, nuthatches, a Carolina wren, red-bellied woodpeckers, and, of course, the local squirrels. The guest room is decorated in country primitive, totally private with own bath. Patty is a spinner and weaver. At no extra cost to guests, included are fresh air, delightful sounds of birds, an occasional hoot of an owl, an array of stars, plus the feeling of embracing the universe.

Host: Patty Peery
Rooms: 1 (PB) $50
Full Breakfast
Credit Cards: None
Notes: 2, 7, 10, 11, 12

WEST ALEXANDRIA

Twin Creek Country Bed & Breakfast

5353 Enterprise Road, 45381
(937) 787-3990; (937) 787-4264; (937) 787-3279

This 1830s farmhouse has been remodeled to offer a quiet getaway for families and couples. The entire house, upper or lower level, or individual rooms are available. There are three bedrooms, two bathrooms, a furnished kitchen, and a living room. The owners live 100 yards away. Guests can roam the 170 acres, which include 70 acres of woods. Restaurants and antique shops are nearby. Local catering is available. Suitable for two families at once. Close to the I-70/I-75 interchange.

Hosts: Dr. Mark and Carolyn Ulrich
Suites: 2 (PB) $79-89
Full Breakfast
Credit Cards: A, B, C, D
Notes: 2, 5, 7, 8, 12

WILMOT

Hasseman House Bed & Breakfast

925 US 62, P.O. Box 215, 44689
(330) 359-7904; FAX (330) 359-7159

At the door to Ohio's Amish country is the Hasseman House Bed and Breakfast. This charming and warm, early 1900 Victorian bed and breakfast invites guests to unpack their bags and relax. Furnished with antiques, the bed and breakfast is indeed a step back into a bygone era. The Hasseman House features four cozy rooms complete with private baths and air conditioning. Guests will fall in love with the intricate woodwork and original stained glass. Amish restaurant and shops are nearby. Walk-ins are welcome!

NOTES: Credit cards accepted: A MasterCard; B Visa; C American Express; D Discover; E Diner's Club; F Other; 2 Personal checks accepted; 3 Lunch available; 4 Dinner available; 5 Open all year; 6 Pets welcome;

Hosts: Milo and Kathryn Miller
Rooms: 4 (PB) $69-110
Full Breakfast
Credit Cards: A, B, D
Notes: 2, 5, 7, 11, 12

WORTHINGTON

The Worthington Inn

649 High Street, 43085
(614) 885-2600; FAX (614) 885-1283

Historic inn, built in 1831 and refurbished in 1983 and 1990. Ohio's second oldest inn. Four-star Mobil rating. Has 26 exquisitely appointed hotel suites furnished with stunning period antiques. Highly acclaimed restaurant featuring regional American cuisine. Banquet facilities accommodate 150 guests. A stay at the Worthington includes cocktails upon arrival, twice-daily housekeeping, and full breakfast. Details large and small taken care of professionally and personally. One mile south of I-270 at the corner of High and New England.

Hosts: Stephen and Susan Hanson
Rooms: 26 (PB) $150-215
Full Breakfast
Credit Cards: A, B, C, D
Notes: 3, 4, 5, 7, 8, 9, 10, 11, 12, 14

America's Finest B&B

ZANESFIELD

Myeerah's Inn

2875 Sandusky Street, 43360
(937) 593-3746

French country decorated inn in the historical village of Zanesfield. Gourmet breakfast. Near caverns, hiking, skiing, golf, horseback riding. Luncheon/dinner by reservation for larger groups.

Rooms: 3 (1 PB; 2 SB) $55
Full Breakfast
Credit Cards: None
Notes: 2, 5, 9, 12, 13

ZOAR

The Cider Mill Bed & Breakfast

198 East Second Street, P.O. Box 438, 44697
(330) 874-3240

The Cider Mill was originally a barn used by the community of Separatists to make and store cider. It has been converted to living quarters featuring a three-floor spiral staircase. Furnished with antiques and decorated country style. Built in 1863, it has received a historic marker and is listed in the national register. Rooms are available with shared or private baths. Reservations are encouraged. Central to outdoor dramas, the Pro Football Hall of Fame, Ohio's largest antique mall, historic sites, golf courses, canoe livery, horse academy, making it quick to travel to entertainment and excellent dining facilities.

Hosts: Vernon and Dorothy Furbay
Rooms: 3 (PB or SB) $60-75
Full Breakfast
Credit Cards: A, B, D
Notes: 2, 5, 7, 12, 13

7 No smoking; 8 Children welcome; 9 Social drinking allowed; 10 Tennis nearby; 11 Swimming nearby; 12 Golf nearby; 13 Skiing nearby; 14 May be booked through a travel agent; 15 Handicapped accessible.

Oklahoma

Oklahoma

ALINE

Heritage Manor

33 Heritage Road, 73716
(405) 463-2563 (phone/FAX); (405) 463-2566
(800) 295-2563; e-mail: heritage@pldi.net
www.cruising-america.com/heritagemanor

Heritage Manor is a country getaway on 80 acres that was settled in the land run of 1893 in northwest Oklahoma. Two pre-statehood homes have been joined together and restored by the innkeepers using a Victorian theme. Beautiful sunrises, sunsets, and stargazing from the rooftop decks. Guests can relax in the hot tub or read a book from the 5,000-volume library. Ostriches, donkeys, and Scotch Highland cattle roam a fenced area. Close to homesteader's 1894 Sod House, selenite crystal digging area, and several other attractions. Lunch and dinner available by reservation. Pets and children welcome by prior arrangements. Smoking permitted in designated areas only.

Hosts: Carolyn and A.J. Rexroat
Rooms: 4 (S3B) $75-150
Full Breakfast
Credit Cards: None
Notes: 2, 5, 9, 10, 11, 12, 13, 15

CHECOTAH

Sharpe House

301 Northwest Second, 74426
(918) 473-2832

Sharpe House is in a one-stoplight town in eastern Oklahoma just eight miles north of Lake Eufaula. The house was built in 1911 and is filled with antiques and family heirlooms. Each room has a paddle fan and air conditioning. Breakfast is served in the formal dining room or on the huge screened porch. Enjoy a few days of peace and quiet and southern hospitality. Inquire about accommodations for pets.

Host: Kay Kindt
Rooms: 3 (PB) $50
Full and Continental Breakfast
Credit Cards: None
Notes: 2, 5, 7, 8, 9, 10, 11, 12

CHICKASHA

Campbell-Richison House Bed & Breakfast

1428 West Kansas, 73018
(405) 222-1754; FAX (405) 224-1190
e-mail: davidratcliff@worldnet.att.net

A red brick three-story home awaits guests with an antique-filled parlor and formal dining room with an antique glass window. Three guest rooms on the second floor provide a welcome retreat to guests or business persons for overnight or extended visits.

Hosts: David and Kami Ratcliff
Rooms: 3 (1 PB; 2 SB) $45-65
Full Breakfast
Credit Cards: A, B
Notes: 2, 5, 7, 8, 9, 10, 12

NOTES: Credit cards accepted: A MasterCard; B Visa; C American Express; D Discover; E Diner's Club; F Other; 2 Personal checks accepted; 3 Lunch available; 4 Dinner available; 5 Open all year; 6 Pets welcome; 7 No smoking; 8 Children welcome; 9 Social drinking allowed; 10 Tennis nearby; 11 Swimming nearby; 12 Golf nearby; 13 Skiing nearby; 14 May be booked through a travel agent; 15 Handicapped accessible.

KENTON

Black Mesa Bed & Breakfast

P.O. Box 81, 73946
(580) 261-7443; (800) 866-3009
e-mail: BMBB1@juno.com
www.ccccok.org/bmbb.html

Two miles north of Kenton at the foot of the Black Mesa (highest point in Oklahoma), this 1910 rock ranch house boasts the best in country hospitality. Whether hiking, rock hounding, fishing, hunting, bird watching, or escaping the routine, rest in a double occupancy or family suite (sleeps eight) at Black Mesa Bed and Breakfast. Group rates available.

Rooms: 2 (PB) $40-60
Full Breakfast
Credit Cards: A, B, D
Notes: 2, 3, 4, 5, 6, 7, 8

OKLAHOMA CITY

Flora's Bed & Breakfast

2312 Northwest Forty-sixth, 73112
(405) 840-3157

In a quiet neighborhood, this home is furnished with antiques and collectibles and includes an elevator. Guests may relax in front of the large wood-burning fireplace or enjoy the outdoors on a 1,500-square-foot balcony with a large spa. There is covered parking, and the hosts enjoy square dancing. Easy access to the National Cowboy Hall of Fame, Remington Park racetrack, Kirkpatrick Center, and other points of interest. Many good eating places in the vicinity. Smoking permitted in designated areas only. Children over 11 welcome.

Hosts: Newton W. and Joann Flora
Rooms: 2 (PB) $55-60
Full Breakfast
Credit Cards: None
Notes: 2, 5, 8, 9, 10, 12, 14, 15

South Dakota

CANOVA

Skoglund Farm

Route 1, Box 45, 57321
(605) 247-3445

Enjoy the prairie: cattle, fowl, peacocks, a home-cooked evening meal, and full breakfast. Visit nearby attractions: Little House on the Prairie, Corn Palace, Doll House, and Prairie Village. Relax, hike, and enjoy a family farm. Rate includes evening meal and breakfast: $30 for adults; $20 for teens; $15 for children. Children five and under free.

Hosts: Alden and Delores Skoglund
Rooms: 5 (SB) $30
Full Breakfast
Credit Cards: None
Notes: 2, 3, 4, 5, 6, 8, 9, 10, 11, 12, 14

CHAMBERLAIN

Cable's Riverview Ridge

HC69 Box 82A, 57325
(605) 734-6084
www.bbonline.com/sd/riverviewridge/

Contemporary home built on a bluff overlooking a scenic bend in the Missouri River. On the Lewis and Clark Trail. Full breakfast and secluded country peace and quiet are all available. Just three and one-half miles north of downtown Chamberlain on Highway 50. Enjoy outdoor recreation; visit museums, Indian reservations, and casinos; or just make this a home away from home. Smoking is permitted in designated areas only.

Hosts: Frank and Alta Cable
Rooms: 3 (1 PB; 2 SB) $60-75

Full Breakfast
Credit Cards: A, B
Notes: 2, 5, 8, 9, 11, 12

CUSTER

Custer Mansion Bed & Breakfast

35 Centennial Drive, 57730
(605) 673-3333
e-mail: cusmanbb@qwtc.net
www.qwtc.net/~cusmanbb/custer.html

Historic 1891 Victorian Gothic house of seven gables is listed in the national register. A blend of Victorian elegance, country charm, and western hospitality. Awake to aroma of delicious home-cooked breakfast. Two honeymoon or anniversary suites, one with Jacuzzi, and one family suite. Near all of Black Hills attractions: Mount Rushmore, Custer State Park, Crazy Horse Memorial, National Caves. Recommended by *Bon Appétit* and Mobil Travel

Custer Mansion

South Dakota

Guide. Member of BBISD. Two-night minimum stay during peak season.

Hosts: Bob and Pat Meakim
Rooms: 5 (PB) $70-98
Family Suite: $120
Full Breakfast
Credit Cards: None
Notes: 2, 5, 7, 8, 10, 11, 12, 13, 14

FREEMAN

Farmers Inn

28193 US Highway 81, 57029
(605) 925-7580

The Farmers Inn is in a rural setting along US 81. It is a midwestern four-square built in 1914 furnished with antiques. Features a fitness center, sauna, and crafts. Accommodations include a three-room Victorian suite with refrigerator, the Country Room with two single beds, the Native American Room with double bed and private balcony, and an attic hideaway with double whirlpool tub. The rooms are furnished with telephones, TVs, and private baths and are air conditioned.

Hosts: MarJean and Russell Waltner
Rooms: 4 (PB) $40-65
Full Breakfast
Credit Cards: None
Notes: 2, 3, 4, 5, 7, 8, 9, 10, 11, 12

GETTYSBURG

Harer Lodge Bed & Breakfast

Rural Route 1, Box 87A, 57442
(605) 765-2167; (800) 283-3356
www.bbonline.com/sd/harerlodge/

This modern cedar lodge has a miniature golf course, miniature horses, and farm animals. Five lovely guest rooms have fresh flowers, private baths, bathrobes, and coffee and cookies when guests arrive. Native American tepee

is available for campers, and a separate honeymoon cottage with an oversized Jacuzzi is available. TV, VCR, and lots of privacy. Country store with crafts, antiques, and a sweet shop is in a cream station/store restored on premises. Pheasant and duck hunting. Boating and fishing at beautiful Lake Oahe. Member of Chamber of Commerce and inspected by South Dakota Department of Health and BBISD. Smoking is permitted in designated areas only. Inquire about accommodations for pets and social drinking.

Hosts: Norma Hockesson Harer and Don Harer
Rooms: 5 (PB) $45-65
Cottage: 1 (PB) $85
Full Breakfast
Credit Cards: A, B
Notes: 2, 3, 4, 5, 8, 11, 12, 14

KEYSTONE

The Anchorage Bed & Breakfast

24110 Leaky Valley Road, 57751
(605) 574-4740; (800) 318-7018
e-mail: AnchrageBB@aol.com
www.bbonline.com/sd/TheAnchorage

The Anchorage is a peaceful harbor in an exciting Black Hills vacation. Private cottage on 20 secluded acres. Borders national forest, Centennial Trail. Hike to Mount Ruchmore! Minutes from lakes, Custer State Park, Crazy Horse Memorial, Keystone, and Hill City. Satisfying full breakfast with hosts. Hot tub in the pines. Member BBISD.

Hosts: Jim and Lin Gogolin
Rooms: 1 (PB) $95
Full Breakfast
Credit Cards: A, B, D
Notes: 2, 5, 7, 8, 9, 10, 12, 13, 14

NOTES: Credit cards accepted: A MasterCard; B Visa; C American Express; D Discover; E Diner's Club; F Other; 2 Personal checks accepted; 3 Lunch available; 4 Dinner available; 5 Open all year; 6 Pets welcome; 7 No smoking; 8 Children welcome; 9 Social drinking allowed; 10 Tennis nearby; 11 Swimming nearby; 12 Golf nearby; 13 Skiing nearby; 14 May be booked through a travel agent; 15 Handicapped accessible.

Bed & Breakfast Inn

208 First Street; P.O. Box 662, 57751
(605) 666-4490; (888) 833-4490
FAX (605) 666-4290
www.bbonline.com/sd/keystone

Just three miles from Mount Rushmore. A cozy, comfortable, and historic home in Old Keystone. AAA-rated. Families welcome. Extra charge for pets. Picnic facilities and hot tub in the courtyard. Guests can relax and listen to the creek babble in the backyard and/or go fishing. Within walking distance to downtown shops and dining.

Hosts: Susanne and David Dennis
Rooms: 6 (PB) $55-80
Full Breakfast
Credit Cards: A, B, C, D
Notes: 2, 5, 6, 7, 8, 9, 10

LEAD

Deer Mountain Bed & Breakfast

HC 37, Box 1214, 57754
(605) 584-2473; FAX (605) 584-3045
e-mail: vonackerman@dgt.net

Unique log home. Skiing and snowmobiling minutes away. Near historic Deadwood gambling town. Mount Rushmore, hunting, fishing, Homestake Gold Mine all nearby. Hot tub, pool table, videos, fireplace, and game rooms

Deer Mountain

for guests' enjoyment. Box lunches available upon request. Inquire about accommodations for pets. Smoking is permitted in designated areas only.

Hosts: Vonnie and Bob Ackerman
Rooms: 4 (2 PB; 2 SB) $65-75
Full Breakfast
Credit Cards: A, B, D
Notes: 2, 5, 8, 9, 11, 12, 13, 14

RAPID CITY

Abend Haus Cottages

Abend Haus Cottages & Audrie's Bed & Breakfast

23029 Thunderhead Falls Road, 57702-8524
(605) 342-7788
www.audriesbb.com

The Black Hills "inn place." Ultimate in charm and Old World hospitality, this country home and six-acre estate is surrounded by thousands of acres of national forest. Thirty miles from Mount Rushmore and seven miles from Rapid City. Each quiet, comfortable suite and cottage has a private entrance, private bath, hot tub, patio, cable TV, and refrigerator. Free trout fishing, biking, and hiking on-site.

Hosts: Hank and Audry Kuhnhauser
Rooms: 6 (PB) $95
Cottages: 4 (PB) $145
Full Breakfast
Credit Cards: None
Notes: 2, 5, 7, 9, 10, 11, 12, 13

NOTES: Credit cards accepted: A MasterCard; B Visa; C American Express; D Discover; E Diner's Club; F Other; 2 Personal checks accepted; 3 Lunch available; 4 Dinner available; 5 Open all year; 6 Pets welcome;

Black Forest Inn Bed & Breakfast Lodge

23191 Highway 385, 57702-6032
(605) 574-2000; (800) 888-1607
FAX (605) 574-2798; e-mail: barkley@iw.net

Guests can relax peacefully in a beautiful mountain lodge in the heart of the Black Hills on Highway 385. Ten tastefully decorated rooms with private baths, antiques, and turned-down beds. Delicious full breakfast. Two cozy fireplaces, hot tubs, deck, game room. Near Pactola and Sheridan Lakes, Black Hills attractions, hiking, fishing, golfing, hunting, skiing, and snowmobiling. Honeymoons, anniversaries, retreats, and reunions. Rates are seasonal.

Hosts: Bob and Betty Barkley
Rooms: 10 (PB) $60-150
Full Breakfast
Credit Cards: A, B
Notes: 2, 5, 7, 8, 9, 11, 12, 13, 14

Carriage House Bed & Breakfast

721 West Boulevard, 57701
(888) 343-6415; www.carriagehouse-bb.com

The stately, three-story pillared Colonial house is on the historic, tree-lined boulevard of Rapid City. Fine antique furnishings reflect an era of Victorian romance. Experience warm and gracious hospitality reminiscent of days gone by. Scenic Mount Rushmore is only 26 miles away. Downtown Rapid City is within walking distance.

Hosts: Jay and Janice Hrachovec
Rooms: 5 (PB) $89-149
Full Breakfast
Credit Cards: A, B, C
Notes: 2, 4, 5, 7, 9, 10, 11, 12, 13, 14

Hayloft Bed & Breakfast

9356 Neck Yoke Road, 57702
(605) 343-5351; e-mail: Hayloft4bb@aol.com

Awarded "Governor's Great Service Award" in 1997. Nestled snugly at the foot of the beautiful Black Hills. Peaceful and quiet, and yet only five miles from Rapid City and within minutes of Mount Rushmore. Decorated in elegant antique decor, each room has a distinct personality and charming presentation. From the Honeymoon Suite, with a canopied bed, two-person heated whirlpool, antique stove, and romantic atmosphere, to the Green Loft Room with six skylights, two double beds and decorated with a cheerful green color scheme. Featured in the *Country Inns Magazine,* the *Rapid City Journal,* and the *Olathe Kansas Sun.*

Hosts: Berdell and Jim Dunworth
Rooms: 8 (PB) $95-115
Full and Continental Breakfast
Credit Cards: A, B, D
Notes: 2, 3, 4, 5, 7, 9, 10, 11, 12, 13, 14

Madison Ranch

8800 Nemo Road, 57702
(605) 342-6997

Honored with an Award of Excellence, this turn-of-the-century working horse ranch is in the beautiful Black Hills. Surrounded by timber and wildlife, the ranch once served as a rodeo guest lodge, hosted rodeos, and movie productions. It features a private museum of heirloom rodeo memorabilia, western and Indian artifacts. Boarding available for guest horses. Member of and inspected by BBISD.

Hosts: Stanley and Marilynn Madison
Rooms: 4 (S2B) $65-70
Full Breakfast
Credit Cards: None
Notes: 2, 7, 9, 11, 12

Willow Springs Cabins

11515 Sheridan Lake Road, 57702
(605) 342-3665

Private one-room log cabins in the beautiful Black Hills National Forest. This secluded setting offers privacy like no other retreat. Each cabin is charmingly decorated with many antique treasures and extras. Breakfast is wonderful, featuring freshly ground coffee, juices,

7 No smoking; 8 Children welcome; 9 Social drinking allowed; 10 Tennis nearby; 11 Swimming nearby; 12 Golf nearby; 13 Skiing nearby; 14 May be booked through a travel agent; 15 Handicapped accessible.

baked goods, and egg dishes. Hiking, swimming, private hot tub, and fishing abound. Featured in *Vacations* magazine as one of America's Best Romantic Inns.

Hosts: Joyce and Russell Payton
Cabins: 2 (PB) $95-110
Full Breakfast
Credit Cards: None
Notes: 2, 5, 7, 8, 9, 10, 11, 12, 13, 14

SIOUX FALLS

Steever House

Steever House Bed & Breakfast

46850 276th Street, Lennox, 57039
(605) 647-5055; www.steeverhouse.com

Surrounded by gently rolling farmland under a vast prairie sky, this restored Queen Anne home welcomes guests to the plains of eastern South Dakota. Porch offers spectacular sunsets and celestial theater, or cozy up to the fireplace, or relax in the Jacuzzi. Private parties and fine dining by reservation. Queen-size beds, cable TV. Just two miles off I-29 and 10 minutes from all the amenities of Sioux Falls.

Hosts: Sara and John Steever
Rooms: 3 (PB) $65-85
Full Breakfast
Credit Cards: None
Notes: 2, 4, 5, 6, 7, 8, 9, 12

VERMILLION

The Goebel House Bed & Breakfast

102 Franklin, 57069
(605) 624-6691

A friendly old home built in 1916 and furnished with antiques and collectibles. Vermillion is home of the nationally known Shrine to Music Museum and the Univer-sity of South Dakota. Four bedrooms have both private and shared baths. Each room is individually decorated with mementos of the past.

Hosts: Don and Pat Goebel
Rooms: 4 (2 PB; 2 SB) $50-65
Full Breakfast
Credit Cards: None
Notes: 2, 5, 9, 10, 11, 12

WEBSTER

Lakeside Farm Bed & Breakfast

Rural Route 2, Box 52, 57274
(605) 486-4430

Guests are invited to sample a bit of country life at Lakeside Farm. Feel free to explore the grove, barns, and pastures, or just relax with a cup of tea in the farmhouse. Accommodations for four to five guests on the second floor. The second-floor bathroom and shower serve both guest rooms. Children are welcome. In northeastern South Dakota with museums featuring

Lakeside Farm

pioneer and Native American culture. Fort Sisseton nearby. Nearby trails marked for snowmobiling. Swimming in summer only. Smoking is not permitted. Alcoholic beverages are not permitted.

Hosts: Glenn and Joy Hagen
Rooms: 2 (SB) $45
Full Breakfast
Credit Cards: None
Notes: 2, 5, 8, 11, 12

YANKTON

Mulberry Inn

512 Mulberry Street, 57078
(605) 665-7116

This beautiful inn was built in 1873 and offers the ultimate in comfortable lodging with historic charm. Included in the National Register of Historic Places. Features parquet floors, six guest rooms furnished with antiques, two parlors with marble fireplaces, and a large porch for evening relaxation. In a quiet residential

Mulberry Inn

area, and within walking distance to the Missouri River, downtown, and fine restaurants. Only minutes from the beautiful Lewis and Clark Lake and Gavins Point Dam. Full breakfast at additional cost.

Host: Millie Cameron
Rooms: 6 (2 PB; 4 SB) $37-55
Continental Breakfast
Credit Cards: A, B
Notes: 2, 5, 7, 8, 10, 11, 12

7 No smoking; 8 Children welcome; 9 Social drinking allowed; 10 Tennis nearby; 11 Swimming nearby; 12 Golf nearby; 13 Skiing nearby; 14 May be booked through a travel agent; 15 Handicapped accessible.

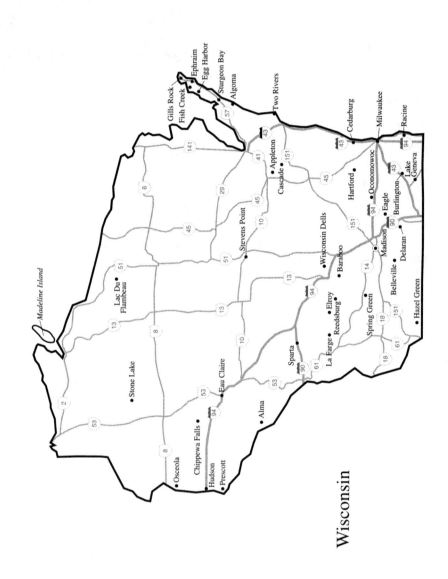

Wisconsin

Wisconsin

Amberwood Inn

N7136 Highway 42 Lakeshore Drive, 54201
(920) 487-3471; www.amberwoodinn.com

Lake Michigan beachfront. Private wooded acreage on the shores of Lake Michigan, less than five miles from Door County. Large luxury suites, each with private bath, fireplace, and double French doors with private decks opening to the beach. Whirlpool tub, wet bars, refrigerators, Finnish sauna, and hot tub. Sleep to the sound of the waves; awaken to a sunrise over the water. Smoking in designated areas only. Inquire about accommodations for children.

Hosts: Mark and Karen Rittle
Rooms: 5 (PB) $80-115
Full Breakfast
Credit Cards: A, B
Notes: 2, 5, 9, 10, 11, 12, 15

ALMA

Laue House Inn

P.O. Box 176, 54610
(608) 685-4923

The comfortable, cozy, and affordable Laue House Inn is the best remaining example of domestic Italianate architecture in Buffalo County. Placed in the National Register of Historic Places in 1979. Step back in time and enjoy the moderately priced rooms of one of Alma's oldest and most elegant houses. There are six guest rooms with TVs and air conditioning. Player piano in the lounge to sing along with and coffee bar for chatting by the fireplace.

Rooms: 6 (SB) $25-40
Continental Breakfast
Credit Cards: None
Notes: 2, 6, 7, 8, 9, 10, 11, 12

APPLETON

The Gathering Place

808 West Front Street, 54914-5465
(920) 731-4418; e-mail: gatherpl@execpc.com
www.execpc.com/~gatherpl/

Architecturally designed and built in 1939, this charming English country home is on the quiet and historic Front Street. Surrounding area has three parks, scenic river views, and first hydro-electrically powered home in the world. Details abound in this cozy, comfortable home. Come to be pampered and enjoy a bountiful breakfast. Scones are a favorite.

Hosts: Madelyn and Dennis Olson
Rooms: 3 (1 PB; 2 SB) $80-100
Full Breakfast
Credit Cards: None
Notes: 2, 5, 7, 10, 11, 12, 14

The Solie Home

914 East Hancock Street, 54911
(920) 733-0863

An early 1900 stucco home tastefully redecorated keeping within the integrity of its time. Of particular interest to visitors are the sculptured plaster walls and woodwork in the living and dining rooms. The home is on a quiet street in a quaint residential neighborhood. Lovely

NOTES: Credit cards accepted: A MasterCard; B Visa; C American Express; D Discover; E Diner's Club; F Other; 2 Personal checks accepted; 3 Lunch available; 4 Dinner available; 5 Open all year; 6 Pets welcome; 7 No smoking; 8 Children welcome; 9 Social drinking allowed; 10 Tennis nearby; 11 Swimming nearby; 12 Golf nearby; 13 Skiing nearby; 14 May be booked through a travel agent; 15 Handicapped accessible.

full breakfast includes fresh fruits, a delicious entrée, and always Carole's freshly baked coffee cakes and muffins. Relax and enjoy good-natured, gracious hospitality. Children over 12 welcome.

Host: Carole Solie
Rooms: 3 (SB) $65-105
Full Breakfast
Credit Cards: None
Notes: 2, 5, 7, 10, 11, 12, 13

BARABOO

Pinehaven Bed & Breakfast

E13083 Highway 33, 53913
(608) 356-3489

This chalet-style inn overlooks a scenic valley and small private lake. Each distinctly different guest room has a queen-size bed or twin beds; some have wicker furniture or antiques. The common room has a fireplace, TV/VCR, game table, and baby grand piano. Take a stroll in this inviting setting. Ask about the private guest cottage. Area activities include Devils Lake State Park, Circus World Museum, the Wisconsin Dells, International Crane Foundation, and ski resorts. Excellent restaurants nearby. Inquire about accommodations for children.

Hosts: Lyle and Marge Getschman
Rooms: 4 (PB) $79-135
Full Breakfast
Credit Cards: A, B
Notes: 2, 5, 7, 9, 11, 12, 13

BELLEVILLE

Abendruh Bed & Breakfast Swiss Style

7019 Gehin Road, 53508
(608) 424-3808

Experience bed and breakfast Swiss style. This highly acclaimed Wisconsin bed and breakfast offers true Swiss charm and hospitality. The serenity of this peaceful retreat is one of many treasures that keep guests coming back. Spacious guest rooms adorned with beautiful family heirlooms. Sitting room with high cathedral ceiling and cozy fireplace. An Abendruh breakfast is a perfect way to start a new day or end a peaceful stay.

Host: Mathilde Jaggi
Rooms: 2 (PB) $50-70
Full Breakfast
Credit Cards: None
Notes: 2, 5, 7, 10, 11, 12, 13, 14

BURLINGTON

The Hillcrest Inn & Carriage House

540 Storle Avenue, 53105
(414) 763-4706; FAX (414) 763-7871
e-mail: hillcrest@ols.com
www.ols.com/~hillcrest

On four wooded acres, this stately 1908 Edwardian home offers accommodations which are romantic, luxurious, and private. Walk the paths through English flower gardens or sit on the porch to enjoy the magnificent view of the countryside and waterways. Rooms are available in the main house and in the elegant carriage house. Period antiques, lovely decor, and queen-size beds in each room, with fireplaces, and double whirlpools in selected rooms. Only minutes from Lake Geneva.

The Hillcrest Inn

Hosts: Mike and Gayle Hohner
Rooms: 6 (PB) $90-170
Full Breakfast
Credit Cards: A, B
Notes: 2, 5, 7, 9, 10, 11, 12, 13

CASCADE

Timberlake Inn

311 Madison Avenue (Highway 28), 53011-0367
(888) 528-8481
e-mail: brlkin@timberlakeinn.com
www.timberlakeinn.com

Stagecoach Inn

This 1895 village landmark features comfortable rustic nostalgia all near southeastern Wisconsin's parks, Elkhart Raceway, sport fishing, Kohler Center, and antiquing—small-town hospitality yet just 45 minutes north of Milwaukee. Reasonably priced; six unique rooms each with queen-size beds, private baths (one with Jacuzzi), and a guest kitchen. A sumptuous country-style (you won't go away hungry) breakfast is included at guests' convenient time (the hosts will make it "to go" if needed). Group rates available year-round. Smoking permitted in designated areas only. Children 10 and older welcome.

Hosts: Rick and Juanita Levandowski
Rooms: 6 (PB) $75-100
Full Breakfast
Credit Cards: A, B, D
Notes: 2, 5, 9, 10, 11, 12, 13, 14

CEDARBURG

Stagecoach Inn Bed & Breakfast

W61 N520 Washington Avenue, 53012
(888) 375-0208; FAX (414) 375-6170
www.stagecoach-inn-wi.com

The inn, listed in the national register, is housed in a restored 1853 stone building in downtown Cedarburg. The rooms are furnished with antiques. Suites include whirlpools and fireplaces. Guests enjoy a complimentary wine social in the pub on the first floor across from a chocolate shop. The inn is conveniently within the historic district; walking distance to parks, antique shops, winery, and a variety of excellent restaurants. A truly memorable getaway. A Continental plus breakfast is served.

Hosts: Liz and Brook Brown
Rooms: 12 (PB) $75-140
Continental Breakfast
Credit Cards: A, B, C, D, E
Notes: 2, 5, 7, 9, 10, 11, 12, 13, 14

The Washington House Inn

W62 N573 Washington Avenue, 53012
(414) 375-3550; (800) 554-4717
FAX (414) 375-9422; e-mail: whinn@execpc.com

A country Victorian bed and breakfast in the heart of Cedarburg's historic district. Rooms feature antiques, whirlpool baths, and fireplaces. All room rates include an afternoon social hour featuring local wines and cheeses and a homemade Continental plus breakfast. The inn is conveniently near the Cedar Creek Settlement and many other fine shops. The Washington House Inn bestows comfort and privacy while offering the ultimate in bed and breakfast accommodations. Some rooms are handicapped accessible.

Host: Wendy Porterfield
Rooms: 34 (PB) $75-205
Continental Breakfast
Credit Cards: A, B, C, D, E
Notes: 2, 5, 10, 11, 12, 13, 14

7 No smoking; 8 Children welcome; 9 Social drinking allowed; 10 Tennis nearby; 11 Swimming nearby; 12 Golf nearby; 13 Skiing nearby; 14 May be booked through a travel agent; 15 Handicapped accessible.

CHIPPEWA FALLS

McGilvray's Victorian Bed & Breakfast

312 West Columbia Street, 54729
(715) 720-1600; (888) 324-1893
www.mcgilvraysbb.com

Step into the wicker-filled screened-in porch and guests will be stepping back into the turn of the century. Built in 1893 by Angus McGilvray this 100-year-old home is decorated and furnished with lovely antiques typical of the era. The style is Neoclassicism and Georgian Revival with a portico featuring two-story columns. McGilvray's is in a quiet west hill neighborhood filled with historic homes. Warm hospitality and a scrumptious breakfast awaits guests.

Rooms: 3 (PB) $60-85
Full Breakfast
Credit Cards: None
Notes: 2, 5, 7, 9, 10, 11, 12, 13

DELAVAN

Allyn Mansion Inn

511 East Walworth Avenue, 53115
(414) 728-9090; FAX (414) 728-0201
e-mail: joeron@allynmansion.com
www.allynmansion.com

Allyn Mansion Inn

This meticulously restored 1885 national register mansion in Wisconsin's Southern Gateways region offers an authentic Victorian setting. Guests are encouraged to enjoy the entire house with its spacious rooms and fine antique furnishings. Read by one of the 10 marble fireplaces, play the grand pianos, peruse the collections of Victoriana, have a good soak in a copper bathtub, or swap stories with the hosts on restoration or antiquing.

Rooms: 8 (5 PB; 3 SB) $100-125
Full Breakfast
Credit Cards: A, B
Notes: 2, 5, 7, 10, 11, 12, 13

EAGLE

Eagle Centre House

Eagle Centre House Bed & Breakfast

W370 S9590 Highway 67, 53119
(414) 363-4700; e-mail: info@eagle-house.com
www.eagle-house.com

A replicated 1846 Greek Revival stagecoach house sets high on a hill amidst 20 scenic acres in the Kettle Moraine. Five spacious bedchambers offer private, adjoining baths. Two boast double whirlpool tubs. Guests will find themselves amidst a vast collection of authentic antique furnishings. In the dining room savor a full breakfast served on period china. Woodburning stoves in the taproom and parlor warm guests in season. ("We're also air-conditioned.")

Rooms: 5 (PB) $95-155
Full Breakfast
Credit Cards: A, B, C
Notes: 2, 5, 7, 9, 11, 12, 13, 14

NOTES: Credit cards accepted: A MasterCard; B Visa; C American Express; D Discover; E Diner's Club; F Other; 2 Personal checks accepted; 3 Lunch available; 4 Dinner available; 5 Open all year; 6 Pets welcome;

EAU CLAIRE

Otter Creek Inn

2536 Highway 12, P.O. Box 3183, 54702-3183
(715) 832-2945; FAX (715) 832-4607
e-mail: hansen@werewolf.net
www.werewolf.net/~hansen

Be pampered! Each antique-filled guest room
has a double whirlpool, private bath, telephone,
air conditioner, cable TV, and many have a fireplace. The breakfast menu allows a choice of
entrées and breakfast in bed. This spacious inn
(more than 6,000 square feet) is a three-story
English Tudor with country Victorian decor.
Nestled on a wooded acre adjacent to, but high
above, the Otter Creek, the inn is less than one
mile from numerous restaurants and shops. In-
ground pool. AAA-rated.

Hosts: Randy and Shelley Hansen
Rooms: 6 (PB) $79-169
Full Breakfast
Credit Cards: A, B, C, D, E, F
Notes: 2, 5, 7, 9, 10, 11, 12, 13

Otter Creek Inn

EGG HARBOR (DOOR COUNTY)

The WildFlower

7821 Church Street, P.O. Box 34, 54209
(920) 868-9030

Charming and intimate—this new home has
blended contemporary amenities with antique
decor. Fireplaces illuminate queen- or king-
size beds. Romantic candlelit double whirlpool
or refreshing shower-for-two. Enjoy cool bay
breezes from own private balcony or stroll the

wildflower path to village activities. Heart-
smart breakfast basket delivered to guests'
door. Hors d'oeuvres served at 5:00 P.M. Gift
shoppe on lower level featuring antiques, collectibles, and home decor.

Host: Judy LaMacchia
Rooms: 3 (PB) $90-145
Continental Breakfast
Credit Cards: A, B, D
Notes: 2, 5, 9, 11, 12, 13, 15

ELROY

East View Bed & Breakfast

33620 County P Road, 53929
(608) 463-7564
www.outspokinadventures.com/eastview

The bed and breakfast is about 1,100 feet
above sea level, which gives it a fantastic view
in all directions. About four miles from the
start of Elroy-Sparts, "400," and Omaha Bike
Trails, little over 35 minutes from the Wisconsin Dells, Wildcat Mountain, Amish community, canoeing on the Kickapoo River, fishing
on the Wisconsin River. Snowmobiling in area.

Hosts: Dom and Bev Puechner
Rooms: 3 (PB) $65-75
Full Breakfast
Credit Cards: A, B, C
Notes: 2, 5, 7, 8, 12, 13, 14

EPHRAIM

Eagle Harbor Inn

9914 Water Street, P.O. Box 588, 54211
(920) 854-2121; (800) 324-5427

On the Main Street of historic Ephraim in Door
County, Eagle Harbor is a gracious, antique-
filled country inn. This bed and breakfast is
across from the lake and close to the boat
ramp, golf course, park, beach, and cross-country ski trails, offering delightful full breakfasts.
Beautiful new indoor pool and fitness spa and
gathering room for meetings and weddings.

7 No smoking; 8 Children welcome; 9 Social drinking allowed; 10 Tennis nearby; 11 Swimming nearby;
12 Golf nearby; 13 Skiing nearby; 14 May be booked through a travel agent; 15 Handicapped accessible.

Luxurious one- and two-bedroom whirlpool suites with two-way fireplace and kitchen.

Hosts: Nedd and Natalie Neddersen
Rooms: 9 (PB) $89-149
Full Breakfast
Credit Cards: A, B, D
Notes: 2, 5, 7, 8, 9, 10, 11, 12, 13, 14, 15

Hillside Hotel

9980 Highway 42, P.O. Box 17, 54211
(414) 854-2417; (800) 423-7023

This beautifully restored 1890s country-Victorian inn overlooks Eagle Harbor on Green Bay. Special to this inn are the full, delightful breakfasts and afternoon teas; feather beds; a spectacular view from the 100-foot veranda and most guest rooms; antique furnishings; and a large, private beach. The hosts also have two deluxe housekeeping cottages available for guests. Near galleries, shops, water sports, and cultural events for visitors to enjoy. Hillside is listed in the National Register of Historic Places.

Rooms: 12 (SB) $73-94
Full Breakfast
Credit Cards: A, B, D
Notes: 2, 7, 8, 9, 10, 11, 12, 13, 15

FISH CREEK

Thorp House Inn & Cottages

4135 Bluff Lane, P.O. Box 490, 54212-0490
(920) 868-2444

Find history and romance nestled in the heart of a charming waterfront village. Gracious antique-filled guest rooms feature private baths (one with whirlpool), air conditioning, guest library, fireplaced parlor, and delicious home-baked breakfasts. Cottages feature wood-burning fireplaces, country antiques, kitchens, decks, and full baths (some with whirlpools). "Inspiration for Lavyrle Spencer's best-selling *Bittersweet*"— *McCall's* magazine. Write or call for detailed brochure. Smoking is not permitted in the inn. Children are welcome in cottages.

Hosts: Christine and Sverre Falck-Pedersen
Rooms: 4 (PB) $85-165
Cottages: 6 (PB)
Continental Breakfast
Credit Cards: None
Notes: 2, 5, 7, 9, 10, 11, 12, 13

GILLS ROCK

Harbor House Inn

12666 Highway 42, 54210
(414) 854-5196

A 1904 Victorian bed and breakfast with Scandinavian country wing and a new lighthouse suite overlooking quaint fishing harbor. Bluffs and sunsets. Within walking of ferry to islands, shops, and restaurant. Sauna, whirlpool, bike rentals, and private beach. Continental plus breakfast.

Hosts: David and Else Weborg
Rooms: 15 (PB) $54-149
Continental Breakfast
Credit Cards: A, B, C
Notes: 2, 6, 7, 8, 11, 12, 15

HARTFORD

Jordan House

81 South Main Street, 53027
(414) 673-5643

This warm and comfortable Victorian home, furnished with beautiful period antiques, is

NOTES: Credit cards accepted: A MasterCard; B Visa; C American Express; D Discover; E Diner's Club; F Other; 2 Personal checks accepted; 3 Lunch available; 4 Dinner available; 5 Open all year; 6 Pets welcome;

only 40 miles from Milwaukee. Near the attractions of majestic Holy Hill Shrine, Horicon Wildlife Refuge, and Pike Lake State Park. Walk to the state's largest antique auto museum, which features Kissel automobiles, or browse through the many antique shops and do some downtown shopping.

Rooms: 4 (1 PB; 3 SB) $55-65
Full Breakfast
Credit Cards: A, B
Notes: 2, 5, 8, 10, 11, 12, 13

Jefferson-Day House

HAZEL GREEN

Wisconsin House Stage Coach Inn

2105 Main Street, P.O. Box 71, 53811-0071
(608) 854-2233

The inn is a historic, country-furnished bed and breakfast. Built in 1846 as a stagecoach inn, it now offers six guest rooms and two guest suites. Just 10 minutes from Galena, 12 minutes from Dubuque, and 15 minutes from Platteville, the inn is convenient to all the attractions of the tri-state area.

Hosts: Ken and Pat Disch
Rooms: 8 (6 PB: 2 SB) $55-115
Full Breakfast
Credit Cards: A, B, C, D
Notes: 2, 4, 5, 7, 8, 9, 11, 12, 13, 14

HUDSON

Jefferson-Day House

1109 Third Street, 54016
(715) 386-7111; www. jeffersondayhouse.com

This 1857 home offers antique collections, five air-conditioned rooms, all with double whirlpools, gas fireplaces, and four-course fireside breakfasts. Complimentary spirits and appetizers are served. The pleasing decor and friendly atmosphere will relax guests, while the nearby St. Croix River, Octagon House Museum, and Phipps Center for the Arts will

bring enjoyment. Thirty minutes from Minneapolis, St. Paul, and the Mall of America. Children over 12 inquire.

Hosts: Tom and Sue Tyler
Rooms: 5 (PB) $99-179
Full Breakfast
Credit Cards: A, B, C, D, E
Notes: 2, 5, 6, 7, 9, 10, 11, 12, 13, 14

Phipps Inn

1005 Third Street, 54016
(715) 386-0800

Described as the "grand dame" of Queen Anne houses, the Phipps Inn can be found on Hudson's historic Third Street. Step back 100 years to a more graceful era of leaded-glass windows and finely crafted furnishings. Guests are encouraged to sip their morning coffee in the

Phipps Inn

---

7 No smoking; 8 Children welcome; 9 Social drinking allowed; 10 Tennis nearby; 11 Swimming nearby; 12 Golf nearby; 13 Skiing nearby; 14 May be booked through a travel agent; 15 Handicapped accessible.

parlor around a glowing fire. A lavish breakfast is served in the dining room or in guests' room. The Phipps Inn was named the Wisconsin's 1994 Property of the Year and has appeared on the cover of four magazines.

Hosts: Todd M. Jadwin and Susan A. Jadwin
Rooms: 6 (PB) $119-189
Full Breakfast
Credit Cards: A, B, C, D
Notes: 2, 5, 9, 10, 11, 12, 13

LAC DU FLAMBEAU

Ty-Bach

3104 Simpson Lane, 54538
(715) 588-7851

For a relaxing getaway any time of the year, share this modern home on the shore of a tranquil northwoods lake with 80 acres of woods to explore. Guest quarters include a large living area and a deck overlooking Golden Pond. Visit the area attractions: the cranberry marshes, the Native American museum, pow-wows, professional theater, wilderness cruises, and more. Golf is 12 miles away. Guests are pampered with delicious country breakfasts served at flexible times. Closed March and April. Inquire about pets being welcome.

Hosts: Kermit and Janet Bekkum
Rooms: 2 (PB) $65-75
Full Breakfast
Credit Cards: None
Notes: 2, 7, 9, 10, 11, 12, 13

Ty-Bach

LA FARGE

Trillium

Route 2, Box 121, 54639
(608) 625-4492

One's own private cottage on this farm amid 85 acres of fields and woods near a tree-lined brook. Experience Wisconsin in a thriving Amish farm community just 35 miles southeast of La Crosse. Children under 12 stay free.

Host: Rosanne Boyett
Cottage: 1 (PB) $75-85
Full Breakfast
Credit Cards: None
Notes: 2, 5, 7, 8, 9, 10, 11, 12, 13

LAKE GENEVA

Eleven Gables Inn on Lake Geneva

493 Wrigley Drive, 53147
(414) 248-8393; www.lkgeneva.com

Nestled in evergreens amid giant oaks in the Edgewater historic district, this quaint lakeside carpenter Gothic inn offers privacy in a prime area. The romantic bedrooms, bridal chamber, and unique country cottages all have fireplaces, baths, TVs, wet bars, kitchenettes, or cocktail refrigerators. Some of the accommodations have charming lattice courtyards, balconies, and private entrances. A private pier provides exclusive water activities for guests. Bike rentals are available. This charming "Newport of the Midwest" community provides visitors with fine dining, boutiques, and entertainment year-round. Call about rates and special packages.

Host: A. Milliette
Rooms: 12 (PB)
Full Breakfast weekends
Continental Breakfast midweek
Credit Cards: A, B, C, D, E
Notes: 5, 7, 8, 9, 10, 12, 14

NOTES: Credit cards accepted: A MasterCard; B Visa; C American Express; D Discover; E Diner's Club; F Other; 2 Personal checks accepted; 3 Lunch available; 4 Dinner available; 5 Open all year; 6 Pets welcome;

T. C. Smith Inn
Historic Bed & Breakfast

865 Main Street, 53147
(414) 248-1097; (800) 423-0233
wwte.tcsmithinn.com

Experience classic elegance and recapture the majesty of 19th-century ambiance. Listed in the National Register of Historic Places. Downtown lake-view inn, complete with oriental carpets, period antiques, and European paintings. Eight spacious guest chambers with private baths, most with whirlpools and fireplaces. Delicious buffet breakfast served. Magnificent honeymoon suites with Grecian-style marble and walnut 6-by-10-foot lighted whirlpool spa. A garden, a fountain, and neoclassical statues grace the large courtyard surrounding the 1845 historical mansion. Veranda, rooftop, balcony, gazebo overlook the restored European formal gardens.

Hosts: The Marks Family
Rooms: 8 (PB) $95-395
Full Breakfast
Credit Cards: A, B, C, D, E
Notes: 2, 5, 6, 7, 8, 9, 10, 11, 12, 13, 14

MADISON

Annie's Bed & Breakfast

2117 Sheridan Drive, 53704
(608) 244-2224 (phone/FAX)
www.bbinternet.com/annies

Since 1985, when guests want the world to go away, they come to Annie's Bed and Breakfast. This quiet little inn on Warner Park offers a beautiful view and deluxe accommodations. Enjoy the romantic gazebo surrounded by butterfly gardens or the lily pond by the terrace for morning coffee, followed by a sumptuous breakfast. Guests have a whole floor of space, including two bedrooms with a connecting bath, a whirlpool room, pine-paneled library with a beautiful fireplace, and dining room with

Annie's

a large nature aquarium. Six minutes to downtown and campus. Children over 12 welcome.

Hosts: Anne and Larry Stuart
Suite: $128-189
Full Breakfast
Credit Cards: A, B, C, E
Notes: 2, 5, 7, 9, 10, 11, 12, 13

Arbor House:
An Environmental Inn

3402 Monroe Street, 53711
(608) 238-2981; www.arbor-house.com

The inn is across the street from the University Arboretum with its 1,200 acres ideal for biking, walking, and bird watching. While preserving the charm of this nationally registered historic home, the award-winning inn is evolving into a model for urban ecology. Whirlpools and TVs in most guest rooms. Full gourmet breakfast served weekends; Continental plus breakfast on weekdays. Guests are treated to a Gehl's iced cappuccino welcoming beverage upon arrival, as well as a canoeing pass, use of mountain

Arbor House

7 No smoking; 8 Children welcome; 9 Social drinking allowed; 10 Tennis nearby; 11 Swimming nearby; 12 Golf nearby; 13 Skiing nearby; 14 May be booked through a travel agent; 15 Handicapped accessible.

bikes, and Aveda personal care products. Corporate rate and meeting space are available.

Hosts: John and Cathie Imes
Rooms: 8 (PB) $85-205
Credit Cards: A, B, C
Notes: 2, 5, 7, 8, 9, 10, 11, 12, 13, 15

Collins House Bed & Breakfast

704 East Gorham, 53703
(608) 255-4230

The Collins House captures the essence of Madison, from its restored Prairie-style architecture to its lakefront location and capitol-university proximity. Experience this midwestern, down-to-earth ambiance while enjoying a host of indulgences: famous full breakfasts (such as oatmeal pancakes with brown sugar pecan sauce and sautéed apples; creamy scrambled eggs with asparagus and shiitake mushrooms), fresh homemade pastries, and signature chocolate truffles from the bakery, whirlpools, and lake sunset. The staff are eager to share their love of Madison and make every stay memorable. Inquire about accommodations for pets.

Hosts: Barb and Mike Pratzel
Rooms: 5 (PB) $85-140
Full Breakfast
Credit Cards: A, B, D
Notes: 2, 5, 7, 8, 9, 10, 11, 13

Mansion Hill Inn

424 North Pinckney Street, 53703
(608) 255-3999; (800) 798-9070
FAX (608) 255-2217

Eleven luxurious guest rooms, each with a sumptuous bath. Whirlpool tubs, stereo with headphones, hand-carved marble fireplaces, minibars, and elegant Victorian furnishings help to make this restored mansion Madison's only four-diamond inn. Private wine cellar, VCRs, and access to private dining and an athletic club are available upon request. Turndown service. Evening refreshments are available in the parlor. The ideal spot for a perfect honey-

moon. Listed in the National Register of Historic Places.

Host: Janna Wojtal
Rooms: 11 (PB) $140-320
Continental Breakfast
Credit Cards: A, B, C
Notes: 2, 5, 7, 9, 11, 12, 13, 14

MILWAUKEE

The Crane House

346 East Wilson Street, 53207
(414) 483-1512

Beautiful 1896 Victorian home in historic Bay View district. Less than 10 minutes from downtown and airport. Furnished with heirlooms and mix of contemporary and antique pieces. Lush perennial garden. Full breakfast is served. Off-street parking is available. Central air conditioning. Please write or call for brochure.

Hosts: Paula Tirrito and Steven Skavroneck
Rooms: 4 (S2B) $65-83
Full Breakfast
Credit Cards: A, B, D
Notes: 2, 5, 7, 8, 9, 10, 11, 12

OCONOMOWOC

The Inn at Pine Terrace

351 East Lisbon Road, 53066
(414) 567-7463; (800) 421-4667

This 1879 elegantly restored Victorian mansion, listed in the National Register of Historic Places, features soaring ceilings, handmade furniture, whirlpool baths, elaborate wall coverings, detailed woodwork, and an in-ground pool. Its convenient location midway between Madison and Milwaukee makes it equally inviting to business travelers and those seeking a romantic retreat. Often called "the Newport of the Midwest," the area offers all-seasons sports, walking tours, shopping sprees, and much more. Continental plus breakfast. Limited handicapped accessibility.

Innkeeper: Shirley W. Hinds
Rooms: 13 (PB) $65.51-142-58
Continental Breakfast
Credit Cards: A, B, C, D, E
Notes: 2, 5, 6, 8, 9, 10, 11, 12, 13, 14

OSCEOLA

Pleasant Lake Bed & Breakfast

2238 60th Avenue, 54020-4509
(715) 294-2545; (800) 294-2545
e-mail: pllakebb@centuryinter.net
www.pleasantlake.com

Enjoy a romantic getaway in one of the history-filled rooms on beautiful Pleasant Lake. While there, guests may take a leisurely walk in the woods, watch the birds and other wildlife, enjoy the lake in the canoe or paddleboat, sit around the bonfire, and watch the moon and stars reflecting on the lake. Then relax in one of the whirlpools and enjoy a fireplace or curl up with a book in guests' private sunroom. Limited handicapped accessibility.

Hosts: Richard and Charlene Berg
Rooms: 8 (PB) $80-140
Full Breakfast
Credit Cards: A, B
Notes: 2, 5, 7, 8, 9, 11, 12, 13

Pleasant Lake

PRESCOTT

The Arbor Inn

434 North Court, 54021
(715) 262-4522; (888) 262-1090
FAX (715) 262-5644

In Prescott, Wisconsin's most westerly city, this 1902 inn sits high overlooking the St. Croix River and is reminiscent of an English country cottage. The inn boasts grapevine breakfast porches, four antique-filled guest rooms with private baths, hand-pieced quilts and a lavish morning repast served at the time guests desire. Open year-round, the Arbor Inn is 45 minutes from the Mall of America and close to golf, ski hills, or state parks.

Hosts: Marvin and Linda Kangas
Rooms: 4 (PB) $125-159
Full Breakfast
Credit Cards: A, B, C
Notes: 2, 5, 7, 9, 10, 11, 12, 13

RACINE

Lochnaiar Inn

1121 Lake Avenue, 53403-1924
(414) 633-3300; FAX (414) 633-3678
e-mail: lochinn@execpc.com

Majestically atop a bluff overlooking Lake Michigan, the Lochnaiar Inn with it's unparalleled panoramic view, offers a grand experience. A stay in this historic English Tudor home, restored to its original splendor, features all the amenities. Featured in the May 1992 issue of *Chicago Magazine* as one of the eight best in the Midwest, the Lochnaiar Inn features all private baths, some with whirlpool or deep Empress tubs, suites with fireplaces, cable TV, small meeting rooms, and much more. Preferred by Racine's major corporations for their special guests, guests can be assured of a comfortable and relaxing stay. Fishing and sailing charters available. Full breakfast served weekends; Continental plus breakfast served weekdays. Personal checks accepted in advance. Smoking permitted in designated areas only. Children 12 and older welcome.

Hosts: Craig and Alice Geisler
Rooms: 8 (PB) $80-175
Full and Continental Breakfasts
Credit Cards: A, B, C
Notes: 5, 9, 10, 11, 12, 13

7 No smoking; 8 Children welcome; 9 Social drinking allowed; 10 Tennis nearby; 11 Swimming nearby; 12 Golf nearby; 13 Skiing nearby; 14 May be booked through a travel agent; 15 Handicapped accessible.

REEDSBURG

Parkview Bed & Breakfast

211 North Park Street, 53959
(608) 524-4333; e-mail: parkview@jvlnet.com
www.parkviewbb.com

In Reedsburg's historic district, this 1895 Queen Anne Victorian home has fish ponds, a windmill, and playhouse enhancing the grounds. Across from City Park and one block from downtown. Discover the original woodwork and hardware, tray ceilings, suitor's window, and built-in buffet inside this cozy home. Wisconsin Dells, Baraboo, Spring Green, and bike trails are nearby. Inquire about accommodations for children.

Hosts: Tom and Donna Hofmann
Rooms: 4 (2 PB; 2 SB) $65-85
Full Breakfast
Credit Cards: A, B, C
Notes: 2, 5, 7, 9, 10, 11, 12, 13, 14

RIVER FALLS

Knollwood House Bed & Breakfast

N8257-950th Street, 54022
(715) 425-1040; (800) 435-0628
e-mail: jjtost@juno.com

The Knollwood House (est. 1886) is unique in that it has so many amenities to offer guests. An outdoor pool, golf green (three tees), hot tub, sauna, groomed hiking trails which overlook the valley, large shaded yard with many flower gardens and birds, two llamas which guests can take for a hike. Twenty minutes from the Great River Road, riding stable nearby. Massage therapy is available. Children over 10 welcome.

Hosts: Jim and Judy Tostrud
Rooms: 4 (2 PB; 2 SB) $95-180

Full Breakfast
Credit Cards: None
Notes: 2, 5, 7, 9, 10, 11, 12, 13

SPARTA

The Franklin Victorian Bed & Breakfast

220 East Franklin Street, 54656
(608) 269-3894; (800) 845-8767
www.spartan.org/fvbb

This turn-of-the-century home welcomes guests to bygone elegance with small-town quiet and comfort. The four spacious bedrooms, two with a shared bath and two with private baths, provide a perfect setting for ultimate relaxation. Enjoy a full home-cooked breakfast served before starting the day of hiking, biking, skiing, canoeing, antiquing, or exploring this beautiful area. Canoe rental and shuttle service for bikers and canoeists available. Children over 10 welcome.

Hosts: Lloyd and Jane Larson
Rooms: 4 (2 PB; 2 SB) $75-95
Full Breakfast
Credit Cards: A, B
Notes: 2, 5, 7, 9, 10, 11, 12, 13, 14

Justin Trails Country Inn/Nordic Ski Center

7452 Kathryn Avenue, 54656
(608) 269-4522; (800) 488-4521
FAX (608) 269-3280

A country inn specializing in recreation, relaxation, and romance. Separate buildings: Paul Bunyan log cabin with two bedrooms, *Little House on the Praire* log cabin, and the Granary, a wood-frame cottage, each with a whirlpool and fireplace; dinners by reservation. Two suites in 1920 farmhouse on farm. Ralph Lauren linens. Four-course breakfasts. Near famous Elroy-Sparta Bike Trail. Cross-country skiing, snowshoeing, and snowtubing and disc or Frisbee golf on premises. Ski lessons and ski rentals.

NOTES: Credit cards accepted: A MasterCard; B Visa; C American Express; D Discover; E Diner's Club; F Other; 2 Personal checks accepted; 3 Lunch available; 4 Dinner available; 5 Open all year; 6 Pets welcome;

Hosts: Donna and Don Justin
Rooms: 7 (PB) $80-300
Full Breakfast
Credit Cards: A, B, C, D, E
Notes: 2, 4, 5, 6, 7, 8, 10, 11, 12, 13, 14

SPRING GREEN

Bettinger House Bed & Breakfast

Highway 23, Plain, 53577
(608) 546-2951

This 1904 brick home, once owned by the host's midwife grandmother, is near the world-famous House on the Rock, Frank Lloyd Wright's Taliesin, and the American Players Theatre. A home-cooked full breakfast is served every morning.

Hosts: Marie and Jim Neider
Rooms: 5 (2 PB; 3 SB) $55-75
Full Breakfast
Credit Cards: None
Notes: 2, 5, 7, 8, 9, 10, 11, 12, 14

STEVENS POINT

Dreams of Yesteryear Bed & Breakfast

1100 Brawley Street, 54481
(715) 341-4525; e-mail: dreams@coredcs.com
www.coredcs.com/~dreams

Designed by J. H. Jeffers, this bed and breakfast was built in 1901 and is lavish in Victorian

Dreams of Yesteryear

detail. Period furniture is evident throughout. The hosts love to visit with guests and talk about this elegant home and its furnishings. The home is listed in the National Register of Historic Places, and its restoration was featured in *Victorian Homes* magazine. Children over 12 welcome.

Hosts: Bonnie and Bill Maher
Rooms: 6 (PB) $55-135
Full Breakfast
Credit Cards: A, B, C, D
Notes: 2, 5, 7, 9, 10, 11, 12, 13, 14

STONE LAKE

The Lake House

The Lake House Bed & Breakfast

N5793 Division on the Lake, 54876
(715) 865-6803

Right on lovely Stone Lake, this spacious Wisconsin inn offers a choice of four country-style bedrooms. In the summer, guests may swim in the clear water or relax on a perfect sand beach. Each room comes with free use of a canoe during the visit. Experience a sunset and watch the loons from the deck or screened gazebo. A lavish full breakfast is served daily and a refrigerator is on-site for guest's use.

Hosts: Maxine (Max) Mashek and Terri Weldon
Rooms: 4 (2 PB; 2 SB) $55-75
Full Breakfast
Credit Cards: A, B
Notes: 2, 5, 7, 9, 10, 11, 13, 15

7 No smoking; 8 Children welcome; 9 Social drinking allowed; 10 Tennis nearby; 11 Swimming nearby; 12 Golf nearby; 13 Skiing nearby; 14 May be booked through a travel agent; 15 Handicapped accessible.

STURGEON BAY

The Scofield House Bed & Breakfast

908 Michigan Street, P.O. Box 761, 54235
(920) 743-7727; (888) 463-0204
e-mail: scofhse@mail.wiscnet.net
www.scofieldhouse.com

Described as "Door County's most elegant bed and breakfast." Victorian Queen Anne, circa 1902. Very ornate interior with inlaid floors and ornamented woodwork. Six guest rooms, each with private bath, double whirlpool, fireplace, cable TV, VCR, stereo, movie library. High Victorian decor throughout with fine antiques. Air conditioned. Full breakfast and afternoon sweet treats and teas. Color brochure. Mobil three-star and AAA three-diamond. Featured in *Chicago Tribune, Country Inns*, and *Midwest Living, Wisconsin Trails*.

Hosts: Bill and Fran Cecil
Rooms: 6 (PB) $95-198
Full Breakfast
Credit Cards: None
Notes: 2, 5, 7, 9, 10, 11, 12, 13

The Scofield House

White Lace Inn

16 North Fifth Avenue, 54235
(920) 743-1105
www.whitelaceinn.com

The White Lace Inn is a romantic getaway featuring four restored turn-of-the-century homes

White Lace Inn

surrounding lovely gardens and a gazebo. The 18 wonderfully inviting guest rooms and suites are furnished with antiques, four-poster and Victorian beds, in-room fireplaces in some rooms, and double whirlpool tubs in others. Readers' choice of *Midwest Living* magazine readers and *Wisconsin Trails*. Inquire about accommodations for children.

Hosts: Bonnie and Dennis Statz
Rooms: 18 (PB) $99-199
Continental Breakfast
Credit Cards: A, B, C, D
Notes: 2, 5, 7, 9, 10, 11, 12, 13, 15

TWO RIVERS

Red Forest Bed & Breakfast

1421 25th Street, 54241
(920) 793-1794; (888) 250-2272

The Red Forest Bed and Breakfast is on Wisconsin's east coast. Minutes from Manitowoc, Wisconsin's port city of the Lake Michigan car ferry. Also midway from Chicago and the Door County Peninsula. The hosts invite guests to step back in time to 1907 and enjoy the gracious three-story, Shingle-style home, highlighted with stained-glass windows and heirloom antiques. Inquire about accommodations for children.

NOTES: Credit cards accepted: A MasterCard; B Visa; C American Express; D Discover; E Diner's Club; F Other; 2 Personal checks accepted; 3 Lunch available; 4 Dinner available; 5 Open all year; 6 Pets welcome;

Red Forest

Hosts: Kay and Alan Rodewald
Rooms: 4 (2 PB; 2 SB) $69-89
Full Breakfast
Credit Cards: A, B, C, D
Notes: 2, 5, 7, 9, 10, 11, 12, 13, 14

WISCONSIN DELLS

Thunder Valley Inn

W15344 Waubeek Road, 53965
(608) 254-4145

Scandinavian hospitality in a country setting. Homemade breads, rolls, and jams will delight the guests. Real old-fashioned comfort. Summer evening family fiddling, and Chautauquas.

Stroll the farmstead, pet the animals, or relax with a good book and cider or Norsk coffee. Near the famous Wisconsin Dells. Rated one of 10 Midwest best. Children welcome.

Hosts: Anita, Kari, and Sigrid Nelson
Rooms: 6 (PB) $45-95
Full Breakfast
Credit Cards: A, B
Notes: 5, 7, 8, 9, 10, 11, 12, 13, 15

The White Rose Bed & Breakfast Inn

910 River Road, 53965
(608) 254-4724; (800) 482-4724
www.thewhiterose.com

As a romantic retreat or family fun getaway, guests' comfort and relaxation is the inn's pleasure. The White Rose Bed and Breakfast Inn invites guests to visit its gardens, relax in the parlor, or experience rich indulgence at the Secret Garden Café, at the lower level of the Victorian bed and breakfast, offering the famous international cuisine of the Cheese Factory Restaurant. Doubles, queen-size, and suites available, all with private baths. Heated outdoor pool.

Rooms: 5 (PB) $75-130
Credit Cards: A, B, C
Notes: 2, 3, 4, 5, 7, 8, 9, 11, 12, 13, 14, 15

7 No smoking; 8 Children welcome; 9 Social drinking allowed; 10 Tennis nearby; 11 Swimming nearby; 12 Golf nearby; 13 Skiing nearby; 14 May be booked through a travel agent; 15 Handicapped accessible.

Canada

●Thompson

●Winnipegosis

10

●Grandview
Riding Mountain ●

8

Hecla—
Hecla Island—

10
10
Neepawa
Stonewall
●

Minnedosa ●
Rivers ~
Portage la Prarie
10
●Grand Marais

1
1

●Beausejour

●Winnipeg

2
59

2
●Souris
●Boissevain

75

Killarney ●
●Letellier

Manitoba

Manitoba

BEAUSEJOUR

Bed & Breakfast of Manitoba

434 Roberta Avenue, Winnipeg, R2K 0K6
(204) 661-0300; FAX (204) 663-8114
e-mail: paulac@escape.ca
www.bedandbreakfast.mb.ca

Bender's Bed & Breakfast. Just 30 minutes east of Winnipeg, wake to the sound of birds and enjoy a heart breakfast featuring homemade jams and the famous New Bothwell cheese. Guests receive complimentary tea or coffee on arrival. On a quiet bay, this home features air conditioning, fireplace, private sitting room, and sunroom overlooking the fountain and gorgeous gardens. Curl up with a book from the extensive library, tour the town on bicycles, or just relax and smell the flowers. Golf courses, "U-pick" berry farms, and many local attractions offer appealing options for anyone. $50 Canadian.

BOISSEVAIN

Dueck's Cedar Chalet

Box 370, R0K 0E0
(204) 534-6019; (204) 534-8011
FAX (204) 534-6939

This chalet offers a Jacuzzi suite with cedar deck entrance. Private bedroom, refrigerator, tea, coffee, TV, telephone. Special hideaway for honeymoons and anniversaries. Additional spacious cedar lodge with loft, kitchenette, bedroom, TV, telephone, fireplace, and large private cedar deck. Great for weddings and group activities. Enjoy the yard with flower garden and gazebo. Don't miss Boissevain's unique shops and outdoor art gallery, nearby International Peace Garden, and Turtle Mountain Provincial Park. Open year-round. Lunch and dinner available upon request. Inquire about accommodations for pets.

Suites: 3 (PB) $65-75
Credit Cards: None
Notes: 2, 5, 7, 8, 9, 10, 11, 12, 13, 14, 15

GRAND MARAIS

Bed & Breakfast of Manitoba

434 Roberta Avenue, Winnipeg, R2K 0K6
(204) 661-0300; FAX (204) 663-8114
e-mail: paulac@escape.ca
www.bedandbreakfast.mb.ca

Inn Among the Oaks. In cottage country, welcome to this rustic two-story home, built of cedar and local pine, hidden amongst the oaks and saskatoon bushes. Enjoy the secluded yard, swim in the outdoor pool, or take a relaxing soak in the indoor hot tub. Spacious, comfortable bedrooms. Tasty breakfasts in the airy sunlit dining room. Enjoy Lake Winnipeg's beautiful sandy beaches and marshes rich in opportunity for eco-tourism. Beautiful cross-country ski trails and snowmobiling in winter. German, some French spoken. $50 Canadian.

NOTES: Credit cards accepted: A MasterCard; B Visa; C American Express; D Discover; E Diner's Club; F Other; 2 Personal checks accepted; 3 Lunch available; 4 Dinner available; 5 Open all year; 6 Pets welcome; 7 No smoking; 8 Children welcome; 9 Social drinking allowed; 10 Tennis nearby; 11 Swimming nearby; 12 Golf nearby; 13 Skiing nearby; 14 May be booked through a travel agent; 15 Handicapped accessible.

GRANDVIEW

Bed & Breakfast of Manitoba

434 Roberta Avenue, Winnipeg, R2K 0K6
(204) 661-0300; FAX (204) 663-8114
e-mail: paulac@escape.ca
www.bedandbreakfast.mb.ca

Morranville Bed and Breakfast. This spacious contemporary home is nestled between the Riding Mountains to the south and the Duck Mountain to the north. Close to the highest point in Manitoba, Mount Baldy, as well as lakes, hiking trails, fishing, cross-country ski trails, and groomed snowmobile trails. Summer or winter there's always something to do. Three bedrooms with a shared bathroom are offered to guests. Fireplace, ample parking, and country peace and quiet available. $45 Canadian.

HECLA ISLAND

Solmundson Gesta Hús

Hecla Provincial Park, P.O. Box 76, R0C 2R0
(204) 279-2088
e-mail: holtz@mb.sympatico.ca
www.heclatourism.mb.ca

The guest house is within Hecla Provincial Park on 43 acres of private property. Enjoy luxurious European-style hospitality in a newly renovated and completely modern, comfortable home in an original Icelandic settlement. Relax on the veranda and enjoy the beautiful view of Lake Winnipeg. Enjoy the tranquil and peaceful atmosphere while petting the dogs and cats or feeding the ducks. The host is a commercial fisherman, so feast on the catch of the day along with garden-fresh vegetables for the evening meal.

Hosts: Dave and Sharon Holtz
Rooms: 4 (1 PB; 3 SB) $45-75
Full Breakfast
Credit Cards: A, B
Notes: 2, 4, 5, 6, 7, 8, 9, 10, 11, 12, 13, 14

KILLARNEY

Bed & Breakfast of Manitoba

434 Roberta Avenue, Winnipeg, R2K 0K6
(204) 661-0300; FAX (204) 663-8114
e-mail: paulac@escape.ca
www.bedandbreakfast.mb.ca

Country Comfort Bed and Breakfast. Quiet country location off Highway 3 between Killarney and Boissevain. Offers private entrance, featuring two bedrooms with facilities for up to 10 persons. Includes living and recreational facilities. Excellent lodging for hunters; includes freezer, refrigerator, and microwave. Children welcome. Close proximity to International Peace Garden, Boissevain art murals, Bottineau Ski Park, golf courses, many parks and lakes for water sports, fishing, skating, tobogganing, snowmobiling, cross-country skiing. Excellent hunting in area (birds and deer). Advance reservations appreciated. $50 Canadian.

LETELLIER

Bed & Breakfast of Manitoba

434 Roberta Avenue, Winnipeg, R2K 0K6
(204) 661-0300; FAX (204) 663-8114
e-mail: paulac@escape.ca
www.bedandbreakfast.mb.ca

Fraser House. Antiques and delicate decor enhances this 1916 Victorian home. Two spacious guest rooms. Experience a gourmet breakfast served in the dining room adjacent to the parlour. The front veranda, back yard patio, fish pond, and flower gardens provide total tranquility and relaxation. Additional meals served upon request. Ten miles north of the U.S. border, off Highway 75. French spoken. Open year-round. Young and old are welcomed guests. $50-60 Canadian.

NOTES: Credit cards accepted: A MasterCard; B Visa; C American Express; D Discover; E Diner's Club; F Other; 2 Personal checks accepted; 3 Lunch available; 4 Dinner available; 5 Open all year; 6 Pets welcome;

MINNEDOSA

Bed & Breakfast of Manitoba

434 Roberta Avenue, Winnipeg, R2K 0K6
(204) 661-0300; FAX (204) 663-8114
e-mail: paulac@escape.ca
www.bedandbreakfast.mb.ca

Fairmount Bed and Breakfast. Fairmount is a 1914 farmhouse sitting on the edge of a slough (prairie waterway) in Minnedosa's beautiful pothole country. A wonderful place to see both woodland and wetland birds. Unwind while watching sheep graze on the pastures by the water, or spend some time hiking and skiing at Riding Mountain National Park, only 25 minutes up Highway 10. It specializes in country cooking, using products from own and surrounding farms. Spanish spoken. $50 Canadian.

PORTAGE LA PRAIRIE

Bed & Breakfast of Manitoba

434 Roberta Avenue, Winnipeg, R2K 0K6
(204) 661-0300; FAX (204) 663-8114
e-mail: paulac@escape.ca
www.bedandbreakfast.mb.ca

Evergreens Farm. Ideal for families, this large self-contained guest house is a fully equipped clean and modern mobile home. Equipped with a full kitchen, laundry facilities, and full bath, guests can enjoy their privacy and independence with the hosts a shout away. The large yard with flower gardens, the picnic and barbeque area, and the screened-in patio allow guests to enjoy their vacation days to the fullest. Only 15 minutes for Portage La Prairie, and less than an hour from Winnipeg. Well-behaved pets welcome. $75 Canadian.

NEEPAWA

Bed & Breakfast of Manitoba

434 Roberta Avenue, Winnipeg, R2K 0K6
(204) 661-0300; FAX (204) 663-8114
e-mail: paulac@escape.ca
www.bedandbreakfast.mb.ca

The Garden Path Bed and Breakfast. Enjoy Manitoba's most beautiful town while staying at this two and one-half story brick Heritage home. Mature landscaped gardens on peaceful, spacious grounds. Close to all town attractions and facilities. House features include fireplace, antiques, crafts, piano, bay windows, hardwood floors. Three attractively decorated guest rooms on second floor. Full buffet breakfast. Warm hospitality, inviting atmosphere create a unique experience. Baseball, cat, and gardening languages spoken. Multiple bookings; 10 percent discount. MasterCard and Visa accepted. $60 Canadian.

RIDING MOUNTAIN

The Lamp Post

Box 27, R0J 1T0
(204) 967-2501 (phone/FAX)
e-mail: info@thelamppost.mb.ca

Guests are invited to stay at this comfortable home where they can relax and enjoy the best home booking a few minutes from beautiful Riding Mountain National Park. Local activities include hunting and sightseeing (bear, elk, moose, deer, ducks, and geese), fishing, skiing, and the hosts offer their assistance and local knowledge to ensure guests have a great adventure and fun times. Highly rated for comfort, quiet, and spacious accommodations. May be booked through Manitoba Bed and Breakfast Association.

Hosts: Stewart and Thelma Spafford
Rooms: 4 (1 PB; 3 SB) $50-60
Full Breakfast
Credit Cards: B
Notes: 2, 3, 4, 5, 6, 7, 8, 9, 10, 11, 12, 13, 14

7 No smoking; 8 Children welcome; 9 Social drinking allowed; 10 Tennis nearby; 11 Swimming nearby; 12 Golf nearby; 13 Skiing nearby; 14 May be booked through a travel agent; 15 Handicapped accessible.

RIVERS

Cozy River Inn

Box 838, R0K 1X0
(204) 328-4457 (phone/FAX)

Enjoy a taste of country living close to town at this guest house one kilometer east of Rivers on Highway 25. Two individual theme rooms with full baths and entrances in a well-treed yard. Continental breakfast includes home-made muffins, bread, jam, and fruit. Smoke-free environment. Lake Wahtopanah provides excellent summer and winter activities; great hunting area. Several fine restaurants, golf course, tennis courts. Close to Brandon. Call ahead for reservations. Open year-round. Canada Select three-and-one-half-star-rating.

Hosts: Lynn and Jake Kroeger
Rooms: 2 (PB) $60
Continental Breakfast
Credit Cards: B
Notes: 2, 5, 7, 8, 9, 10, 11, 12, 13

SOURIS

Bed & Breakfast of Manitoba

434 Roberta Avenue, Winnipeg, R2K 0K6
(204) 661-0300; FAX (204) 663-8114
e-mail: paulac@escape.ca
www.bedandbreakfast.mb.ca

Inn the Wright. This historic home has been an elegant feature of the Souris landscape since it was built in 1896. Directly across from the town's most famous landmark, the swinging bridge, 114 Sowden Street has been embraced as a municipal historic site, not only for its remarkable Italianate architecture, but also for its equally remarkable inhabitants. Beautiful original cedar woodwork runs throughout the house and up the curving banister to the three guest rooms and one guest suite. Start each day with a fresh home-baked breakfast. Open May 1 through November 1 (off-season by special request). $50 Canadian.

STONEWALL

Bed & Breakfast of Manitoba

434 Roberta Avenue, Winnipeg, R2K 0K6
(204) 661-0300; FAX (204) 663-8114
e-mail: paulac@escape.ca
www.bedandbreakfast.mb.ca

Six Pines Ranch. Enjoy the peace and serenity of country living while only 15 minutes from the Winnipeg International Airport and 30 minutes to downtown Winnipeg. Guests are invited to stay at this turn-of-the-century home that was built in 1911. The hosts offer three beautifully restored, comfortable bedrooms. Enjoy breakfast in the antique setting dining room. Relax in the smoking parlour and go through some early century books. Or take a tour and see the various farm animals in the breathtaking, treed 35-acre pasture with the horses. In the evening, relax and enjoy nightly bonfires under the stars. Enjoy home-cooked, country-style meals. $69 Canadian.

THOMPSON

Anna's Bed & Breakfast

204 Wolf Street, R8N 1J7
(204) 677-5075
e-mail: info@annasbnb.mb.ca

A spacious, self-contained suite on the main floor with two twin beds, a full kitchen, private bath, den with cable TV/VCR, private tele-phone, private parking and private entrance. Anna and Robert invite guests to share their comfortable home and warm Dutch hospitality. Come and enjoy the "Heart of the North." A full breakfast is served. Complimentary snacks in the evening. Scenic touring is available by car. May be booked through Bed and Breakfast Manitoba Reservation Service.

Hosts: Anna and Robert Doorenbos
Rooms: 1 (PB) $50 Canadian
Full Breakfast
Credit Cards: None
Notes: 2, 4, 5, 7, 9, 11, 12, 13, 14

NOTES: Credit cards accepted: A MasterCard; B Visa; C American Express; D Discover; E Diner's Club; F Other; 2 Personal checks accepted; 3 Lunch available; 4 Dinner available; 5 Open all year; 6 Pets welcome;

WINNIPEG

Bed & Breakfast of Manitoba

434 Roberta Avenue, Winnipeg, R2K 0K6
(204) 661-0300; FAX (204) 663-8114
e-mail: paulac@escape.ca
www.bedandbreakfast.mb.ca

Algonquin Park Bed and Breakfast. In a quiet and well-landscaped area and embellished with fine traditional furniture, guests' stay will be one of comfort and pleasure. Enjoy a full breakfast every morning in the kitchen eating area or in the formal dining room. TV and fireplace for cozy winter evenings, and huge deck complete with gazebo overlooking the English-style garden to delight guests in the summer. Close to golf courses, Bird's Hill Park, shopping center, Casino Regent, and many restaurants. Adults-only facility. Private bath. $60 Canadian.

Andrews. Beautiful river property in older treed neighborhood. Close to bus, restaurants, and attractions. Enjoy bedroom suite with private bath and private TV lounge. Cruise the river in hosts' canoe, enjoy the flowers, or relax in the gazebo. Bike, exercise equipment available. Home-baked breakfasts. Close to airport, bus depot, VIA Rail, Trans-Canada Highway city route. Discounts for long stays. $55 Canadian.

Anne's Garden. Enjoy home-baked breakfast, tea, coffee, and snacks anytime in living room or patio overlooking beautifully treed yard. Quiet surroundings for bird watching, reading, or relaxing. Close to University of Manitoba, The Forks, golf course, and Fort Whyte Nature Centre. English, German, and Spanish spoken. Near Pembina Highway. $55 Canadian.

Bannerman East. Enjoy this lovely Georgian home, evening tea, and quiet walks in St. Johns Park or along the Red River. Close to Seven Oaks House, the planetarium, concert hall, and Rainbow Stage. $48 Canadian.

Bright Oakes. Spacious home on one-half acre of parklike grounds near the Red River. Close to St. Vital Park, University of Manitoba, good restaurants, and St. Vital Shopping Center. Easy access to the mint, St. Boniface Hospital, and downtown. English, French, and Polish spoken. $50 Canadian.

Bunny Hollow. Enjoy a quiet Victorian retreat in the heart of the city of Winnipeg. Nestled beside the historic St. Boniface district and walking distance to many of Winnipeg's historical and cultural attractions. Frequent bus service close by. In summer, enjoy the large sunroom, deck, and gardens. In winter, the cozy fireplace is just right. Select breakfast items—omelets, waffles, quiche, fruit plate, and homemade breads are just the beginning. Visa accepted. Friendly cat in residence. $50 Canadian.

Cozy Nook. Welcome to this cozy, yet modern and spacious bungalow. Quiet residential neighborhood close to University of Manitoba and major routes south to the U.S. and east to Ontario. Large shopping center with cinema nearby, with easy access to downtown, the Royal Canadian Mint, and many attractions and restaurants. Workspace facilities for the business traveller. The home-cooked breakfast is prepared to guests' choice and taste. French and some Spanish spoken. $45-55 Canadian.

Elsa's Hide-a-Way. Enjoy the seclusion of the pleasant backyard, indoor and outdoor hot tubs, and outdoor swimming pool. Easy access from the Perimeter, off Pembina Highway. Near University of Manitoba, parks, shopping mall, and restaurants. German spoken. $50 Canadian.

Fraser's Grove Bed and Breakfast. Privacy plus the comforts of home. This split-level home allows guests the choice of room with en suite bath (and shower) and private sitting room, or lower level suite with family room and fireplace. In a quiet residential area. Great

7 No smoking; 8 Children welcome; 9 Social drinking allowed; 10 Tennis nearby; 11 Swimming nearby; 12 Golf nearby; 13 Skiing nearby; 14 May be booked through a travel agent; 15 Handicapped accessible.

for walks or bike rides along the Red River or in nearby Fraser's Grove Park. Ten minutes to downtown, near golf courses, Rainbow Stage. Nearby express bus route, shopping, restaurants. Convenient to beaches of Lake Winnipeg. $55 Canadian.

Mary Jane's Place. Enjoy a relaxed atmosphere in this unique three-story home with beautiful oak interior. Excellent transit service, near downtown, will pick up at the airport. Quick access to The Forks Market, zoo, hospital, and Dalnavert Museum. $45-65 Canadian.

Meadow Lake Bed and Breakfast. Wonderfully quiet and relaxing suburban location, yet so close to downtown. There are a lake and a meadow for year-round walks and winter tobogganing. Comfortable great room with fireplace, TV/VCR, wide selection of movies and books for guests' use. Close to Club Regent Casino, golf course, fitness center, restaurants, and major shopping center. Main-floor accommodations. Breakfast includes a selection of homemade breads and jams, waffles, and crêpes. Transportation and tours can be arranged. German and some Spanish spoken. $55 Canadian.

Niagara House. A 1926 vintage home in River Heights. Close to airport; direct bus routes to downtown and Polo Park shopping center; easy access to perimeter and Trans-Canada Highway. Assiniboine Park nearby, as well as local shops, recreational facilities, and playground. Enjoy a relaxing stay in an atmosphere enhanced by surroundings. Children and pets welcome. Baby-sitting available. $45 Canadian.

Oakdale Bed and Breakfast. A charming mix of contemporary home with antique furnishings in a quiet residential neighborhood. Large private backyard with deck. Direct bus route to city center; easy access to airport, perimeter, and Trans-Canada Highway. Close to Assiniboine Park and zoo, golf courses, most major

shopping centers. Enjoy breakfast in the great room. German spoken. $50 Canadian.

Prairie Comfort. Come for a relaxing stay in this quiet, quaint, cozy home. Guests enjoy use of living room and TV. In Fort Garry near Pembina Highway. Quick access to excellent city transit service to downtown and University of Manitoba. Near golf course, Crescent Park, and Fort Whyte Nature Centre. $45 Canadian.

Ravelston Manor. Old World hospitality with the contemporary romantic features. One guest at a time. The beautifully appointed bedroom with private en suite bath is on the main floor, and the lower level complete with wood-burning fireplace and jetted hot tub is for guests' exclusive use. Bring own wine and favorite CDs to set the mood. Complimentary hors d'oeuvres; will arrange for flowers upon prior arrangement. $50 Canadian.

Roads & Rainbows. Minutes from key historical sites, museums, the Forks, downtown shopping, the new baseball park, fabulous restaurants, and yearly festivals events. Delightfully decorated, mixing old and new and blending handicrafts and collectibles. A breakfast of guests' choice will welcome guests each morning. $50 Canadian.

Shar-A-Cuppa Bed and Breakfast. Relax in the cozy bilevel home with two guest rooms, three-piece bath, and private family room with fireplace on the lower level. There is also a deck off the dining area and a patio by the garden. $55 Canadian.

Southern Rose Guest House. Experience the charm of decades past with a touch of southern hospitality. Enjoy morning breakfast in the formal dining room or on the wraparound cedar sun deck. Getaway to yesterday! Red brick exterior, warm woods, burnished brass-trimmed leaded glass, flickering fireplace, and live greenery. The yard provides a retreat to read, converse, or enjoy the afternoon sun. Play horseshoes, volleyball, or relax in redwood hot tub. Close to Polo Park shopping mall, The Forks, casino, good restaurants, zoo, airport, Winnipeg Convention Centre, and bicycle route. Just off express bus route. $50 Canadian.

Villa in the Woods. Large custom-built home with lots of cozy sitting rooms and a deck that surrounds the whole house. Two guest rooms. Both have private en suite bath with jetted tubs. King-size room also has private whirlpool bath. Hospitality with class and distinction. Sumptuous, luxurious surroundings—just what your looking for. $85-95 Canadian.

Waterloo Bed and Breakfast. The unsurpassed accommodation alternative, this modern, newly furnished home awaits guest in a prestigious mature neighborhood just minutes from downtown and airport, Polo Park Shopping Centre, Corydon Avenue, and most attractions. Newly furnished, completely private quarter with separate entrance, en suite four-piece bath, and own living room with TV/VCR/CD player. Guests' choice of home-cooked or Continental breakfast includes homemade cakes and jams. Wheelchair accessible. $55 Canadian.

Ellie's Bed & Breakfast

77 Middle Gate, R3C 2C5
(204) 772-5832; FAX (204) 783-1462

Enjoy a stay in historic Armstrong's Point. A peaceful and picturesque cul-de-sac in the heart of Winnipeg. Hosts are well traveled and love to cook. Superb omelets plus, bread, scones, muffins, cinnamon buns, jams, and jellies—all homemade. "Make us your home away from home." Near bus service and all major attractions. Take the river walk to The Forks Market. Will pick up guests traveling by air, bus, or train for additional charge.

Hosts: Peter and Eugenia Ellie
Rooms: 3 (3 SB) $50-60
Full Breakfast
Credit Cards: None
Notes: 2, 3, 4, 7, 8, 9

Mary Jane's Place

144 Yale Avenue, R3M 0L7
(204) 453-8104

Enjoy stay in a relaxed atmosphere in a unique three-story brick home nestled in the heart of Winnipeg's historic area of Crescentwood. Enjoy a leisurely walk in the neighborhood and view historic housing, the Assinaboine River, Little Italy, and Wellington Crescent's walking and jogging trail. The home has an oak interior, beautiful fireplaces, stained- and beveled-glass accents. Close to the airport, downtown, and all attractions. Easy to find from all directions. Hosts cater to guests' breakfast needs. Close to three bus routes.

Hosts: Jack and Mary Jane
Rooms: 4 (1 PB; 3 SB) $45-65 Canadian
Full Breakfast
Credit Cards: None
Notes: 5, 7, 8, 9, 10, 11, 12

Twin Pillars

235 Oakwood Avenue, R3L 1E5
(204) 452-4925 (phone/FAX)
e-mail: tls@escape.ca

Ten minutes from downtown, near all major bus routes; walk to Osborne Village, River Walk, near shops, restaurants, theatre. Enjoy a stay in a beautiful turn-of-the-century home with lovely verandas across from park. Air conditioned. Continental plus breakfasts. Sightseeing information; baby-sitting available with prior notification. Linens and towels are washed with hypo-allergenic products. Smoking permitted in designated areas. Kid's pool available for swimming.

Hosts: Bev Suek and Joe Taylor
Rooms: 4 (4 SB) $48-55
Continental Breakfast
Credit Cards: None
Notes: 2, 5, 6, 8, 9, 10, 12

7 No smoking; 8 Children welcome; 9 Social drinking allowed; 10 Tennis nearby; 11 Swimming nearby; 12 Golf nearby; 13 Skiing nearby; 14 May be booked through a travel agent; 15 Handicapped accessible.

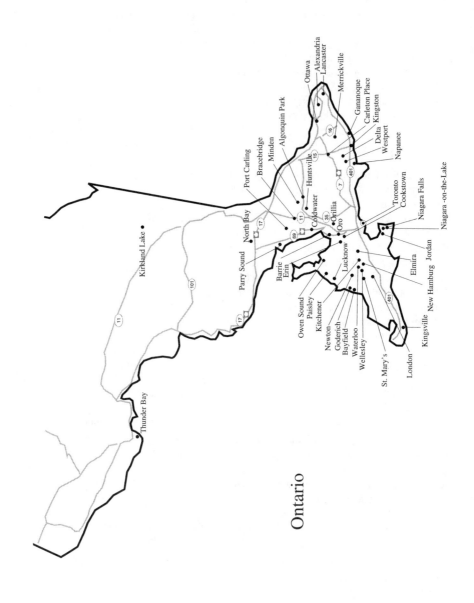

Ontario

Ontario

Maple Lane Guest Home Bed & Breakfast

#21320, Glen Robertson Road, K0C 1A0
(613) 525-3205; (905) 666-0517
www.bbcanada.com/1068.html

Century home on 100 acres (built in 1856 by Scottish settler) with beamed kitchen, pine floors, antiques, and canopied beds. Truly a peaceful setting, tucked away down a lane of maples. Entertainment and Glengarry historical attractions, etc. are nearby. Great location—midway between Ottawa and Montreal and close to U.S. and Québec borders. Come sample the bilingual hospitality plus music, fun, and laughter. It's an ideal adult getaway—where the past and present blend.

Hosts: Audrey and Ed MacDonald
Rooms: 4 (1 PB; 2-3 SB) $55-65
Full Breakfast
Credit Cards: None
Notes: 3, 4, 7, 12, 14

ALGONQUIN PARK

Arowhon Pines

Algonquin Park, Box 10001, Huntsville, P1H 2G5
(705) 633-5661; (416) 483-4393 (winter)

Rates include three meals per day and use of all recreational facilities: canoes, sailboats, sailboards, hiking trails, tennis courts, sauna, swimming in pristine waters, and games room. Open June through mid-October. Smoking is not permitted in some cabins. BYOB. Breakfast, lunch, and dinner are included in room rates.

Hosts: Eugene and Helen Kates
Rooms: 50 (PB) $120-230
Full Breakfast
Credit Cards: A, B
Notes: 2, 3, 4, 8, 10, 11, 12, 14

BARRIE

Cozy Corner

2 Morton Crescent, L4N 7T3
(705) 739-0157

An elegant city home. Old World curtsy and just nice folks make guests feel spoiled and pampered. Two spacious suites, Jacuzzi, queen-size bed, duvet, arm chairs, coffee table, private TV. Two other bright and comfortable double bedrooms, writing desk, double dresser, private TV. The location in the centre of Lakelands, marvel at the pristine beauty of the surroundings, clean air and abundant forests. Chef Kirby (retired) in residence.

Hosts: Charita and Harry Kirby
Rooms: 2 (S1B) $65
Suite: 2 (PB) $110
Full Breakfast
Credit Cards: B
Notes: 4, 5, 7, 9, 10, 11, 12, 13, 14

Round Table Bed & Breakfast

59 Kinzie Lane, L4M 5Z8
(705) 739-0193; FAX (705) 739-0145

Homey in-town location, one hour north of Toronto, in historical Huronia cottage country house surrounded by white picket fence and English gardens. TV room, TV in each guest room, fireplace, hot tub, and bicycles. Preserves (jams and pickles) for sale. Twin and

NOTES: Credit cards accepted: A MasterCard; B Visa; C American Express; D Discover; E Diner's Club; F Other; 2 Personal checks accepted; 3 Lunch available; 4 Dinner available; 5 Open all year; 6 Pets welcome; 7 No smoking; 8 Children welcome; 9 Social drinking allowed; 10 Tennis nearby; 11 Swimming nearby; 12 Golf nearby; 13 Skiing nearby; 14 May be booked through a travel agent; 15 Handicapped accessible.

queen-size beds. Cot available. Cat and dog in residence. Reduced rates for long-term stay (one week or more). Dinner available by reservation only. Children over eight welcome. Smoking permitted outside only.

Host: Diane C. Murray
Rooms: 2 (1 PB; 1 SB) $65
Full Breakfast
Credit Cards: None
Notes: 2, 5, 6, 7, 9, 10, 11, 12, 13

Century House

BAYFIELD

The Little Inn of Bayfield

Main Street, P.O. Box 100, N0M 1G0
(519) 565-2611; (800) 565-1832

Originally a stagecoach stop, the inn has been welcoming guests to this picturesque lakeside village since the 1830s. This designated Heritage inn is replete with fireplaces, en suite whirlpools, sauna, games, and books. Fine dining has long been a tradition, with superb meals and imaginative menus. Guests have a perfect base from which to explore the countryside and attend the Stratford and Blyth Festivals. There is much to do any time of the year. pets welcome with prior arrangements. Smoking permitted in designated areas only.

Hosts: Patrick and Gayle Waters
Rooms: 30 (PB) $110-225
Cards: A, B, C, E
Notes: 2, 3, 4, 5, 8, 10, 11, 12, 13, 14, 15

BRACEBRIDGE

Century House Bed & Breakfast

155 Dill Street, P1L 1E5
(705) 645-9903; e-mail: cnturybb@muskoka.com

"Accommodation for gentlefolk" in this charming, air-conditioned, restored century-old home in the province's premier recreational lake district, a two-hour drive north of Toronto. Sandy's breakfasts are creative and generous. Waffles with local maple syrup are a specialty. Century House is close to shopping, beaches, and many craft stu-

dios and galleries. Enjoy the sparkling lakes, fall colors, studio tours, and cross-country skiing in the winter. A friendly dog is in residence.

Hosts: Norman Yan and Sandy Yudin
Rooms: 3 (SB) $65-70
Full Breakfast
Credit Cards: B
Notes: 5, 7, 10, 11, 12, 13, 14

CARLETON PLACE

Stewart's Landing Bed & Breakfast

137 Montgomery Park Road, Rural Route 1, K7C 3P1
(613) 257-1285; FAX (613) 257-5828
www.bbcanada.com/1419.html

Right on Mississippi Lake, only three minutes from Carleton Place and 30 minutes from Ottawa. It takes 22 minutes to reach the Corel Centre. Enjoy comfortable smoke-free rooms with lake views. Pedal boating, canoeing, swimming all at the door. Relax on the deck, sip afternoon tea, listen to the loons laugh and watch swallows dip over the lake. Several towns and historical attractions are close by. A full gourmet country breakfast will make taste buds tingle. Warm hospitality makes this spot truly "Close to Heaven."

Hosts: Allen and Peggie Stewart
Rooms: 4 (1 PB; 3 SB) $55-65
Full Breakfast
Credit Cards: None
Notes: 2, 3, 4, 5, 7, 11, 12

NOTES: Credit cards accepted: A MasterCard; B Visa; C American Express; D Discover; E Diner's Club; F Other; 2 Personal checks accepted; 3 Lunch available; 4 Dinner available; 5 Open all year; 6 Pets welcome;

COLDWATER

Inn the Woods

4240 Sixth Line North, Oro-Medonte, L0K 1E0
(705) 835-6193; (800) 289-6295
e-mail: robet.shannon@sympatico.ca

Inn the Woods was designed for comfort, privacy, and relaxation. It combines a peaceful scenic ambiance with the nearby availability of quaint shops, fine restaurants, mountain trails, scenic country roads, fishing streams, and golf courses. A warm welcome awaits guests at this three-level Colonial-style home—on the fringe of Copeland Forest Preserve in a tranquil wooded setting in the heart of the Medonte Hills ski country. Lunch and dinner available upon request.

Hosts: Betty and Bob Shannon
Rooms: 5 (5 SB) $55-75
Full Breakfast
Credit Cards: A, B, C
Notes: 2, 5, 7, 8, 9, 12, 13, 14

COOKSTOWN

Victoria House Bed & Breakfast

36 Victoria Street East, L0L 1L0
(705) 458-0040 (phone/FAX)
e-mail: pine@bconnex.net

In the picturesque village of Cookstown with its many antique and craft shops, this comfortable, well-kept home offers two spacious, very private guest rooms with queen-size beds and en suite baths. Enjoy the garden, decks, and living room with fireplace, TV, VCR, and piano. Easy walk to quaint Cookstown or a short drive to lakes, cottage country, golf, skiing, outlet mall; approximately one hour to downtown Toronto. Highway 400/89/27.

Hosts: Gisele and Alfred Baues
Rooms: 2 (PB) $65
Full Breakfast
Credit Cards: None
Notes: 2, 6, 7, 9, 12, 13

DELTA

Denaut Mansion Country Inn

5 Mathew Street, K0E 1G0
(613) 928-2588 (phone/FAX)
www.denautmansion.com

Restored 1849 stone mansion features art work, pottery, and carpets from around the world. Each room with en suite bath. Imaginatively presented, simply prepared three-course set menu dinners served in the candlelit dining room or enclosed verandah. Licensed. Pool, air conditioning, walking, canoeing, golf, antiquing, hosts' own mapped loop cycle routes. Set on 11 wooded acres in a village setting in the Rideau Lakes, one-half hour from I-81 and the Ivy Lea Bridge. Colour brochure. Continental plus breakfast. Cross-country skiing nearby.

Hosts: Deborah and David Peets
Rooms: 5 (PB) $110-135 Canadian
Continental Breakfast
Credit Cards: A, B
Notes: 4, 5, 7, 8, 11, 12, 13

Denaut Mansion Country Inn

ELMIRA

The Evergreens

Rural Route 1, N3B 2Z1
(519) 669-2471

Welcome to a quiet bed and breakfast nestled among the evergreens. Enjoy long walks through the forest, swimming in the pool, or cross-country skiing in winter. Two comfortable bedrooms with two guest bathrooms, and breakfast with homemade baking and preserves. In Mennonite country, with Elmira, St. Jacobs, and Elora nearby. North of Elmira, east off Regional Road 21 on Woolrich Road

---

7 No smoking; 8 Children welcome; 9 Social drinking allowed; 10 Tennis nearby; 11 Swimming nearby; 12 Golf nearby; 13 Skiing nearby; 14 May be booked through a travel agent; 15 Handicapped accessible.

3. Smoking is not permitted in home. Open year-round.

Hosts: Rodger and Doris Milliken
Rooms: 2 (SB) $50
Full Breakfast
Credit Cards: None
Notes: 2, 5, 6, 7, 8, 9, 11, 12, 13

GANANOQUE

The Victoria Rose Inn

279 King Street West, K7G 2G7
(613) 382-3368

This stately mansion, with a commanding central tower, was built by the first mayor in 1872. Nine elegant nonsmoking guest rooms with private bath and air conditioning. Two charming guest rooms with shared bath in annex. The honeymoon suite has a marble fireplace and Jacuzzi. Guests are welcome to enjoy the parlor, veranda, patio, and two acres of garden. The ballroom is an ideal location for a family reunion, special party, or business meeting. The Rose Garden Cafe is open April through October for lunch, afternoon tea, and dinner. Close to an excellent selection of restaurants, the summer playhouse, boat tours, and interesting shopping.

Hosts: Liz and Ric Austin
Rooms: 11 (9 PB; 2 SB) $75-155
Full Breakfast
Credit Cards: A, B, C
Notes: 3, 4, 5, 7, 10, 11, 12, 13

GODERICH

Colborne Bed & Breakfast

72 Colborne Street, N7A 2V9
(519) 524-7400; (800) 390-4612
FAX (519) 524-4943
e-mail: kathryn.darby@odyssey.on.ca

This turn-of-the-century home is in Canada's prettiest town, within walking distance of beaches, shopping, restaurants. The bed and breakfast has 10-foot ceilings, foot-high baseboards, stained-glass windows. Enjoy the guest

parlour with fireplace, TV, VCR. The sun porch is enclosed and furnished in wicker. A full distinctive breakfast is offered. All four bedrooms have en suite bathrooms, one twin-, one double-, and two king-size beds, some with gas fireplaces and whirlpool tubs.

Host: Kathryn Darby
Rooms: 4 (PB) $60-95
Full Breakfast
Credit Cards: None
Notes: 3, 5, 7, 9, 10, 11, 12

Kathi's Guest House

Rural Route #4, N7A 3Y1
(519) 524-8587; FAX (519) 524-2969

Welcome to this farm amongst rolling hills. Close to Lake Huron, about 12 kilometers east of Goderich, near Benmiller. Enjoy the privacy of the guest house which has two bedrooms for guests' convenience. A nice place for two couples who share friendship together or young families with children. A crib is available. A full country-style breakfast is served. The host has friendly pets. English and German spoken. Open year-round. Reservations preferred. Deposit required. Special rates for longer stays.

Hosts: Kathi Beyerlein
Rooms: 2 (PB) $60
Full Breakfast
Credit Cards: None
Notes: 5, 8, 11, 12, 13

HUNTSVILLE

Fairy Bay Guest House

228 Cookson Bay Crescent, P1H 1B2
(705) 759-1492; (888) 813-1101
FAX (705) 789-6922
e-mail: hosts@fairybay.ca; www.fairybay.ca
www.muskoka.com/tourism/fairybay

Relax at this charming lakeside country inn. Eight large elegant rooms with en suite baths are equipped for comfortable reading and sleeping. Big windows overlook the lovely treed garden, bird feeders, white-sand beach, and a

NOTES: Credit cards accepted: A MasterCard; B Visa; C American Express; D Discover; E Diner's Club; F Other; 2 Personal checks accepted; 3 Lunch available; 4 Dinner available; 5 Open all year; 6 Pets welcome;

picturesque, quiet bay. Delicious breakfasts are served by the gracious hosts. Guests may use the two lounges, kitchenette, barbecue, bicycles, dock, and various watercraft. Nearby are five golf courses, Algonquin Park, walking trails, tennis, Pioneer village, fine dining, shopping, driving tours, skiing, and snowmobiling.

Hosts: Rick and Lori Stirling
Rooms: 8 (PB) $105-180
Full Breakfast
Credit Cards: A, B
Notes: 2, 5, 7, 8, 9, 10, 11, 12, 13, 14

JORDAN

The Vintner's Inn

3845 Main Street, L0R 1S0
(905) 562-5336; (800) 701-8074
www.vintnersinn.on.ca.

Elegant country inn in renovated winery building. All rooms have Jacuzzi, fireplace, telephone, and antique appointments. On the same property as an award-winning premium winery and one of Canada's finest regional restaurants, Cave Spring Cellars and On The Twenty, respectively. Village of Jordan has a number of artisan and antique shops. Thirty minutes to Niagara-on-the-Lake, Niagara Falls, and in the heart of Ontario's wine country.

Host: Helen Young
Rooms: 16 (PB) $199-275 Canadian (approx. $145-165 U.S.)
Continental Breakfast
Credit Cards: A, B, C, E
Notes: 3, 4, 5, 7, 8, 9, 10, 12, 14

KINGSTON

Painted Lady Inn

181 William Street, K7L 2E1
(613) 545-0422; www.aracnet/paintedldy

This stately Victorian offers seven elegant rooms, all with private baths, queen-size beds, antiques, and central air. Romance comes alive in luxury rooms with Jacuzzis and fireplaces.

Always lively conversation over scrumptious gourmet breakfasts—waffles, omelets, French toast. Inn is close to restaurants, pubs, Queen's University, Fort Henry, and Thousand Island boats. After a busy day, guests relax on a charming veranda or on sunny balcony. Parking. Four blocks to Lake Ontario.

Host: Carol Franks
Rooms: 7 (PB) $95-155 Canadian
Full Breakfast
Credit Cards: A, B, C
Notes: 2, 5, 7, 9, 10, 11, 12

KINGSVILLE

Kingswood Inn

101 Mill Street West, N9Y 1W4
(519) 733-3248; FAX (519) 733-8734
e-mail: kingswd@mnsi.net
www.lsol.com/kingswood

The ultimate in luxury. This 1859 octagonal manor was built by the founder of Kingsville. Five elegant guest rooms feature fine linens, robes, private baths. Air conditioned. Antiques and canopied beds. Master suite with fireplace and two-person whirlpool. Large drawing room and library with fireplace, TV, VCR, for guest use. Three acres of beautifully landscaped grounds and large in-ground pool. Close to several wineries, Point Pelee National Park, Colasanti's Tropical Gardens, Jack Miner's Bird Sanctuary, and fine dining. Just 45 minutes from Detroit.

Hosts: Barb and Bob Dick; Helen and Jay Koop
Rooms: 5 (PB) $95-280 Canadian
Full and Continental Breakfast
Credit Cards: A, B
Notes: 2, 5, 7, 9, 10, 11, 12, 14

KIRKLAND LAKE

Bed & Breakfast By The River

53 Athenia Boulevard, P. O. Box 96, P0K 1T0
(705) 642-3424 (phone/FAX)

Experience Kirkland Lake's gold mining culture and history, unspoiled rivers and trails, and

7 No smoking; 8 Children welcome; 9 Social drinking allowed; 10 Tennis nearby; 11 Swimming nearby; 12 Golf nearby; 13 Skiing nearby; 14 May be booked through a travel agent; 15 Handicapped accessible.

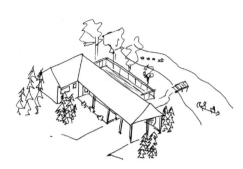

Bed & Breakfast By The River

northern hospitality. Enjoy a panoramic view of the beautiful Blanche River while dining on the gourmet breakfast. Open May through October, reasonable tax-free rates, fireplace, and waterside dock. Culver Park (25 acres), golf, tennis, horse riding, community complex, museum of Northern history, and home of Sir Harry Oakes on the Mile of Gold all close by. A smoke-free and pet-free adult accommodation.

Hosts: Pat and Bill Klass
Rooms: 2 (2 SB) $85-95
Full Breakfast
Credit Cards: B
Notes: 7, 9, 10, 11, 12

KITCHENER

Aram's Roots and Wings Bed & Breakfast

11 Sunbridge Crescent, N2K 1T4
(519) 743-4557; FAX (519) 743-4166

Country living right in the city. Roots and Wings is in the north end of Kitchener on the boundary with Waterloo. Ten minutes from St. Jacobs, universities, and most activities in the Kitchener/Waterloo area. Recreational facilities include a heated pool, Jacuzzi, and walking trails. Ultra whirlpool baths in two bathrooms. Delicious breakfasts start guests on their day's adventures.

Host: Fay Teal-Aram
Rooms: 4 (2 PB: 2 SB) $65-80

Full Breakfast
Credit Cards: A, B
Notes: 5, 6, 8, 9, 10, 11, 12, 15

LANCASTER

MacPine Farms

Box 51, K0C 1N0
(613) 347-2003; FAX (613) 347-2814
e-mail: macpine@glen-net.ca
www.bbcanada.com/688.html

Welcome to MacPine Holstein Farm on the shores of the St. Lawrence River, south of 401, a half-mile east of Lancaster 814 exit, 10 miles from Québec border. Enjoy this modernized century home. Shaded by large old pine trees. Five-minute walk to the cottage on the river, where guests can swim, canoe, paddleboat, relax, and watch the ocean ships go by. Attractions: golf, fishing, boating, nature trails, china outlet, and craft and antique shops. Visit Montréal, Cornwall, or Ottawa. Smoke-free in home; smoking permitted outside only. Children are welcome. Full Breakfast.

Hosts: Guelda and Robert MacRae
Rooms: 3 (SB) $40-50
Full Breakfast
Credit Cards: None
Notes: 2, 5, 7, 8, 9, 11, 12, 13

LONDON

Clermont Place

679 Clermont Avenue, N5X 1N3
(519) 672-0767; FAX (519) 672-2449

A modern home in a parklike setting with its own heated outdoor pool. Central air conditioning, three attractive bedrooms sharing a four-piece bath. A full Canadian breakfast is served in the dining room, by the pool, or in the gardens. Four free tennis courts behind the house; two public golf courses five minutes away. Forty minutes from the Stratford Shakespeare Festival. Close to the University of Western Ontario and University Hospital in northeast London. Cross-country skiing in area.

NOTES: Credit cards accepted: A MasterCard; B Visa; C American Express; D Discover; E Diner's Club; F Other; 2 Personal checks accepted; 3 Lunch available; 4 Dinner available; 5 Open all year; 6 Pets welcome;

Hosts: Doug and Jacki McAndless
Rooms: 3 (SB) $55-65
Full Breakfast
Credit Cards: B, C
Notes: 2, 3, 4, 5, 7, 9, 10, 11, 12, 13

Hilltop

82 Compton Crescent, N6C 4G1
(519) 681-7841

Modern air-conditioned home on quiet crescent in South London. Easy access to Highway 401, downtown London as well as Stratford Huron County Playhouse and Port Stanley. Offers twin and double rooms, each with private bath. Dining room overlooks the city. Outdoor pool available to guests. Nonsmoking adults. No pets.

Host: Beverley Corlett
Rooms: 2 (PB) $60 Canadian
Full Breakfast
Credit Cards: None
Notes: 5, 7, 11

LUCKNOW

Perennial Pleasures Guest Home

558 Rose Street, N0G 2H0
(519) 528-3601

A warm welcome awaits guests at this comfortable, modern bungalow. Attractively decorated, comfortable rooms. Freedom of the

Perennial Pleasures

house and bright, colorful gardens. Perennials for sale. Lucknow is centrally positioned for numerous day trips for antiquing; walking, biking, or swimming at Lake Huron; see Mennonite way of life with farms selling fruit, vegetables, and crafts. Inquire about accommodations for pets.

Host: Mrs. Joan Martin
Rooms: 3 (S2B) $45
Full Breakfast
Credit Cards: None
Notes: 2, 3, 4, 5, 7, 8, 9, 10, 11, 12, 13, 15

MERRICKVILLE

Millisle

Millisle Bed & Breakfast

205 Mill Street, P.O. Box 341, K0G 1N0
(613) 269-3627; FAX (613) 269-4735

Forty-five minutes south of Ottawa, adjacent to the Rideau River and Locks. Three-minute walk to center of village. A restored, turreted Heritage Victorian home (1858). Bedrooms furnished with antiques. Bathrooms private, one with whirlpool for two, two with Victorian claw-foot tubs, and one with shower only. Full breakfast served in Heritage dining room. Dinner package available with nearby restaurant, in a Heritage building. Thirty minutes from U.S. border. Cross-country skiing nearby.

Hosts: Kathy and Derry Thompson
Rooms: 5 (PB) $68 Canadian

7 No smoking; 8 Children welcome; 9 Social drinking allowed; 10 Tennis nearby; 11 Swimming nearby; 12 Golf nearby; 13 Skiing nearby; 14 May be booked through a travel agent; 15 Handicapped accessible.

Full Breakfast
Credit Cards: A, B, C
Notes: 2, 4, 5, 7, 9, 11, 12, 13, 14

MINDEN

The Stone House

Rural Route 2, K0M 2K0
(705) 286-1250

Rustic elegance in secluded, mature woods.
Four styles of accommodation, each offering
full privacy. The Stone House has two bedrooms, kitchen, and full bath. Large fieldstone
fireplace in living room. The Roof Garden is an
airy chalet-style studio with two sun decks, full
bath, and kitchen. The Gingerbread Cottage
has a full bath and a screened porch. The Sugar
Cabin has full bath and screened porch. Laundry facilities available, and coffee and tea
always on tap. Swimming, boating, and whitewater rafting within one mile. Two hours from
Toronto. Open May 15 to October 15. Personal
checks accepted in advance. Call about pets.
Hearty gourmet breakfast served.

Host: Phyllis Howarth
Rooms: 5 (2 PB; 3 SB) $65-75
Continental Breakfast
Credit Cards: None
Notes: 7, 9, 10, 11, 12

NAPANEE

Fairview House
Bed & Breakfast

373 Dundas Street West, P.O. Box 114, K7R 3S5
(613) 354-5142; FAX (613) 354-0609
e-mail: lucas@king.igs.net

Fairview House, built in 1860s by a United
Empire Loyalist, is one of Napanee's finest Victorian-style homes. Once a grand estate, it has
recently been restored to its original charm and
splendor with each guest's comfort in mind.
Pine floors, plastered crown mouldings, ceiling
fans, and Victorian furnishings await in each
guest bedroom. Victorian period furnishings,

modern conveniences, gracious lawns, landscaping, and seasonal facilities, such as an in-
ground pool, offer guests complete comforts.

Host: Mr. Shaune E. Lucas
Rooms: 3 (3 SB) $45-65 Canadian
Continental Breakfast
Credit Cards: None
Notes: 5, 7, 8, 10, 11, 12

NEW HAMBURG

The Waterlot Restaurant and
Bed & Breakfast

17 Huron Street, N0B 2G0
(519) 662-2020; FAX (519) 662-2114
e-mail: waterlot@sympatico.ca
www3.sympatico.ca/waterlot

The Waterlot opened in the fall of 1974 and
from the outset it has been committed to quality of ambiance and service. Two large and
comfortably appointed rooms share a memorable marbled shower, bidet, water closet, wet
vanity, and sitting area. Suite has a private bath
and a living area. The Waterlot is one of
Ontario's finest dining establishments. Twelve
miles from world-renowned Stratford Shakespeare Festival May through November.

Host: Gordon and Leslie Elkeer
Rooms: 3 (1 PB; 2 SB) $70-110 Canadian
Continental Breakfast
Credit Cards: A, B, C, E
Notes: 2, 3, 4, 5, 7, 8, 9, 10, 11, 12, 13

The Waterlot

NEWTON

Country Charm

Rural Route #1, Road #129, Emg. #6841, N0K 1R0
(519) 595-8789

Come and enjoy bed and breakfast in the hosts' large Mennonite country home just one kilometer south of Newton. Relax around a campfire (weather permitting) or watch the sunset near the creek. There are a sawmill and a buggy shop at the cross-roads. Skideu Trail, bakery, and cheese factory are favorite spots for guests' enjoyment. Open year-round. "Share a memory with us."

Hosts: Marlene and Ezra Streicher
Rooms: 3 (1 PB; 2 SB) $45
Full Breakfast
Credit Cards: None
Notes: 2, 4, 5, 7, 8, 10, 11, 12, 13

NIAGARA FALLS

Gretna Green

5077 River Road, L2E 3G7
(905) 357-2081; www.bbcanada.com/262.html

This tourist home offers bright, comfortable rooms with en suite bathrooms. All guest rooms are air conditioned and have TV. Families are welcome. This is "a home away from home" where guests are treated to a full, home-

Gretna Green

cooked breakfast that includes muffins, scones, jams, and jellies. Niagara has much to offer: the falls, Skylon Tower, IMAX Theatre, the Floral Clock, the rose gardens, and museums. Bike rentals available. Personal checks accepted for deposit only. Smoking permitted in designated areas only.

Hosts: Stan and Marg Gardiner
Rooms: 4 (PB) $45-75
Full Breakfast
Credit Cards: None
Notes: 8, 10, 12

NIAGARA-ON-THE-LAKE

The Old Bank House

10 Front Street, P.O. Box 1708, L0S 1J0
(905) 468-7136 (phone/FAX)

A gracious 19th-century country inn in the heart of the old town, while overlooking Lake Ontario. Eight tastefully decorated rooms/ suites, air conditioned. Parking. In-season rates include a gourmet breakfast. Attractive off-season rates. A luxury cottage also available upon request. Daily and off-season rates available.

Hosts: Judy and Misha
Rooms: 8 (6 PB; 2 SB) $100-140
Full Breakfast
Credit Cards: A, B, C
Notes: 2, 5, 7, 12, 14

7 No smoking; 8 Children welcome; 9 Social drinking allowed; 10 Tennis nearby; 11 Swimming nearby; 12 Golf nearby; 13 Skiing nearby; 14 May be booked through a travel agent; 15 Handicapped accessible.

NORTH BAY

Hummingbird Hill
Bed & Breakfast

254 Edmond Road, Astorville, P0H 1B0
(705) 752-4547; (800) 661-4976
e-mail: mabb@vianet.on.ca
www.bbcanada.com/955.html
www.on-biz.com/hummingbirdhill/

Unique geodesic dome cedar home has outdoor
hot tub, sauna, screened cedar gazebo, extensive gardens and pond. Bird watching, privacy.
Elegant, spacious accommodations, Victorian
Room with en suite, Ivy Room with en suite,
and the Loft with shared luxury bath with fireplace. Meals are gourmet, heart smart, low
calorie, and vegetarian. Country living at its
best. All inclusive spa and gourmet packages.

Hosts: Marianne and Gary Persia
Rooms: 3 (1 PB; 1 SB) $60-75
Full Breakfast
Credit Cards: B
Notes: 2, 3, 4, 5, 7, 8, 9, 10, 11, 12, 13, 14, 15

Hummingbird Hill

ORILLIA

Betty and Tony's Waterside
Bed & Breakfast

677 Broadview Avenue, L3V 6P1
(800) 308-2579; FAX (705) 326-2262
e-mail: tony.bridgens@encode.com
www.bbcanada.com/9.html

Betty and Tony's

A modern air-conditioned home in the Lakelands of Ontario, with lawns running down to
the 300-mile-long Trent-Severn Waterway.
Fishing, swimming, docking for up to 40-foot
cruisers, a paddleboat, canoe, and bikes are
available. English hosts serve breakfast on
Wedgwood bone china. Charming large rooms,
guest lounge, books. Nearby are Casino Rama,
Stephen Leacock Museum, city parks, and
beach. Ice-fishing in the canal.

Hosts: Betty Bridgens, B. Ed. and Tony Bridgens,
    P. Eng.
Rooms: 3 (1 PB; 2 SB) $60-95 Canadian
Full Breakfast
Credit Cards: A, B, E
Notes: 2, 3, 4, 5, 6, 7, 8, 9, 10, 11, 12, 13

The Verandahs

4 Palm Beach Road, Rural Route 2, Hawkestone,
    L0L 1T0
(705) 487-1910 (phone/FAX)

Beautiful Victorian-style home with verandas
on large landscaped lot 200-feet from Lake
Simcoe. Bright, comfortable interior with welcoming ambiance. Guest sitting room with
fireplace, TV, books, and games. Ultra-com-
fortable beds with goose-down duvets. Hearty
homemade breakfasts. Summer season May 15
to October 15. Walk to beach and boat launch.
Short drive to summer theatre, great restaurants, boat tours. Winter season December 28
to March 31. Close to skiing, snowmobiling
and ice fishing for winter enjoyment. Inquire
about accommodations for children.

NOTES: Credit cards accepted: A MasterCard; B Visa; C American Express; D Discover; E Diner's Club;
F Other; 2 Personal checks accepted; 3 Lunch available; 4 Dinner available; 5 Open all year; 6 Pets welcome;

Hosts: Pearl and Norm Guthrie
Rooms: 3 (PB) $80
Full Breakfast
Credit Cards: A, B
Notes: 2, 7, 9, 11, 12, 13

ORO

Siberi*inn Bed & Breakfast

Rural Route 2, Hawkestone, L0L 1T0
(705) 487-6456; FAX (705) 487-6459
e-mail: siberinn@barint.on.ca
www.barint.on.ca/~siberinn

Relax in the peaceful setting of the panoramic hardwood forest. Take in the fresh air and picturesque natural surroundings. Enjoy affection from the Siberian Huskies who run the place. Year-round outdoor recreation. Hiking trails and skiing from the doorstep. Best snow around! Guest lounge with fireplace. Wrap-around veranda. Only 10 minutes west of Orillia, on the scenic 10th Line of Oro.

Hosts: Mike Pidwerbecki and the Siberian Huskies
Rooms: 2 (PB) $65-80 Canadian ($45-55 U.S.)
Full Breakfast
Credit Cards: None
Notes: 5, 7, 12, 13

Siberi*inn

OTTAWA

Albert House Inn

478 Albert Street, K1R 5B5
(613) 236-4479; (800) 267-1982
www.alberthouseinn.on.ca

Albert House Inn

Gracious Victorian inn built in 1875 by a noted Canadian architect. Each room is individually decorated and has private facilities, telephone, TV, and air conditioning. Guest lounge with fireplace. Famous Albert House breakfast. Parking is available, but inn is within walking distance to most attractions.

Hosts: Cathy and John Delroy
Rooms: 17 (PB) $80-125
Full Breakfast
Credit Cards: A, B, C, E
Notes: 5, 9, 13, 14

Auberge McGEE'S Inn (Est. 1984)

185 Daly Avenue, K1N 6E8
(613) 237-6089; (800) 2MCGEES
FAX (613) 237-6201
www.coatesb.demon.co.uk/McGees

Fifteen years of award-winning hospitality. McGEE'S is a smoke-free upscale bed and breakfast inn in downtown Ottawa. Each room features a telephone equipped with computer modem hook up, enabling guests to direct-dial long distance (a savings of 30 percent) and receive messages on personal voice mail. Two Jacuzzi en suite theme rooms. Walking distance of Congress Centre, Parliament, University of

7 No smoking; 8 Children welcome; 9 Social drinking allowed; 10 Tennis nearby; 11 Swimming nearby; 12 Golf nearby; 13 Skiing nearby; 14 May be booked through a travel agent; 15 Handicapped accessible.

Ottawa, Rideau Canal, trendy Byward Market. Ten-minute drive to ski hills. AAA-approved. Meeting rooms for 24 people. Full breakfast.

Hosts: Anne Schutte and Mary Unger
Rooms: 14 (PB) $78-170 Canadian
Full Breakfast
Credit Cards: A, B, C
Notes: 5, 7, 8, 9, 11, 12, 13

Australis Guest House

Australis Guest House

35 Marlborough Avenue, K1N 8E6
(613) 235-8461 (phone/FAX)
e-mail: waters@intranet.ca
www.bbcanada.com/1463.html

This guest house is the oldest established and still operating bed and breakfast in Ottawa. On a quiet, tree-lined street one block from the Rideau River and Strathcona Park, it is a 20-minute walk to the Parliament buildings. The home boasts leaded windows, fireplaces, oak floors, and unique, eight-foot, stained-glass windows. The spacious rooms, including one with private bathroom, feature many collectibles from different parts of the world. The hearty, delicious breakfasts help start the day right. Winner of the Ottawa Gold Award, Star of the City for services to tourism, recommended by *Newsweek* and *Travel Scoop*. Carol Waters is co-author of *The Breakfast Companion*.

Hosts: Brian and Carol Waters
Rooms: 3 (1 PB; 2 SB) $62-78

Full Breakfast
Credit Cards: None
Notes: 5, 7, 10, 11, 12, 13

Bye-the-Way

310 First Avenue, K1S 2G8
(613) 232-6840

Modern, comfortable, and elegant, Bye-the-Way bed and breakfast offers all the conveniences of gracious living in downtown Ottawa. A few minutes' walking distance from the Rideau Canal, city attractions, Carleton University, and world-class museums. The host is happy to guide first-time visitors around Ottawa. Central air conditioning, smoke- and pollen-free.

Hosts: Krystyna, Rafal, and Adam
Rooms: 4 (2 PB; 2 SB) $70-80
Suite: $80
Full Breakfast
Credit Cards: A, B, E, F
Notes: 2, 5, 7, 8, 9, 10, 11, 12, 13, 14

Bye-the-Way

Gasthaus Switzerland Inn

89 Daly Avenue, K1N 6E6
(613) 237-0335; (888) 663-0000
FAX (613) 594-3327; e-mail: switzinn@magi.com
http: //infoweb.magi.com/~switzinn/

The Gasthaus Switzerland Inn, in the heart of Canada's capital, offers guests traditional Swiss hospitality. Twenty-two well-appointed air-conditioned rooms, some with fireplace, private bath/Jacuzzi en suite, cable TV, tele-

NOTES: Credit cards accepted: A MasterCard; B Visa; C American Express; D Discover; E Diner's Club; F Other; 2 Personal checks accepted; 3 Lunch available; 4 Dinner available; 5 Open all year; 6 Pets welcome;

phone, a smoke-free environment, limited free parking, and a Swiss country breakfast buffet. Recommended by CAA, AAA, Canada Select, and Tourism of Ontario. Honeymoon/romantic getaway suite featuring king-size canopied poster bed, a double Jacuzzi.

Hosts: Josef and Sabina Sauter
Rooms: 22 (PB) $68-188
Full Breakfast
Credit Cards: A, B, C, E
Notes: 5, 7, 10, 11, 12, 13

Lovat

OWEN SOUND

Sunset Farms Bed & Breakfast

Rural Route 6, 398139 28th Avenue East, N4K 5N8
(519) 371-4559; e-mail: moses@bmts.com
www.bmts.com/~moses/

Well-traveled hosts own and operate Owen Sound's longest-established bed and breakfast. Forty picturesque acres just five minutes from the city's center. Ideal for day trips to Manitoulin Island, Georgian Bay touring, and bicycle trips. Bruce Trail access nearby. Gorgeous during autumn. Antique-furnished unique home. Gardens, patios, and pond for outdoor enjoyment. Artistically presented breakfasts featuring garden-fresh produce and flowers. Inquire regarding bringing children and pets.

Hosts: Bill and Cecilie Moses
Rooms: 4 (1 PB; 3 SB) $45-95
Full and Continental Breakfast
Credit Cards: None
Notes: 5, 7, 9, 10, 11, 12, 13, 14

PAISLEY

Lovat Bed & Breakfast

Rural Route 2, N0G 2N0
(519) 353-5534; FAX (519) 353-4195

Come stay at this log home built in the late 1800s. Sleeping accommodations include three bedrooms as well as a fourth bedroom for a family. In winter there are cross-country skiing, snowmobiling, and toboggan hills in the area. Summer is great with an outdoor barbecue. Spend the day on the beach; only 15 to 30 minutes from Lake Huron areas. Guests can travel to Tobermory and enjoy a cruise aboard the MS *Chi-Cheemaun*. Open year-round. Hot tub (new for 1998).

Hosts: Jim and Gail Dalman
Rooms: 4 (SB) $50
Full Breakfast
Credit Cards: None
Notes: 2, 3, 4, 5, 7, 8, 9, 11, 12, 13

PARRY SOUND

Victoria Manor

43 Church Street, P2A 1Y6
(705) 746-5399; e-mail: victoria@zeuter.com

Welcome an era of gracious living in the restored Victorian home. Enjoy our antiques, relax in the cosy library, front parlor or screened veranda. A full breakfast is served in the dining room. We are in the heart of Parry Sound, only a few minutes' walk from the Festival of the Sound, Rainbow Theatre, 30,000 Islands Cruise, shopping, restaurants, and Georgian Bay beaches. Snowmobile and cross-country ski trails and golf are a short drive away. Open year-round. Inquire about accommodations for children.

Hosts: Sharon and John Ranney
Rooms: 5 (1 PB; 4 SB) $60-95
Full Breakfast
Credit Cards: None
Notes: 2, 5, 7, 9, 10, 11, 12, 13

7 No smoking; 8 Children welcome; 9 Social drinking allowed; 10 Tennis nearby; 11 Swimming nearby; 12 Golf nearby; 13 Skiing nearby; 14 May be booked through a travel agent; 15 Handicapped accessible.

PORT CARLING

DunRovin

Box 304, P0B 1J0
(705) 765-7317; e-mail: dunrovin@muskoka.com
www.bbcanada.com/615.html

Warmth and charm of a cottage with comforts of home. Lovely wildflower gardens. Large deck overlooking Lake Muskoka. Swim or boat in protected bay. Relax on private boathouse, swing in hammock. Comfortable guest area, hot tub in winter. Queen-size bedroom with romantic half-canopied bed with an en suite. Twin bedroom with great lake view, duvets, and private bath. Heart-healthy breakfasts served upstairs in the great room or on the deck. Two hours north of Toronto.

Hosts: Wilsie and Bob Mann
Rooms: 2 (PB) $80-90 Canadian
Full Breakfast
Credit Cards: None
Notes: 2, 5, 7, 9, 10, 11, 12, 13

DunRovin

ST. MARYS

Eagleview Manor Bed & Breakfast

178 Widder Street East, P.O. Box 3183, N4X 1A8
(519) 284-1811

Step back in time at this gracious, smoke-free Queene Anne Victorian home which is perched on a hill overlooking quaint St. Marys, with two rivers, five bridges, waterfalls, and the Canadian Baseball Hall of Fame. There is a grand sweeping staircase, large rooms, three shared guest bathrooms, Jacuzzi, fireplaces, antique quilts, stained-glass windows, formal oak dining room, guest parlor, menu breakfast, tea table, and in-ground swimming pool. Minutes from Stratford and London.

Hosts: Bob and Pat Young
Rooms: 3 (3 SB) $65-80
Full Breakfast
Credit Cards: A, B
Notes: 2, 5, 7, 8, 9, 10, 11, 12, 13, 14

THUNDER BAY

Pinebrook Bed & Breakfast

Rural Route 16 Mitchell Road, P7B 6B3
(807) 683-6114; FAX (807) 683-8641
e-mail: pinebrok@baynet.net
www.bbcanada.com/1184.html

Warm and friendly cedar chalet. Ten minutes from downtown. Welcoming. Quiet. On 43 rolling acres of meadows and pine forest along more than one-half mile of private river frontage. It is truly a place to rest and relax. Sumptuous meals. Jacuzzi. Three bathrooms. Fireplace room. Sauna by river. Canoeing. Fishing. Meadows and forest trails. Mountain bikes. Library and video library. Children and pets welcome. A home away from home. Smoking permitted outside only.

Hosts: Sara Jeffrey and Armin Weber
Rooms: 4 (1 PB; 3 SB) $45-75 Canadian
Full Breakfast
Credit Cards: A, B, C
Notes: 3, 4, 5, 6, 7, 8, 9, 11, 12, 13

TORONTO

Amblecote

109 Walmer Road, M5R 2X8
(416) 927-1713; FAX (416) 927-0838
e-mail: info@amblecote.com
www.amblecote.com

A restored historical Edwardian home, built in the English cottage style. Wonderful neighbor-

---

NOTES: Credit cards accepted: A MasterCard; B Visa; C American Express; D Discover; E Diner's Club; F Other; 2 Personal checks accepted; 3 Lunch available; 4 Dinner available; 5 Open all year; 6 Pets welcome;

hood. Quiet street yet minutes from the subway, museums, Casa Loma, Yorkville. Plenty of restaurants, café, and shopping within walking distance. The house is furnished with antiques and Persian rugs. The guest rooms are appointed with period furniture and provide comfort and tranquility from another era.

Rooms: 5 (2 PB; 3 SB) $70-95 Canadian
Full or Continental Breakfast
Credit Cards: A, B, C
Notes: 5, 7, 9, 11

Annex House Bed & Breakfast

147 Madison Avenue, M5R 2S6
(416) 920-3922 (telephone/FAX)

Enjoy comfortable bed and breakfast facilities at Annex House, a restored turn-of-the-century Georgian home in the heart of downtown Toronto, with private parking. The tranquility and beauty of the Annex area offers a pleasant 10-minute walk to shops, sights, and restaurants. The best shopping is close by, at Yorkville, Yonge and Bloor Streets, and on Spadina Avenue. Sightseeing opportunities include Casa Loma, the Royal Ontario Museum, McLaughlin Planetarium, historic University of Toronto, and Queen's Park. Subways and buses are three minutes away, making the whole of the city instantly accessible.

Host: Carol (Ricciuto) Davey
Rooms: 3 (PB) $85
Full Breakfast
Credit Cards: None
Notes: 5, 7, 8, 9, 10

Bed & Breakfast Association of Downtown Toronto

P.O. Box 190, Station B, M5T 2W1
(416) 410-3938 (9:00 A.M.-6:00 P.M. Mon-Fri)
   (8:30 A.M.-12:00 P.M. Sat-Sun)
FAX (416) 368-1653
e-mail: bnbtoronto@globalserve.net
www.bnbinfo.com

Representing Toronto's largest selection of fully inspected and privately owned Victorian

homes in downtown Toronto. All within 10 minutes of the major tourist attractions. Let the hosts be a guide to the international flavor of Toronto's interesting neighborhoods. Guests can choose a range of accommodations from elegant suites with fireplaces and whirlpool baths to simple, warm guest rooms for the more budget minded. For reservations, free brochure, or any other information one might need, please contact Linda Lippa. There are 50 accommodations with private and shared baths. Full and Continental breakfasts served. All rates include breakfast, taxes, and parking. Visa accepted. $65-120.

Howland at Bloor. An 1800s Georgian two-story flat in the heart of the Annex neighborhood. Walking distance to the Royal Ontario Museum, university, shopping, and great local restaurants. Only a five-minute walk to the Bloor and university subway stations. The home features original moldings, high Georgian ceilings, and much more. The host offers a guest room with TV and private baths. Full breakfast. $75-90.

Howland Street. Renovated Victorian home in the university neighborhood known as the Annex. With its great local restaurants, it is within walking distance to the Royal Ontario Museum, university, public transit to famous Yorkville for shopping, and easy access to the city center. Host offers a second-floor guest room with private bathroom and TV. Full breakfast. $75-90.

Jarvis at Bloor. Beautiful Victorian home in a great downtown neighborhood, only steps from Bloor and Yonge Streets, the shopping center of the city. Only a minute's walk to transit and theaters. Two guest rooms offered. The guest room in the main home has a private bath and the guest room in the coach house has a private bath with a single tub with jets. Breakfast is served in the main house. $75-115.

7 No smoking; 8 Children welcome; 9 Social drinking allowed; 10 Tennis nearby; 11 Swimming nearby; 12 Golf nearby; 13 Skiing nearby; 14 May be booked through a travel agent; 15 Handicapped accessible.

King Street West. Beautiful 1800s Victorian home overlooking the lake. On the King street-car line, only 15 minutes from Eaton Centre, and a short walk to the Canadian National Exhibition grounds. Also nearby is a walkway over the expressway to Sunnyside Park on the lake. This home is full of Old World charm, stained-glass windows, hardwood flooring, and floor-to-ceiling bookcases in the library. Hostess offers two suites for guest rooms. Private baths, queen-size beds, and kitchenettes. $55-75.

Oriole Parkway. Wonderful and spacious 1920s home in one of the more elite neighborhoods of the city. Only a 15-minute walk to the Yonge and Davisville subway or 10 minutes down to St. Clair and Avenue Roads. There is also a bus right out front. Beautifully decorated. Relax in a spacious sitting area in front of the fireplace or outside on the deck. Three guest rooms with private and shared baths. All rooms have TVs. $65-85.

Phoebe Street. Lovely new brownstone in the heart of Queen Street West Village, known for its trendier shopping and cafés. Only steps from Spadina and Queen, easy access to public transit, and a 10-minute walk from Eaton Centre and theaters. Two second-floor guest rooms, each with private bath. $55-85.

St. George. Beautiful early 1900s Edwardian home in the heart of the Annex neighborhood, only a 10-minute walk to the university, Royal Ontario Museum, Yorkville, and Casa Loma. Also only a five-minute walk to the Dupont subway stop, making easy access to the rest of the city's attractions. This home features Old World charm, antiques, nooks with leaded bay windows, and fireplaces throughout. Four guest rooms, with two common baths. $65-90.

Seaton Street. Spacious restored Victorian home in downtown, only a 10-minute walk to Eaton Centre and Pantages Theatre, and a minute's walk to public transit. This home fea-

tures antiques, pine and hardwood flooring throughout, and has been totally renovated. The hosts offer a third-floor suite. It has a sitting area with fireplace, private bath with a large single tub with jets, and lots of light from large skylights. $120.

Shaw Street. This quaint home is only a five-minute walk to the Bloor subway line at Ossington station, and only 10 minutes to public transit to the city center, to the Royal Ontario Museum, University of Toronto, and Yorkville Village. This immaculate home, with hardwood flooring and antiques throughout, offers a second-floor guest room with a private bath. Continental breakfast. $50-70.

Soho at Queen. A beautiful brownstone, only steps from Spadina Avenue and Queen Street, a trendy area for shopping and wonderful eateries. Only a 10-minute walk to the Sheraton Centre and Metro Convention Centre, and to the Royal Alexandra and Princess of Wales theaters. A spacious second-floor guest room with an en suite bath is offered. Continental plus breakfast. Parking not included in rates. $60-80.

Bed & Breakfast Homes of Toronto

P.O. Box 46093, College Park, M5B 2L8
(416) 363-6362

Alcina's. (416) 656-6400; www.bbcanada. com/1104.html. This gracious, old Victorian brick house is on a shady tree-lined street in the exclusive Wychwood Park neighborhood. Enjoy casual elegance: indoors, soft furnishings and oak; outdoors an old-fashioned English Garden. Close to Spadina House and ever-popular Casa Loma. Subway, bus, and streetcar are all in walking distance. Casual eateries can be found locally. Continental breakfast. Parking available. Resident cat, Cina. Seasonal rates. Smoking allowed in back yard seating area. $65-80.

NOTES: Credit cards accepted: A MasterCard; B Visa; C American Express; D Discover; E Diner's Club; F Other; 2 Personal checks accepted; 3 Lunch available; 4 Dinner available; 5 Open all year; 6 Pets welcome;

Colwood. (416) 234-9988; FAX (416) 234-1554; e-mail: jgartner@idirect.com; www. bbcanada.com/1100.html. Stunningly renovated traditional home in a prestigious area close to both the airport and downtown; both 10 to 15 minutes away by car. It is near and easily accessible to all major highways. Public transit with direct access to the subway is a short walk. A full range of amenities and restaurants are nearby as are James Gardens and the Humber River park system with its bike and walking trails. The home is bright and sunny with an outdoor swimming pool set amid a beautiful landscaped garden. Breakfasts are served in the dining room or on the deck; tea and coffee are complimentary. Rooms are air conditioned and have ceiling fams. On-site parking is free. Smoke-free. Resident Labrador retriever. $75-105.

Feathers May and Max. (416) 534-1923 or (416) 534-2388; www.bbcanada. com/1115.html. A charming, spacious Victorian home in the popular Annex, only a five-minute walk from Bathurst subway and Bloor Street. Guests are two blocks away from one of Toronto's most delightful areas of cosmopolitan restaurants and cafés, film and live theaters, bookstores and antique shops. Nineteenth-century European and oriental furnishings, china, delicate tapestries, and an unusual collection of antique puppets lend a unique atmosphere to this interesting and beautifully restored home. Continental breakfast. Discount offered if no breakfast desired. Central air. Color TV in guest rooms. No smoking in house, please. English, Dutch, French, and German spoken. Free parking. $70-80 Canadian.

Greener-Gunn. (416) 698-9061 (phone/fax); e-mail: greener-gunner@sympatico.ca; www.bbcanada.com/1113.html. In the increasingly popular Beaches area of Toronto, east of downtown, this home offers guests friendly hospitality and a good homemade breakfast in a relaxed, casual atmosphere, served in the dining room or, weather permitting, just outside on the front deck. A two-minute walk will take guests down to Queen Street, where they can find cafés, boutiques, craft shops, small art and antique galleries, and many fine restaurants and night spots. Downtown is accessible by car in 10 to 15 minutes, or by a leisurely 20-minute trolley-car ride. Front driveway parking. Smoking on the deck only. Bathroom shared by guests. Dog in residence. Seasonal discounts. $50-70 Canadian.

Helga's Place. (416) 633-5951; FAX (416) 636-3050; e-mail: helgaplace@hotmail. com. A country home in the city with wood stoves and fireplace, terrazzo floors, and antiques all surrounded by natural wood. Large front porch overlooks the rock garden in a quiet, well-treed neighborhood. A variety of interesting restaurants, shops, and cinemas are within easy walking distance, while a five-minute walk takes guests to the Bloor subway and easy access to downtown. Generous and nutritious breakfsats are served with dietary preferences being catered to. Parking. Smoking permitted on front porch. Airport pick-up and drop-off can be arranged. $60-80 Candian.

Inverness. (416) 769-2028 (phone/FAX). e-mail: ewleslie@interlog.com; http: //bbcanada.com/2918.com. A country home in the city. Antiques, woodstoves, terrazo floors, and lots of natural wood, create a warm and inviting home. Only a five-minute walk to the subway and to High Park, Toronto's largest and greenest park. Walk to a variety of interesting restaurants, shops, and movies. Either downtown or the airport only a 15-minute car ride. Parking available. Generous, nutrituous breakfsats served by candlelight. $50-70 Canadian.

Kingslake Korners. (416) 491-4759; www.bbcanada.com/477.html. Comfort, relaxation, and hospitality await guests in a cheerful, quiet residential area of north Toronto in a family home setting, 20-30 minutes to downtown, depending on traffic flow. Relax in clean, spacious, and tastefully decorated guest rooms— one with private bath and the other with en suite

---

7 No smoking; 8 Children welcome; 9 Social drinking allowed; 10 Tennis nearby; 11 Swimming nearby; 12 Golf nearby; 13 Skiing nearby; 14 May be booked through a travel agent; 15 Handicapped accessible.

bath, color cable TV and VCR. Children welcome; crib and highchair are available and playground and parks are nearby. Full breakfast is served in the dining room. Special diets can be accommodated. Central air. On-site parking. Smoke-free. Dog and cat in residence; no guest pets, please. $50-60 Canadian.

Martyniuk. (416) 603-2128 (phone/FAX) ; e-mail: martyniukbb@home.com; www.bbcanada.com/1105.html. This home, more than 100 years old, in the Kensington Market area, is quite modest in style and decor, but at prices well below average, it is an excellent choice for the budget traveler, especially for those without cars. The Martyniuk home is exactly one mile from the Eaton Centre, bus terminal, or Elgin and Pantages Theatres. European-style restaurants and Toronto Western Hospital are within walking distance. The full breakfast is served in the kitchen. English, Ukrainian, Polish, and German spoken. Very limited smoking permitted. Ten percent discount from October to March if over seven days. Rooms individually air conditioned. Parking extra $5 per day. $45-55 Canadian.

Morning Glory. (416) 533-6120; www.bbcanada.com/1103.html. This Edwardian home has high ceilings, maple trim, and stained-glass windows. Little Italy and Bloor Street are within walking distance and there is easy access to Chinatown, theaters, concert halls, art galleries, and most other major attractions. Public transportation is very close at hand. A generous, delicious breakfast is served. Convenient highway access; garage available for parking. Smoke-free home. Smoking area on patio. English, French, German, and Dutch spoken. $55-70 Canadian.

Oriole Gardens. (416) 924-4736; www.bbcanada.com/1108.html. Enjoy a warm, friendly atmosphere in this gracious family home on an upscale, tree-lined residential street. A few minutes' walk from St. Clair sub-

way station and Yonge Street buses, and within easy reach of Toronto's major attractions. The location offers an interesting variety of restaurants, pubs, fashion stores, bakeries, bookstores, and cinemas. Historic Casa Loma and Spadina House are approximately 15 to 20 minutes' walking distance. A full and healthy breakfast is served. On-site parking. Cat and dog in residence. $60-85 Canadian.

Sundown. (416) 657-1900; www.bbcanada.com/1102.html. A bright, spacious home on a quiet tree-lined boulevard, a block away from the colorful and lively Corso Italia with its small outdoor bistros and bustling shops. A five-minute streetcar ride takes guests right into the St. Clair W. subway. Minutes to theaters. The generous breakfast consists of hot and cold dishes and is served in the dining room. Cable TV and VCR. Parking. Central air. Smoking on the front veranda. Discounts for long stays. $59-99 Canadian.

Vanderkooy. (416) 925-8765; FAX (416) 925-8557; e-mail: jvanderkooy@ hotmail.com; www.bbcanada.com/ 1107.html. This charming older, traditional home is in an excellent location on a lovely tree-lined street close to Summerhill subway, a choice of good restaurants, and fine boutiques. The house is bright and sunny, with stained-glass windows, and features some original artwork. One of the bedrooms has a private three-piece bathroom and the other has a shared bath. The atmosphere of this home is relaxed and casual. A full breakfast is served on a round oak table overlooking the garden. Parking. Air conditioning. Cat in residence. No smoking. Easy access to all downtown attractions. $70-80 Canadian.

Winchester Square. (416) 928-0827; www.bbcanada.com/1111.html. This recently restored late 1800s three-story brick residence is in Cabbagetown, a quiet downtown Toronto neighborhood of Victorian and Edwardian homes. Round-the-clock public transportation stops a block away, or guests can walk a few

---

NOTES: Credit cards accepted: A MasterCard; B Visa; C American Express; D Discover; E Diner's Club; F Other; 2 Personal checks accepted; 3 Lunch available; 4 Dinner available; 5 Open all year; 6 Pets welcome;

steps to the many charming shops and restaurants or enjoy the gardens and architecture of Heritage homes that make up the heart of Cabbagetown. A healthy Continental breakfast is served. The guest kitchen is conveniently equipped with a dishwasher and laundry facilities for extended stays. Visiting professionals, lecturers, and families take note: Polish is a second language. Air-conditioned suite. Smoking is allowed only on the open-air deck. Free parking. Bathroom shared by only two guest rooms and one en suite. $50-99 Canadian.

Craig House Bed & Breakfast

78 Spruce Hill Road, M4E 3G3
(416) 698-3916; FAX (416) 698-8506
www.bbcanada.com/1222.html

Guests will be welcomed to a large traditional beach home with its beautiful flower gardens from spring to fall. Craig House is in a popular neighbourhood with the air of a small town resort by the lake, a superb location close enough to downtown that guests can be there in 10 minutes by car or by a leisurely street car ride 25 of minutes on the 24-hour public transportation. The guest rooms are on a private second floor. There is a kitchen for the use of guests making light snacks, tea, or coffee. The third floor is a one-bedroom apartment that sleeps four with private bath and TV. Craig House is CAA/AAA-approved.

Host: Dorothy Maguire
Rooms: 4 (2 PB; 2 SB) $65-90
Full Breakfast
Credit Cards: None
Notes: 7, 9, 10, 11, 14

The Homewood Inn

65 Homewood Avenue, M4Y 2K1
(416) 920-7944; FAX (416) 920-4091
e-mail: nickwood@interlog.com
www.interlog.com/~nickwood/homewood.html

Three beautiful Victorian houses converted into a typical English bed and breakfast. Ten minutes walking distance from Eaton Centre

and seven minutes from subway stations. All rooms have color TV and refrigerators. Air conditioning, maid service, free parking, and laundry facilities. Airport bus service. Self-contained and deluxe suites available. Smoking and nonsmoking rooms. Full English breakfast. Guest kitchen available.

Hosts: Nick and Dolores Thompson-Wood
Rooms: 30 (3 PB; 27 SB) $60-90
Full Breakfast
Credit Cards: A, B, C
Notes: 5, 6, 8, 9, 10, 11, 12, 14

Palmerston Inn

322 Palmerston Boulevard, M6G 2N6
(416) 920-7842; FAX (416) 960-9529

Palmerston Inn is an elegant Georgian-style mansion circa 1906. Flanked by large white pillars, it sits majestically on a stately tree-lined boulevard in the heart of one of downtown Toronto's most interesting neighborhoods, close to all amenities. The guest rooms feature traditional furnishings, some period pieces, fresh flowers, bath robes, ceiling fans, clock radios. All double rooms are air conditioned. A full hot breakfast features fresh fruit salad, home baking, and creative egg dishes. Private parking. No smokers.

Hosts: Judy Carr
Rooms: 8 (3 PB; 5 SB) $110-195 Canadian
Full Breakfast
Credit Cards: A, B
Notes: 5, 7, 9, 10, 11, 12, 13, 14

The Red Door Bed & Breakfast

301 Indian Road, M6R 2X7
(416) 604-0544; e-mail: reddor@idirect.com
http: //webhome.idirect.com/~reddoor/

Elegant, spacious accommodation on a quiet, tree-lined residential street. The bedrooms have queen-size beds, air conditioning, TV, clock radio, and comfortable chairs. The bed and breakfast is a five-minute walk from the subway, which will take guests to the centre of downtown in 10 minutes. Guests are served a

7 No smoking; 8 Children welcome; 9 Social drinking allowed; 10 Tennis nearby; 11 Swimming nearby; 12 Golf nearby; 13 Skiing nearby; 14 May be booked through a travel agent; 15 Handicapped accessible.

The Red Door

gourmet breakfast in the spacious dining room and can read and relax in the large, comfortable living room filled with art and antiques.

Hosts: Jean and Paul Pedersen
Rooms: 4 (2 PB; 2 SB) $85-100 Canadian
Full Breakfast
Credit Cards: B
Notes: 2, 5, 7, 10, 11, 12

Vanderkooy Bed & Breakfast

53 Walker Avenue, M4V 1G3
(416) 925-8765; FAX (925) 8557
e-mail: jvanderkooy@hotmail.com

Joan and the resident cat, welcome guests to this charming home where they will enjoy comfortable guest rooms and breakfast served in an open dining room overlooking the garden. A short walk to Summerhill station on the Younge subway line allows easy access to downtown attractions, including the Harbourfront, Skydome, the Eaton Centre, and theaters. Restaurants and shopping districts are all within walking distance. Feel free to watch TV by the fire, enjoy the waterfall and pond in the garden, or relax on the flower-filled deck in the summer. Children over 12 welcome.

Host: Joan Vanderkooy
Rooms: 3 (1 PB; 2 SB) $70-80 Canadian
Full Breakfast
Credit Cards: None
Notes: 5, 7, 9,

WATERLOO

Les Diplomates Bed & Breakfast (Executive Guest House)

100 Blythwood Road, N2L 4A2
(519) 725-3184; (800) 645-9457
e-mail: bmateyk@easynet.ca
www.trqavelinx.com/les_diplomates
www.bbcanada.com/222.html

Classic elegance for executive travellers and romantic getaways. A re-created 19th-century French/English ambiance. Nestled among the serene woods right in the heart of Waterloo. Minutes from universities, Kitchener, St. Jacobs, Farmers Market, and Oktoberfest*ivities*. Very large bedrooms all with en suite/private bathrooms. Full use of spacious parlor and dining room. Caters to special events and elegant smaller weddings. Prices include five-course gourmet breakfast and afternoon Victorian tea. Inquire about accommodations for pets.

Hosts: Hoda and Bob Mateyk
Rooms: 3 (PB) $69-115
Full Breakfast
Credit Cards: A, B
Notes: 2, 5, 7, 8, 9, 10, 11, 12, 13, 14

WELLESLEY

Firella Creek Farm

Rural Route 2, N0B 2T0
(519) 656-2974 (phone/FAX)

Retreat to nature in the heart of Mennonite farming country. Country breakfast with a view of trout pond, stream, and apple orchard. Relax beside the fireplace or explore hiking and cross-country ski trails through ancient forest. Birds, animals, and wildflowers abound. Excellent cycling roads. German and Canadian cuisine served. Air conditioned, smoke-free rooms. On Regional Road 5 between Wellesley and Crosshill, 25 minutes from Stratford, Kitchener, or St. Jacobs Farmers' Market.

Hosts: Adolph and Emily Hafemann
Rooms: 3 (PB) $50-55 Canadian

NOTES: Credit cards accepted: A MasterCard; B Visa; C American Express; D Discover; E Diner's Club; F Other; 2 Personal checks accepted; 3 Lunch available; 4 Dinner available; 5 Open all year; 6 Pets welcome;

Full Breakfast
Credit Cards: None
Notes: 2, 5, 7, 8, 9, 10, 11, 12, 13

WESTPORT

Stepping Stone Bed & Breakfast Inn

328 Centreville Road, Rural Route 2, K0G 1X0
(613) 273-3806; FAX (613) 273-3331
e-mail: stepping@rideau.net
www.steppingstoneinn.com

Retreat to this peaceful, safe haven. Get back to nature. Beautiful seven-room 1840 Victorian Heritage inn on 150 acres. Relax by spring-fed pond and walk through magnificent gardens and nature trails; enjoy horses, cows, birds, skiing, golfing, and swimming. Weddings with memories for a lifetime; intimate/family dinners, mouth-watering gourmet breakfasts; corporate retreats, seminars. Come capture winter, summer, spring, or fall in all their glory. Between Ottawa and Kingston. Cozy cabin sleeps two with private shower in main building.

Host: Madeline Saunders
Rooms: 7 (4 PB: 3 SB) $75-150 Canadian
Full Breakfast
Credit Cards: A, B, C
Notes: 3, 4, 5, 7, 8, 9, 10, 11, 12, 13, 14, 15

7 No smoking; 8 Children welcome; 9 Social drinking allowed; 10 Tennis nearby; 11 Swimming nearby; 12 Golf nearby; 13 Skiing nearby; 14 May be booked through a travel agent; 15 Handicapped accessible.

RECOMMENDATION FORM

As *The Annual Directory of American and Canadian Bed & Breakfasts* gains approval from the traveling public, more and more bed and breakfast establishments are asking to be included on our mailing list. If you know of another bed and breakfast which may not be on our list, give them a great outreach and advertising opportunity by providing us with the following information:

1) B&B Name _____

Host's Name _____

Address _____

City _____ State _____ Zip Code _____

Telephone _____ FAX _____

2) B&B Name _____

Host's Name _____

Address _____

City _____ State _____ Zip Code _____

Telephone _____ FAX _____

3) B&B Name _____

Host's Name _____

Address _____

City _____ State _____ Zip Code _____

Telephone _____ FAX _____

Please return this form to: Barbour Publishing, Inc.
P.O. Box 719, Uhrichsville, OH 44683
(740) 922-6045; FAX (740) 922-5948